A DECOLONIZING EAR

Documentary Film Disrupts the Archive

A Decolonizing Ear

Documentary Film Disrupts the Archive

OLIVIA LANDRY

UNIVERSITY OF TORONTO PRESS
Toronto Buffalo London

ISBN 978-1-4875-4485-0 (cloth)   ISBN 978-1-4875-4486-7 (EPUB)
ISBN 978-1-4875-4673-1 (PDF)

Library and Archives Canada Cataloguing in Publication

Title: A decolonizing ear : documentary film disrupts the archive /
    Olivia Landry.
Names: Landry, Olivia, author.
Description: Includes bibliographical references and index.
Identifiers: Canadiana (print) 20220250715 | Canadiana (ebook)
    20220257043 | ISBN 9781487544850 (hardcover) |
    ISBN 9781487544867 (EPUB) | ISBN 9781487546731 (PDF)
Subjects: LCSH: Sound recordings in ethnology. | LCSH: Visual
    anthropology. | LCSH: Sound archives – Social aspects. | LCSH:
    Documentary films – Social aspects. | LCSH: Archives – Social aspects. |
    LCSH: Decolonization.
Classification: LCC GN348 .L36 2023 | DDC 305.8002/08 – dc23

We wish to acknowledge the land on which the University of Toronto
Press operates. This land is the traditional territory of the Wendat, the
Anishnaabeg, the Haudenosaunee, the Métis, and the Mississaugas of the
Credit First Nation.

University of Toronto Press gratefully acknowledges the support of Lehigh
University, which provided funds toward the publication of this book.

University of Toronto Press acknowledges the financial assistance to its
publishing program of the Canada Council for the Arts and the Ontario
Arts Council, an agency of the Government of Ontario.

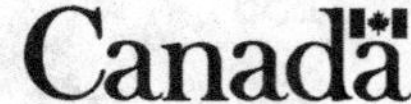

Contents

Illustrations

Acknowledgments

This book could not have come into being without the generous support of the Alexander von Humboldt Foundation. Under the auspices of the Humboldt Foundation, I was able to travel to Berlin to perform research at a time when borders were officially closed due to the pandemic. I am incredibly grateful to Volker Pantenburg for hosting me at the Freie Universität in Berlin, despite the challenging times. He supported the project from its early stages and offered ideas throughout its development. A nod and many thanks also go to his graduate students at the FU, who read and commented on an early version of this book's introduction. Their astute feedback was invaluable. In many ways, this book is deeply marked by Volker's insights and expertise.

Berlin during lockdown was an altogether strange, quiet, and new experience. If it had not been for Randall Halle and Mohammed Bamyeh, I do not know what I would have done. They sustained me with wonderful food, wine, and always stimulating conversation over many a Berlin evening, and I cannot thank them enough. My gratitude towards Randall extends as well to his tremendous scholarly support and inspiration over the years. In this spirit, I must also acknowledge Claudia Breger, my mentor and co-conspirator, and the embodiment of everything I aspire to be as a scholar. To my very dear and close friends and colleagues in academia Erin Noelliste, Ela Gezen, and Nicole Perry, thank you for always being there (on Zoom or by phone) and always, always inspiring. Perhaps in the first place, though, I am grateful to Eric Rentschler and Brad Prager at the *New German Critique* for their encouraging interest in my earlier writing on Philip Scheffner's film *The Halfmoon Files*, which was the thematic and intellectual genesis of this book.

Nothing would be possible without the manifold endorsement of my wonderful colleagues at Lehigh University. From a pre-tenure, semester-long sabbatical and the financial support of a Faculty Research Fund to my appointment as director of the Film and Documentary Studies Program, I have been superbly supported and championed by my colleagues both within my home department of Modern Languages and Literatures and well beyond. I also wish to express my gratitude to my students at Lehigh, especially those who took my experimental undergraduate course "Truth, Lies & Film: Germany through Documentary" in the fall of 2020. Their engagement, enthusiasm, and patience, in particular when I tested out some ideas for this book, were pleasantly surprising and extremely motivating.

It has been a privilege and pleasure to work with Stephen Shapiro at the University of Toronto Press again. He is an extraordinary editor. I also cannot thank enough the two anonymous readers for the press, whose careful and incisive reading of the manuscript proved extremely helpful and whose strong enthusiasm and overall praise were so heartening. At the University of Toronto Press, I have also been the fortunate recipient of the editoral expertise of Janice Evans, who ushered this book through its later stages, and the final copyediting assistance of Terry Teskey. Getting the book to this stage would not have been possible without the marvellous early hand of Alana Dunn, copy-editor extraordinaire – and fantastic friend, to boot!

To my families in Canada and Turkey, whom I have not seen now for over two years, and to my longest and dearest friends in Germany, Britta Füchtenbusch and Neslihan Inalbars-Yılmaz and respective families, I am ever so lucky to have you in my life. From afar, you see me through and give me strength, not to mention immense joy. I am especially obliged to my sister, Christinia Landry, from whom I still learn so much, and who first introduced me to the musical work of Jeremy Dutcher. Most of all, though, I thank my amazing partner Ihsan Ata Topaloğlu. I cannot imagine a world without you, *canım*. I do not exaggerate when I say that you make everything possible.

Procuring materials and permissions was not always an easy task. Heartfelt thanks go to Marlon Fuentes, Adele Horne, Library of Congress, Jeremy Dutcher and Valeo Arts Management, University of Wisconsin-Madison Memorial Library, Wolfgang Fuhrmann, Brian Hochman, Santanu Das, Christopher Li at the Berlin Lautarchiv, Österreichische Mediathek/Technisches Museum Wien, Berlin-Brandenburgische Akademie der Wissenschaften (BBAW), bpk Bildagentur, Deutsches Historisches Museum, Robbi Siegel at Art Resource, Lara Kelingos, and Lehigh University Libraries Interlibrary

Loans and Acquisitions for kindly providing information, materials, and/or permissions.

Some material in chapter 3 appears in "Searching for a Storyteller, Remediating the Archive: Philip Scheffner's *The Halfmoon Files*," *New German Critique* 36, no. 3 (2019): 103–24. I gratefully acknowledge Duke University Press for the permission to reuse this material.

A DECOLONIZING EAR

Documentary Film Disrupts the Archive

The Phonograph on Film

This is a book about what film can do with colonial listening and sound reproduction. *Buschmann spricht in den Phonographen* (Bushman speaking into the phonograph) (figure I.1) is one of the most widely cited examples of early ethnographic film.[1] Filmed on 22 August 1908 in Camel Pan, Ngamiland, in what is present-day Botswana by Austrian anthropologist and ethnographer Rudolf Pöch, this mere 3:36-long film features "Kubi," a sixty-year-old San man, as he speaks into the funnel of the phonograph.[2] With spirited gesticulation, Kubi allegedly narrates a story about a herd of elephants at a nearby watering hole.[3] Early ethnographic films such as this one frequently featured scenes of encounter with the phonograph. Ethnographic filmmakers were eager to capture (or better: to stage for the camera) the European myth of "first contact." Michael Taussig classifies such an image as displaying the double appeal of the colonial encounter – that is, "the fascination of the Other's fascination with the talking machine."[4] Fatimah Tobing Rony calls it the reassuring "contrast between the Primitive and the Modern."[5] Assenka Okslioff adds the description "the 'myth of the primal encounter' with technology."[6] Most recently, Anette Hoffmann offers a deeper account of the scene of the "first encounter" with the technology of the phonograph as the absolute marking of the "Other," an image that Western archives have avidly preserved.[7] The presence of the phonograph came to index the colonial context of intense contact and its expression of difference in the meeting of two worlds, both culturally and technologically.

If German and Austrian anthropologists and ethnologists enthusiastically embraced the possibilities of the phonograph for ethnographic fieldwork as a means to record language and music, then Germans and Austrians also established an early interest in ethnographic filmmaking through the endeavour to in turn capture this very scene of

Figure I.1. Film still from Rudolf Pöch's *Buschmann spricht in den Phonographen* (1908). © Österreichische Mediathek/Technisches Museum Vienna, Austria.

phonographic recording.[8] One medium served the representation of another. Slightly later films such as the black-and-white short 1912 colonial documentary *Deutsch-Ostafrika: Eine große öffentliche Schule in der Provinz Usambara* (German-East Africa: A big public school in the province Usambara) followed suit.[9] Lasting just four minutes, this film documents several brief scenes of a public school in the German colony of what was German East Africa and is now present-day Tanzania, including a final pairing of shots introduced by the intertitle *"Zur Unterhaltung dient der Phonograph Pathé"* ("The phonograph of the Pathé company takes care of entertainment").[10] In these final shots, the schoolchildren appear to eagerly congregate around a table where white Europeans sit decadently drinking champagne and smoking cigars. Atop the table sits a phonograph. Fully embracing and extending the ideal of a scientific ethnographic film archive championed by the French film pioneer duo Félix-Louis Regnault and Charles Comte with their late nineteenth-century protofilmic chronophotography, Pöch and other German-speaking ethnographers such as Richard Neuhass, Hans Schomburgk, Karl Weule, and Robert Schumann made among the most extensive and well-documented ethnographic documentaries of the early decades of the twentieth century.[11]

The trope of the "first encounter" lived on in subsequent German colonial films of the Weimar period (1918–33). In 1930 two feature-length so-called expedition films were released, Martin Rikli and Rudolf Biebrach's *Am Rande der Sahara* (At the edge of the Sahara) and Gernot Bock-Stieber and Lutz Heck's *Mit Büchse und Lasso durch Afrika* (Through Africa with box and lasso). Both contain documentary footage and therein striking scenes of the "first encounter" in which Indigenous African subjects are captured in shock and awe at the presence of the Western magic box that apparently emits sound ex nihilo.[12] It is safe to say that early colonial propaganda film viewers could not get enough of this iconic scene and filmmakers employed it with great fervour. Even a glance to much later German fiction film shows unyielding enthusiasm for the cinematic manufacturing of the colonial scene of encounter and the phonographic imaginary, as evidenced by Werner Herzog's epic adventure drama *Fitzcarraldo* (West Germany, 1982). In Herzog's film, an aspiring Irish rubber baron and lover of opera living in the Peruvian rainforest at the turn of the twentieth century dreams of one day opening an opera house in the small jungle town of Iquitos. His excessively large phonograph on which he plays the music of the contemporary operatic tenor Enrico Caruso becomes a kind of inanimate sidekick that successfully pacifies the Indigenous tribe on whose land Fitzcarraldo trespasses. According to Taussig, the film is "constructed around the fetish of the phonograph."[13] More specifically, the film is constructed around the fetish of the staging of the encounter of the Indigenous subject with the phonograph, what Lutz Koepnick astutely calls "an act of acoustical colonialism." The phonograph represents "the silencing of ominous native sounds with the help of Western harmony and melody, the taming of wild nature through advanced culture and technology."[14] The German context provides particularly fertile ground for exploring the nexus of the phonograph and film. Writing within the context of German studies, I begin this study with a specific cultural-historical paradigm. The direction of this book does, however, go beyond these national origins.

In many ways, the phonograph became *the* instrument and symbol of ethnography tout court. A famous example within film and documentary studies is Robert J. Flaherty's 1922 *Nanook of the North*, about an Inuk man and his struggles to survive in the Canadian Arctic. This film is often considered the first feature-length documentary film *avant la lettre*.[15] In a notable scene, Nanook visits a trading post to sell his fur pelts to a white man, the fur trader. There he encounters a phonograph, apparently for the first time. In this silent documentary, Nanook appears to listen with an expression of excited disbelief. With pronounced physical agitation, he inspects the machine with great curiosity; then he grasps the record and bites into it, not just once, but three times.[16] "Nanook is shown to be ignorant of Western technology," Rony notes. "This conceit of the indigenous person who does not understand Western technology allows for voyeuristic pleasure and reassures the viewer of the contrast between the Primitive and the Modern."[17] Cinema's archive brims with these scenes. Not only did they deliver voyeuristic pleasure to audiences, these colonial scenes taught audiences where interest and pleasure lie. That early cinema shaped and reinforced how we perceive the world is well established; that it did so in part with the help of the phonograph is a line of thought this book pursues. Critical here is the overlap between colonial systems of knowledge and the development of media.

From a media perspective, filmed scenes with the phonograph also served a reflexive purpose for the audiovisual medium. All of the films put forward in the opening pages of this book provide, at the very least, thematic evidence to support Tom Gunning's claim that if the phonograph changed our perception of the human senses by isolating the ear from the eye, then the goal of early cinema, and one advanced by Thomas Edison in particular, was to reunite them. Gunning described this development as follows:

> First, ... the phonograph was the original instrument of a new sort of reproduction, one that extended and transformed our conception of the human senses by recording them as they occurred in real time, and ... could serve as a model for further similar experiments in recording and reproduction. Secondly, and implicitly, it [the goal of early cinema] indicates that the phonograph had in effect separated the human senses, divorcing ear from eye, and that Edison's original intention in pursuing motion pictures was to bring them back together.[18]

The first recording and playback device, the phonograph provided both a prototype and a motivation for the cinematograph. Cinema thus emerged as a paradox. It drew from the model of the phonograph and simultaneously sought to undo its effects by doubling its invention to include the visual. At first, the attempt to reunite the audio and the visual resulted in a kind of enhanced phonography, or phonography with added visuals.[19] Early attempts to produce synchronized sound cinema through a combination of the phonograph and film ultimately proved unfeasible; symbolic attempts nevertheless evidently endured.[20] With distinct intentions, ethnographic film in particular actively sought to achieve this goal of reunion and did not shy away from reinscribing it in cinema directly. For even the silent film *Nanook of the North* insists on the visual reminder of the power of the technology of the phonograph and its reproduced sound. Its scene with Nanook and the phonograph is the most widely discussed one in commentary and scholarship on the film.

I begin this book by examining the history of early sound reproduction as an instrument of ethnography and colonialism. I put forward a radically sceptical stance on listening, on the basis of which I understand some forms of listening as highly mediated acts shaped by both technology and ideology. The extractive mechanism of listening as ethnographic recording has historically sanctioned the oppressive powers, not least knowledge production, of Euro-American empire. The book then asks how we might begin to disturb this history – how might we decolonize listening? It offers a response in the form of several examples of documentary films released between the mid 1990s and the 2000s, which effectively take up and destabilize the joint histories of colonial listening, recording, and reproduction. If early ethnographic films instrumentalize the phonograph to reproduce the colonizing effect of the first encounter, then the later films call our attention to these colonial entanglements of the phonograph. They furthermore conjure the ghost of the phonograph that haunts cinema history and seek to scramble the logic of such a troubling heritage of the colonial past and its archive. Finally, we are reminded that film is an audiovisual medium and therefore equally as mired in the audio as it is in the visual, and just as dramatically shaped by the ear as by the eye – that is, by listening as well as looking.

This book examines a diverse group of films derived from the twentieth and early twenty-first centuries that directly and critically engage with colonial listening and its sound archives. These films include Madhusree Dutta and Philip Scheffner's *From Here to Here* (Germany/India, 2005), Philip Scheffner's *The Halfmoon Files* (Germany, 2007), Marlon Fuentes's *Bontoc Eulogy* (Philippines/US, 1995), and Adele Horne's *The Tailenders* (US, 2006). All offer a critique of the colonial ear and remarkable means of countering it. To be sure, this body of films is narrow; *A Decolonizing Ear* does not present a movement or even a thematic trend in filmmaking. Yet the work these films do and the qualities that hold them together are also singular. These disparate films produced various years apart come together in their efforts to unsettle the colonial ear and to offer possible methods of decolonizing listening through the filmic medium and especially the documentary mode. What binds them further is their direct recourse to and thematization of the sound archive. If, according to Mèhèza Kalibani, the colonial ear serves as a metonymy for "the acoustic representation and construction of colonized native people by the colonizers," then these films all reflexively reappropriate and repurpose these collected and archived acoustic representations, as a means of turning them on their (colonial) ear.[21] To my knowledge, few other films do this.[22]

There is a plethora of studies on the influence of early ethnography on cinema and the corollary of the ethnographic gaze. Consider Fatimah Tobing Rony's *The Third Eye: Race, Cinema, and Ethnographic Spectacle* (1996), Alison Griffith's *Wondrous Difference: Cinema, Anthropology, and Turn-of-the-Century Visual Culture* (2002), Tobias Nagl's *Die unheimliche Maschine: Rasse und Repräsentation in Weimarer Kino* (2009), Paula Amad's *Counter-Archive: Film, the Everyday, and Albert Kahn's Archives de la Planète* (2010), and Katherine Groo's *Bad Film Histories: Ethnography and Early Film History* (2019). All of these present rich and nuanced studies of early ethnographic cinema and its inextricable adherence to the hegemonic or perpetrator gaze of Western imperialism. In particular, Rony's primary study provides an illuminating point of departure for thinking about how ethnography and the ethnographic spectacle have given form to film and in response how film can subvert this by turning the ethnographic gaze back on itself. "The third eye" is shorthand for the reflexive perception that permits access to a vision of oneself as presented from outside. Rony describes the third eye as "another eye" with which "I see how I am pictured as a landscape, a museum display, an ethnographic spectacle, an exotic."[23] The present study imagines how film can do the same for the ear. In other words, it asks how film can raise the possibility for more reflexive modes of listening. I propose a different kind of listening with what one might call a reimagined "third ear."[24] Here the third ear, or the decolonizing ear, like the third eye, seeks to turn the colonial ear back on itself.

In the German context, Nagl's *Die unheimliche Maschine* first alerted us to the entanglement of colonialism, racialized representation, and film. With a focus on cinema of the Weimar period, Nagl's study proffers a critical dialogue between postcolonial critique, theories of racism and racialization, and film studies. It also opens with an image of technological encounter. "Die unheimliche Maschine" (the uncanny machine) names the image of a man in tribal costume and brandishing a spear and shield looking with great hesitance into a camera mounted on a tripod. Shot on the film set for Joe May's *Die Herrin der Welt* (The mistress of the world, 1919) and featuring an actor in costume, the image was published in the magazine *Illustrierte Filmwoche* in the fall of 1919 and caught the attention of a broad public. Similar to the still from Rudolf Pöch's *Buschmann spricht in den Phonographen*, "Die unheimliche Maschine" presents the problematic Ur-scene of the so-called first encounter between "primitive" body and technologies of representation. Nagl employs this image as a point of entry to broadly critique how such staged and constructed ethnographic images of Indigenous and minoritized bodies subsequently influenced cinematic representations. But similar to Rony he also examines the image for traces of resistance through its potential inversion of the gaze.[25]

But whereas looking, not to mention the technological apparatus of the camera, has traditionally been perceived as an act irrevocably inscribed by power structures, listening has on the whole enjoyed the repute of a more attentive experience underpinned by qualities of reflexivity, relationality, and even empathy. For when we listen, do we not open ourselves up to others? Listening, Jean-Luc Nancy claims, is a methexic exercise of participation and sharing in a collaborative straining towards possible meaning.[26] This putative conviction of listening's unimpacted mode of perception can also be found in film studies. Mary Ann Doane has maintained that through listening the audience may experience the ideological truth of the film, which is often contained within the soundtrack. By contrast, the visual track can mislead the viewer.[27] But listening is not a more immersive and subjective act. Lest we be fooled by the apparently inherent differences between looking and listening, Jonathan Sterne reminds us with his much-cited "audiovisual litany" that it is merely an ideological pursuit and ultimately unproductive to position hearing and seeing as embattled opposites.[28] In his tome *The Audible Past*, arguably the seminal text of sound studies, Sterne demonstrates how listening practices are inherently linked to technological invention and development. Similar to looking, listening shoulders a long history of operational and instrumentalized perception. Putting it bluntly, audition is by no means unmediated, neutral, or candid; it is just as entrenched in cultural, historical, and social practices as looking. To speak of the colonial ear is to evoke a regime of listening that is particularly charged. In theory, the colonial ear bears out over unequal power relations and epistemic violence. In practice, the colonial ear is akin to the ethnographic ear. It listens in the service of knowledge production. This listening frequently entails the use of a recording device. Ethnographers perform colonial listening by way of their machines, recording for dissection, salvage, and accretion. Colonial listening may also play out as the imposition by ethnographers and colonizers alike that the colonized listen to certain reproduced sounds. We might say that the colonial ear, like the phonograph itself, has a three-way function of recording, reproducing, and listening to (reproduced) sound. The methods of the colonial ear are purposeful and informed by the processes of modernity, technological development, and Western hegemony. Oppression and domination frame the act of imposition of the phonograph in this context, insofar as voices are recorded without full and cognizant consensus from the subjects; these voices are then reproduced under the new ownership of the ethnographers, and finally dissected for research purposes or, in some cases, circulation.

Drawing on the capacious field of sound studies, *A Decolonizing Ear* finds influence and insight in recent turns against the whiteness of both sound and sound studies to recognize that the "racialized differences in listening history have a history."[29] In different ways, Ronald Radano, Tejumola Olaniyan, Jennifer Lynn Stoever, Gustavus Stadler, Dylan Robinson, meLê yamomo, Mèhèza Kalibani, and Kira Thurman have alerted us to the imbrications of sound, colonialism, race, and power.[30] In their respective works, these scholars consider how Western empiricism and epistemology have shaped sound as well as what Sterne refers to as "regimes of listening practices."[31] They furthermore examine the extent to which historical methods of sonic recording have played a role in colonial systems of oppression and domination. Robinson characterizes (settler) colonial listening as "hungry listening" – that is, a practice of fevered "consumption for knowledge resources."[32] It participates in the conceit that more knowledge means more power and is predicated on the desire to possess and control all means of listening. According to Robinson, throughout history listening has been instrumentalized as a means of consumption, appropriation, and accretion of knowledge for ethnographers working in the name of empire. Enmeshed in the epistemologies and ontologies of coloniality and modernity, listening becomes a highly mediated and even racialized act. Thus, to decolonize listening, in Robinson's words, "involves becoming no longer sure what LISTENING is."[33] In particular, rethinking listening demands a rethinking of the instruments and tools of listening. Technological modernity not only historically coincided with colonialism and racialized power relations but also facilitated its endeavours, from ethnographic to missionary projects. If, as Gunning claimed, the phonograph isolated the senses, then, as Stadler argues, it also reorganized their capacities in a manner that reformulated and even promulgated power relations and violence.[34]

New studies on the extensive colonial instrumentalization of the phonograph and the massive archivization of its recordings in the German context offer further significant contributions to this broader politically resonant turn in sound studies. Britta Lange's opus *Gefangene Stimmen: Tonaufnahmen von Kriegsgefangenen aus dem Lautarchiv 1915–1918* (Captured voices: Sound recordings of prisoners of war from the Sound Archive 1915–1918), which appeared in 2019, serves as both an authority and a critical guide for the present study. Through an intensive scrutiny of the collection of the Königliche Preußische Phonographische

Kommission (Royal Prussian Phonographic Commission, hereafter RPPC) at prisoner-of-war camps in Germany, Lange's book carefully weaves media history with archival studies and sound studies. (To a large extent, the collection comprises recordings made in prisoner-of-war camps designated for colonial soldiers.) She brings these more contemporary disciplinary insights to bear on German colonial history and likewise broadly expands the discursive significance of Germany in the history of sound and sound reproduction. As indicated earlier, German ethnographers maintained a keen investment in the phonograph as a tool of colonial encounter. But the medium itself also generated wide general public interest. From 1900 to 1933, the German-language magazine *Phonographische Zeitschrift* (Phonographic Journal) was published in Berlin and circulated throughout Germany, Austria-Hungary, and beyond. It launched as the "Offizielles Organ des internationalen Vereins für phonographisches Wissen" (official organ of the International Society for Phonographic Knowledge) with the aim to celebrate the invention of the phonograph and its promising utility for the progress of culture.[35] In his foundational article on the phonograph and the history of sound reproduction at the turn of the twentieth century, Eric Ames also draws our attention to the central position of Germany in this evolution. Modernity and sound critically collide in this cultural context.[36]

Germany's first sound archive was the Berliner Phonogramm-Archiv (Berlin Phonogram Archive).[37] Initiated as one of only two of its kind (the other established in Vienna in 1899) at the turn of the twentieth century in 1900 by Carl Stumpf, this archive still holds roughly 16,700 wax cylinder recordings and remains one of the largest and most fully preserved autonomously maintained sound archives of phonographic recordings in the world.[38] Although similar archives with an emphasis on sound recordings were subsequently established in St. Petersburg (1903), in Paris (1911), and in Budapest (1914), none matched the significance and capacity of the Berlin one.[39] The Phonogramm-Archiv comprises mostly recordings of traditional music hailing in large part from Germany's former colonies on the African continent and in the South Seas and extracted primarily between 1900 and 1914.[40] Given the nature of its holdings, in the 1930s the archive came under the wing of the Ethnological Museum of Berlin.

Some recordings made by the RPPC, whose collection serves as an important example for the present study, were absorbed into the Phonogramm-Archiv. These included the musical recordings made in the prisoner-of-war camps. But the vast portion of the RPPC collection formed the basis for what was later to become the Lautarchiv der Humboldt Universität zu Berlin (the sound archive of Humboldt University), affiliated with the Hermann von Helmholtz-Zentrum für Kulturtechnik and established first in 1920 as the Lautabteilung (sound department) attached to the Prussian State Library.[41] The holdings of the Lautarchiv consist chiefly of the speech recordings extracted by the RPPC in the prisoner-of-war camps. These recordings are supplemented with voice portraits of famous figures and European folk music.[42] Both the Phonogramm-Archiv and the Lautarchiv have convoluted histories, which frequently overlap. Jointly constituting the world's largest historical sound collection, these sound archives proffer both a crucial starting place and a collective register for comparison and assessment.

It stands to reason that any scholar in pursuit of the history of sound and sound recording, especially the imbrications of sound, ethnography, colonialism, and power, might perforce begin in Germany, or at the very least eventually find their way there.[43] By virtue of the cinematic objects my own study pursues, which come from far afield geographically, it will move beyond models of the national so rigorously defended by the project of recording, reproducing, and listening practised under the colonial regime. However, the book's pursuit of other horizons should not be read as part of a linear historical progress narrative from the national to the universal. As Thomas Elsaesser has taught us, in any discussion of cinema today we must look both ways: into the future as well as into the past.[44] Germany is not so much a point of origin as it is an important place of cultural, historical and, especially, conceptual reflection. In criss-crossed fashion, this reflection commences in that provenance of many a thought, story, and debate – the archive.

From the (Colonial) Archive

In order to trace the origins of ethnographic sound recording and its archivization as heard through film, we must begin by attending to the archive and its contents. By no means an arbitrary starting place, the Lautarchiv and its RPPC collection are paradigmatic as both entity and concrete institution, not to mention their direct treatment in two of the four films I examine at length in this book.[45] This archive provides an unprecedented and unmatched example of the creation and preservation of sound recordings orchestrated by colonial and military encounters. At the same time, the emblematic themes the Lautarchiv raises provide an instructive conceptual model of colonial listening that extends beyond its own historical and geographical context. By closely examining the formation of the Lautarchiv, we begin to grasp the complex set of ideologies underpinning such an institution. This knowledge guides us to a more general understanding of any colonial sound archive, as it has also emerged in other cultural, geographical, and historical contexts, as an examination of my corpus of films will demonstrate.

As a highly discursive topic, the archive introduces its own rubric of analysis. Already thrown into question in the 1960s with Michel Foucault's radically groundbreaking study *The Archaeology of Knowledge*, the archive has for decades been a contested site of epistemology and power. In the 1990s Jacques Derrida's brief theoretical treatise *Archive Fever* alerted us to the potential of the archive as more than just a dusty repository for official documents classified and ordered together in the service of historiography. More than any other thinker, Derrida maintained the revolutionary potential of the archive alongside the traditional.[46] Do we not continue to feverishly return to the archive in the hope of stumbling upon hidden insights and pieces of unsanctioned knowledge that may have slipped through the grids of order and cracks in intelligibility? We repeatedly search for the aberrances that might point towards other histories. Certainly, the archive cannot be all bad; it often holds as many subversive secrets as it does officialese.

Yet the colonial archive, any colonial archive, is heartily invested in the enterprise of fiction-making and the repression, concealment, and even destruction of evidence. Tackling its obscene obstructions often presents a grave challenge, not least the struggle of detaching oneself from its epistemological vortex. With effort, though, even the colonial archive, to which this book turns, seems to disclose the promise of unexpected yields hiding in its margins. In her study of the Dutch colonial archive, Ann Laura Stoler enjoins the reader not to dismiss the colonial archive but to examine it "along its grain." In Stoler's view, the colonial archive is but the comprisal of "unsure and hesitant sorts of documentation."[47] Clustering fragments of events and bits of information that often do not fit together, the colonial archive, or any archive for that matter, cannot escape what Helen Freshwater describes as the "disquiet and anxieties" of its own arbitrary accretion.[48] Try as it might, the archive cannot write history. Its objects can only be interpreted and reinterpreted; from this site we can fetch mere "partial and provisional truths."[49] This posed a dilemma for colonial dogma because, as Stoler contends, "epistemic uncertainties repeatedly unsettled the imperial conceit that all was in order."[50] Thus, reading along the archival grain permits a perspective of the colonial archive that at least speculatively belies its own ideals of empire. Indeed, the grain is a metaphor for the granular or rough surface of historical events whose frictions cannot be smoothed over.[51] Rather than assuming a position against the grain or against the archive, Stoler encourages us to enter into its "field of force" in order to learn and to understand its inconsistencies.

Despite the felicitous metaphoric parallel that can be drawn between the grain and the grooves of a wax recoding, a practice of reading along the archival grain still requires a palpable extension in the context of the sound archive, where the act of reading documents and literature passes over into listening. This brings us to what Anette Hoffmann and Britta Lange conceptualize as a mode of "close listening."[52] By way of listening closely to the colonial sound archive, one becomes attuned to all the various sounds that get recorded and stored, both intentional and not. Hoffmann's formulation is instructive here: "[Close listening] entails the attempt to grasp as many as possible of the audible features of a recording: for instance, the sound of a pitch pipe (that indicates the speed at which the recording should rotate), the noise of a rotating cylinder or scratched record, the recordist's announcement (the 'acoustic tag'), the language and genre of speech or song (if identifiable), the features of the voice of the speaker and singer, accent, pauses, background noises – in short, *everything* one can hear on a recording."[53] In practice, close listening follows the path of New Criticism's exegetic close reading, but it is also distinct. As the above quote by Hoffmann demonstrates and Lange also clarifies, close listening means listening to as well as beyond the spoken or sung text of the recording to all dimensions of what can be heard, even if those sounds form the noise that would appear to disrupt the speech of the voice.[54] These background noises, which filter through in all manner of timbres and hums, demand our attention. Noises of the machine and noises of the speaker are not dissimilar to the frictions of the archive of which Stoler speaks. Close listening to the colonial sound archive registers the intense contact and interaction within the context of unequal power relations at the site of recording and knowledge production. While much research exists on the topic of the archive, the scholarship that makes up the body of research on the sound archive is still relatively narrow. Hoffmann and Lange's approach to the sound archive is foundational and offers a significant point of departure and sustained engagement for the present study and for my own thinking through a method of decolonial listening.

It is impossible to attend to the matter of the colonial archive in the contemporary German context without addressing the subject of the Humboldt Forum and the surrounding debates regarding its ostensibly revisionist treatment of German colonial history. While not directly situated within this discourse, in its intervention in the sovereign violence of the colonial archive the present study does implicitly contribute to it.[55] Indeed, the transfer of the sound recording collections to this new storehouse in the centre of the German capital places new conditions and imperatives on these objects, their representation, accessibility, and historical positioning. But at this point it is too early to tell what the implications of this rehousing will be.

Media Archaeology and Listening

A turn to the multimedia archive precipitates a turn to the methods of media archaeology. Foucault pursued a method of archaeology in the archive of documents in an effort to define discourses in their specificity and rules of practice.[56] What he proposed is that the historical document in the archive is not simply an inert trace of things once said and done but the very discursive material that structures what we can know.[57] If documents no longer simply reflect history but instead set the very conditions for thought and knowledge as emergent discourses, they disturb the smooth teleology of history founded on a single domain of rationality and form a multiplicity of decentred relations.[58] The media archaeologist follows in Foucault's discursive footsteps. In many ways the pioneer of the field of media archaeology, Friedrich Kittler sought to examine technical media the same way Foucault read the written material of the archives as discrete in their influences and discursive capacities.[59] Media archaeology is against reading media history as some kind of story of progress. Broadly put, media archaeology plumbs the cultural and technological layers of past media to develop a fuller picture of the present. But while Foucault and Kittler are two of the most influential and foundational theorists of the field, media archaeology and its practices travel in many different directions. Attempting to manage the ambit of this heterogeneous discipline, Jussi Parikka enumerates four main themes of media archaeology: "(1) modernity, (2) cinema, (3) histories of the present, and (4) alternative histories."[60] These are useful guideposts as I establish my own pursuit of a media archaeological method.

Following the insights of Wolfgang Ernst in particular, media archaeology not only accompanies the present project back to the sound archive with the objective of uncovering both its materiality and the broader context of the emergence of sound recording, but through the layer of film it also listens intently to the noise of the machines that have provided these recordings. The shift away from visual regimes in favour of acoustic ones is central to Ernst's more recent work. In his words, "after the *acoustic turn* and in an age of technically augmented sonospheres, the cold gaze needs to be supplemented by 'unpassionate listening': listening to the musicality not only emerging from, but taking place *within*, technomathematical media."[61] Ernst's process of close listening thus entails an agonistic attunement to the buzzes, hisses, and hums of media and their machines, an attunement that in turn gives rise to a technological understanding over a cultural or semantic one. But what may appear to be a truncated approach – for what ultimately comes of simply listening to machines? – is in truth a much more complex one. In the case of the films in focus in the later chapters of this study, listening to the machines of the sound archive matters because it reveals the discursive conditions of archival practices of the period. The media archaeological ear in the sound archive draws attention to what Ernst calls the "overriding multimedia practice of global classification, data processing, and information storage leading to early twentieth-century efforts to create a universal science of cultural documentation."[62] In other words and in the context of the present study, the media archaeological ear incites us to consider both the medium specificity of the first recording and playback sound device, the phonograph, and its taxonomic corollary, the sound archive.

Notwithstanding media archaeologists' scrutiny of the past, they should not be mistaken for media historians. In true Foucauldian spirit, the media archaeologist digs up events of the past through their amplification in the present, typically through digital media. If the phonograph brings dead voices to life, digitalization subsequently unfreezes them.[63] Thawing the analogue voices recorded onto wax cylinders at the turn of the twentieth century evokes Jay David Bolter and Richard Grusin's much-cited concept of remediation and its method of repurposing analogue media through new media.[64] If Tom Gunning reads cinema as the reunion of sight and sound, historically rent asunder by the invention of the phonograph, and the early visualizations of the phonograph on film pay tribute to this, then Bolter and Grusin's theory of remediation proposes a more contemporary reunion of media. However, remediation's goal of wresting a sense of liveness and presence through its layering of old and new media sneaks around the codes of media archaeology, for which mediation and processes of remediation are both means *and* ends. While neither media archaeology, nor remediation for that matter, demand a turn to the audiovisual medium of film, certainly this direction facilitates the collective possibilities of awakening analogue voices. Bringing these methodologies into dialogue with film does not present a theoretical sleight of hand, but it does call for a discursive enrichening in attention to the matter of colonial sound recording and listening. Not surprisingly, these media theories do not hold questions of race and power steadily in view. Therefore, I bring them into dialogue with postcolonial and decolonial discourses and reimagine new theoretical relations and collaborations.

Film and the Sound Archive: Towards a Method of Decolonial Listening

As the examples provided at the start of this chapter demonstrate, sites of colonial listening may be perpetuated, remediated, and even performed through film. To be sure, there are just as many, perhaps even more, instances of colonial listening in film as there are instances of decolonial listening, even in the periods from which the examples of decolonial listening in this study derive, namely the late twentieth and early twenty-first centuries. Consider for instance Dietrich Schüller's 1984 treatment of Rudolf Pöch's *Buschmann spricht in den Phonographen*, which does not attempt to critically rework the original material as a means of confronting its colonial heritage, but instead simply synchronizes the moving image with the near-incoherent original sound, taken simultaneously by Pöch himself with separate recording machines.[65] Film certainly does not present an inherently decolonial medium. But many documentary filmmakers do tackle the colonial archive with the aim of laying bare or altering the intentionality of visual and audiovisual materials through appropriation and reconfiguration. Archive-based films, or films produced through what Catherine Russell calls a process of "archiveology," entail the "reus[ing], recycling, appropriation, and borrowing of archival material." These have long been products of a practice of filmmaking that imagines and reimagines objects of collective memory and history at the reconstruction site of the archive in the twenty-first century.[66] Thus, while not an unambiguous medium of decolonizing, film can do things with archival material that few other media can. Just as the archive itself is volatile, not fixed to one particular assignment of meaning or historiography, filming the archive always introduces a new site of possible narration or agitation. Jaimie Baron captures this spirit of volatility, even fugitivity, well:

> Although the archive and its contents are constantly changing, at any given instant the archive is static, waiting for someone to enter and appropriate particular documents and put them into motion, giving them a direction or an intentionality in order to articulate some idea about or relationship to the historical past. Every film that is made and preserved also becomes part of the archive, awaiting new (and frequently unanticipated) use. The freedom to continually use and reuse archival documents means we will never determine a stable, objective truth about the past, but it is that freedom that makes the archive a site not only of repression and limitation but also of possibility.[67]

The power of filming the archive is not simply a matter of recontextualization. According to Baron, filming the archive puts it in motion. Is the medium of film not a medium of motion? Through motion, film gives the archive direction. This direction in turn articulates a relationship between the past and the present. Left untouched and static, the archive maintains a hegemony and its link to the ideological endeavours that first brought it into existence. It remains a conservative bulwark true to its etymology, the Greek *arkhē*, the principle "in the order of commencement as well as in the order of commandment," as Derrida reminds us.[68] When the archive is taken up through film, dust flies; in this eddy of dust the law and order of the archive become disrupted.

Unsettling the law and order of the colonial archive can be a particularly political and significant act of filmmaking. There are many examples of postcolonial films that appropriate colonial ethnographic photographs and footage in an effort to present another message. Most famous is perhaps Dutch filmmaker Vincent Monnikendam's compilation documentary *Moeder Dao, de schildpadgelijkende* (Mother Dao, the turtlelike; 1995). This 35 mm film compiles ninety minutes of found footage of documentary and propaganda films made between 1912 and 1933 in the former Dutch colony of Indonesia. It continues to garner attention as a masterpiece in compilation filmmaking, receiving wide regard and praise. Appropriated and re-edited together with an original soundtrack, the repurposed silent footage performs a counternarrative and a different kind of historiography that challenges the regime of the colonial archive and its epistemes. Another, though less known, example is Gustav Deutsch's *Welt Spiegel Kino* (World mirror cinema; Austria, 2005), which similarly employs footage made in colonial Indonesia and plucked from the Netherlands' vast accrual of artifacts. The audiovisual valences of film provide opportunities for creative subversion. Yet more frequently than not, archive-based appropriation films with an anticolonial purport, such as *Moeder Dao, de schildpadgelijkende*, rely on visual materials as opposed to audio ones. Part of the reason for this is availability of material, but it also hinges on the perception of images and visual material as more ideologically inscribed than audio recordings and therefore more salient as evidence both of colonial devastation and of archival suppression that must be worked through.

Ariella Aïsha Azoulay proposes that image-making under colonialism constitutes "a petty sovereign."[69] The image stands in for the entire colonial enterprise and its afterlife. In Azoulay's words, the image "commands what sort of things have to be distanced, bracketed, removed, forgotten, suppressed, overcome, and made irrelevant for the shutter of the camera to function, as well as for a photograph to be taken, and its meaning accepted."[70] In the audiovisual context, the decolonial treatment of the archival image demands a careful balancing act of reframing without repeating injury through decontextualization or further exploitation. The task of approaching the archival sound recordings through the decolonizing ear in film must similarly work against the constitutional elements of the "petty sovereign," albeit through a different medial process. While this book does not spend significant time on comparing the afterlives of the colonial image and the colonial audio recording in decolonial films, Azoulay's description of the colonial image is illuminating in its medium specificity and merits further thought here. The operation of the shutter of the camera, she claims, is to decide what will be shown and what should be cut out of the frame, including the traces of the operation itself. Sound, on the other hand, cannot be isolated in the same way. The image is always framed, but there is no auditory container.[71] Certainly, at the turn of the twentieth century sound recordings made on a phonograph were not what they might be today. Amplification and even post-recording editing were not possible, or at least very difficult to achieve. Thus, unlike photography or even silent film footage, the likelihood of error was significant. As I will discuss in subsequent chapters, the audio recordings I consider contain both the slips of inadvertent sounds as well as background and machinic noise. Unforeseen words and extralinguistic resonances flood the recordings. Especially over time, the deterioration of these recordings surrenders to the crackling and static that further impede the intended recorded message. Paying close attention to these "unintended" sounds, which could not be contained or excised from the machinic operation of colonial ethnography, opens up novel layers of meaning, knowledge, and experience.

I want to be careful not to suggest that the very products of colonialism and colonial ethnography can be decolonized through their remediation. As we have learned from Eve Tuck and K. Wayne Yang, "decolonization is not a metaphor" and therefore should not be arbitrarily applied to the treatment of objects whose afterlife has no direct political bearing.[72] Instead, *A Decolonizing Ear* points us to films that at the very least question colonial historiography and the authority of the archive, and perhaps even offer radical and creative interventions. These films create sites for unsettling colonial artifacts through their misappropriation and misemployment. Erstwhile intentions are rejected, and with them the regimes of listening that developed alongside hand in glove. In keeping with the insight of decolonial scholars such as Frantz Fanon, Aníbal Quijano, Walter Mignolo, and Catherine Walsh, the site of film as I propose it here as a possible site of decolonizing must be one of complete upheaval of order, all the way to the systems and production of knowledge. If these archived ethnographic sound recordings served as instruments of knowledge production, then listening to them in different ways – that is, in ways unintended by ethnographers and the archons, those keepers of the archive, alike – has the potential to produce other kinds of awareness and knowledge. Throughout, I explore how ethnographic listening was operationally shaped by colonial politics and ideologies of both Western superiority and the unfettered pursuit of knowledge acquisition. Thus, listening for the disruptive, inadvertent sounds – the noise and the inevitable errata of speech deployments – not subsumed under ethnographic categories becomes a means of listening differently, and even decolonially. This is the pursuit of the films explored in this book.

A Decolonizing Ear brings together some exceedingly distinct documentary films. To be abundantly clear, the goal is not to introduce and constitute a new (sub)genre or trend in filmmaking of sound archive-based films. Instead, this study has sought out documentary films that reflexively engage with ethnographic audio recordings and their colonial context as a means of challenging the way Western auditors have been colonially conditioned to listen through the audiovisual medium. Although the study begins in Germany, the films do not all have this cultural and direct historical connection. I began with Indian filmmaker Madhusree Dutta and German filmmaker Philip Scheffner's *From Here to Here* and Scheffner's *The Halfmoon Files* and then asked which other films do something similar. To date, there are not many films that do this kind of archival listening work, but the ones that do are complexly rich and exhilaratingly diverse. Marlon Fuentes's *Bontoc Eulogy* and Adele Horne's *The Tailenders* are US-made documentary films that interrogate different US-colonial sound archives and contexts. However, their grouping is by no means arbitrary; they engage in analogous material treatment of colonial listening. By dint of this comparative study, we also gain new insights into each of these films. These titles may have never been examined together in a singular study before, but here they present a significant aggregate of archive-based films that challenge the sound archive and its colonial underpinnings. These films alert us to how sound and listening have been shaped by a long history of unequal power relations. They alert us to our own conditioned listening.

Referencing the documentary mode provides a means of loosely grouping the films, but they also stretch the boundaries of documentary. Slippery objects, these films do not directly subscribe to standard filmic categories, genres, or modes. *From Here to Here* is an experimental video, *The Halfmoon Files* follows an essayistic mode, *Bontoc Eulogy* has been called a mockumentary or docudrama, while *The Tailenders* might be viewed as a more conventional documentary that plays with expository and poetic modes. Wonderfully open, capacious, and unimposing in its apparent "clumsiness," documentary as a category nonetheless provides some disciplinary uniformity and guidance, not to mention a rich range of scholarship from which to draw.[73] On the strength of their heterodox nature, all of the films considered in later chapters are formally reflexive. They further undermine the expectations of documentary voice-over (in each case provided by the respective filmmaker) by playing with the authority of the all-knowing, male, unaccented voice. These films take for granted neither the audiovisual medium nor the operational edicts of documentary cinema. Unlike early ethnographic documentaries, which exploited the trope of the first contact of phonographic listening and recording, these films take this scene to task in different ways. Their interventional nature bleeds from content to form, if we can still speak in these dualistic terms. Filming the colonial sound archives, *From Here to Here*, *The Halfmoon Files*, *Bontoc Eulogy*, and *The Tailenders* are models of unconventional listening. They also spur reperceptions of film as an *audio*visual medium.

When I began this project, it was unclear what direction it would take; I therefore would tell people simply that I am interested in sinister listening. I would follow up with the clarification that this posits a purposeful mode of audition that objectifies and exploits speaking subjects. Most people I spoke to had trouble with this concept. Is listening not a passive and receptive undertaking, not to mention a gesture of openness and possible vulnerability? Then the conversation would veer towards eavesdropping, that auditory surreptitious keyhole-peeking. Through this example, my interlocutors could begin to understand sinister listening. Given my own area of study as a Germanist, the conversation would quickly turn to the infamous East German Ministry for State Security (Stasi) surveillance machine. Yes, a focus on listening as surveillance, that makes sense, they would concede. In connection with film, the conversation easily moved to popular features. They asked: so, will you be taking up Florian Henckel von Donnersmarck's *Das Leben der Anderen* (The lives of others; Germany, 2006), or perhaps even its famous Hollywood precursor, Francis Ford Coppola's *The Conversation* (US, 1974)? As a result of these conversations, I paused several times at this passage from Jacques Attali's *Noise: The Political Economy of Music*: "Eavesdropping, censorship, recording, and surveillance are weapons of power. The technology of listening in on, ordering, transmitting, and recording noise is at the heart of this apparatus. The symbolism of the Frozen Words, of the Tables of the Law, of recorded noise and eavesdropping – these are the dreams of political scientists and the fantasies of men in power: to listen, to memorize – this is the ability to interpret and control history, to manipulate the culture of a people, to channel its violence and hopes."[74] In particular, the final line of this passage struck a chord. Listening can sustain the power to interpret and control history. While I was not given over to the idea of including the Stasi in my study, nor audio surveillance for that matter, these initial conversations and my own discovery of Attali and his innovative writing on noise did motivate me to think about how colonial listening could at least conceptually compare to eavesdropping by the state. Controlling sound and sound production similarly lies at the heart of colonial listening. Mainly, I drew from these conversations the message that there is a lack of a broader discourse regarding the topic of listening with pernicious – or at the very least questionable – intentions. Even the language to address the topic is absent. There is no equivalent to "gaze" for audition. The "colonial *ear*" must suffice as a signifier of auditory power, control, and subjectivity. With *A Decolonizing Ear*, I hope to contribute to this evolving discourse. I must recognize, however, that this project of decolonizing is not about restitution; rather, it is about unlearning. As a white scholar born and raised in Canada and now based in the United States, my own unlearning has been a critical part of this project.

The lack of clarity accompanying this project was heightened with the planned transfer of the collections formerly contained within the Lautarchiv to the Humboldt Forum starting in 2018, and it exploded with the onset of the global pandemic in 2020. Both events severely restricted access to the archive. In the end, I was unable to perform any significant on-site archival work. I twisted fate to my advantage and developed a project that instead specifically turns to and learns from film. Challenging putative models of listening that have long favoured immersion, sincerity, and empathy, film teaches us how to listen reflexively and critically. In other words, it teaches us how to unlearn dominant practices of listening conditioned by colonial history.

A Note on Composition and Summary of Chapters

A Decolonizing Ear is thematically divided in two parts. The first two chapters serve as a historical and methodological grounding for the subsequent three chapters, which in turn offer close examinations of the films. To begin, I focus my historical scope on the Lautarchiv, for several reasons. First, as one of two internationally significant (colonial) sound archives in Berlin, the Lautarchiv remains fully preserved and operational. Second, the conditions under which the vast majority of the voice recordings of this sound archive were made are well documented and paradigmatic in terms of their colonial, scientific, and military entanglements. Finally, despite its scheduled physical move to the Humboldt Forum, the Lautarchiv's collections will remain independent and unabsorbed by the registers of other museum or national archive holdings. The US-American archives treated in the films *Bontoc Eulogy* and *The Tailenders* are shaped by similar politics and ideologies but are institutionally either scattered or private and narrow. Given their inaccessibility, scant research exists on their histories and holdings. An examination of the Lautarchiv and its features is no arbitrary endeavour, but one from which we may begin to think more broadly about the origins, development, and discursive contribution of any colonial sound archive. Overall, the book and its various parts pursue a balance between the important conceptual similarities of the films in contribution to the broader arc of practices of decolonizing listening and the films' own unique cultural and historical contexts.

Chapter 1 introduces the reader to the formation of a sound archive through the example of the Lautarchiv and its largest collection, the yields of the RPPC during the First World War. Under the direction of Wilhelm Doegen, the goal of the RPPC was to create an archive containing audio recordings of all the languages of the world. With its massive project to record the voices of prisoners of war distributed throughout the numerous camps in Germany, the RPPC exemplifies the colonial drive of appropriation and accrual. The greater part of the recordings was made at colonial prisoner-of-war camps, where colonial soldiers from the Belgian, British, French, and Russian armies were interned. Intensifying this colonial context of violence and unequal power relations was the inescapable reality of war and with it the influence of militarized imprisonment. Colonialism and militarism formed a formidable set of circumstances that served to benefit the researchers. By way of this paradigmatic example, chapter 1 pursues a historical and conceptual analysis of colonial listening that is meant to provide footing for subsequent chapters. It takes broad strokes. We begin in the period of German protocolonialism and with the early rumblings of the colonial ear found in the private journals of eighteenth-century thinker and explorer Alexander von Humboldt. From there, a jump to the disciplinary beginnings of ethnomusicology in Europe takes us to the late nineteenth century and its contemporaneous development with early field ethnography in North America. Finally, the media honing of the colonial ear transpires with the invention of Edison's phonograph in 1877. The latter part of this chapter delves into the discursive breadth of the archive more broadly. From the foundational theoretical writings of Michel Foucault and Jacques Derrida to the work of more contemporary authors, the "archival turn" in scholarship has diverted our attention from the nation-based, unifying structures of the archive to a complex and contingent set of epistemes.

If chapter 1 explores the long history and politics of colonial listening, then chapter 2 asks what can be done to counter this legacy. Bringing together exceedingly different theories and practices, chapter 2 delineates a methodology of decolonizing listening that will be brought to bear on the primary objects of *A Decolonizing Ear*: the films. The insight of Britta Lange and Anette Hoffmann's concept of close listening and Ann Laura Stoler's supplication to "read along the archival grain" – that is, to not dismiss the colonial archive outright but to engage it – serve as a significant starting place. We begin in the archive. But throughout its pages, this chapter puts forth a more radical approach to the sound archive that finds inspiration in the discourse of decoloniality and its call for absolute upheaval, in particular in the way knowledge systems are created. Walter Mignolo famously describes this process as the epistemological "delinking" from the colonial matrix of power.[75] Decolonial listening entails a delinking from the structures of knowledge that have long conditioned the way we perceive sound. Dylan Robinson has powerfully conceptualized normative listening as "hungry listening," the auditory encounter premised on power and acquisition. How can we disrupt hungry listening? Robinson's theory follows closely with practice. A turn to the insurgent strategies of Indigenous artists and their media practices of decolonizing listening provides unexpected but compelling points of tangency. However, the methodology that this chapter lays out settles in an even more unexpected place. The field of media archaeology offers the instructive bridge to a thinking about decolonizing listening and the sound archive through film and media. Media archaeology accounts for what Jussi Parikka refers to as the "epistemic thresholds" of media inception and operation.[76] Here I draw on the illuminations of thinkers such as Siegfried Zielinski, Thomas Elsaesser, and especially Wolfgang Ernst to imagine a mode of media repurposing that adds new layers to Jay David Bolter and Richard Grusin's widely circulated concept of remediation, specifically one that applies to the repurposing of analogue sound recordings in digital (or at least more recent) audiovisual media as a means of both epistemically and materially interrogating the former. The question becomes not simply what we can do about these media artifacts – these bad objects – that derive from colonial ethnography, but additionally what traces of resistance do they already contain? An audiovisual repurposing of these sound recordings brings into relief moments of medial resistance against hegemonic historiography and archival logic.

The chapters that follow respond to the question of how film can be a tool for the decolonization of listening and the sound archive. Chapter 3 is the first of three to treat specific films. Serving as a transition in thinking from the more general to the particular, this chapter takes as its objects of study Madhusree Dutta and Philip Scheffner's shorter film *From Here to Here* and Scheffner's feature-length film *The Halfmoon Files*. Made just two years apart, both films explore the Lautarchiv and the collection amassed by the RPPC. They concentrate on the recordings extracted from the prisoners in the Halbmondlager (hereafter, Halfmoon camp) situated in Wünsdorf, just outside of Berlin. This camp was of particular interest to the RPPC because it interned a diverse group of colonial prisoners of war from the Indian subcontinent and North Africa and was the site from which the largest group of recordings in the collection hailed. Both films focus on the recording of the prisoner Mall Singh, whose identity and fate present a mystery. However, I read this focus as more a point of departure for a broader exploration of the colonial sound archive and its properties. *From Here to Here* and *The Halfmoon Files* are attuned to the recalcitrant effects of noise. Resonating in pervasive hisses and crackles from the early technology of the phonographic record, noise not only indexes the historicity of the recording in its sustained shaping of the listening experience, but also interrupts. If the intention of the ethnographers was to create a crisp and decipherable recording, then the noise of the machine becomes a nuisance. This nuisance resists. As Jacques Attali reminds us, noise bears a rupturing quality.[77] Both films draw this out. In *The Halfmoon Files* the noise of the machine meets the inadvertent noises of the voice. Scheffner presents the coughs, sighs, guffaws, and echolalic utterances of prisoners that trouble the "purity" of the recording. Through the experimental strategies of *From Here to Here* and *The Halfmoon Files*, the colonial sound archive transforms into a reverberating anarchive of noise.

Developing from the insights established in a study of the Lautarchiv and its audiovisual treatment through Dutta and Scheffner's films, chapter 4 turns its attention to the US-American context and various archival spaces. Still, the conceptual framework of the sound archive set in motion in chapter 1 becomes instructive in a close analysis of Marlon Fuentes's personalized docudrama *Bontoc Eulogy* and its handling of the colonial sound archive. Indeed, the broader context of colonial listening opens up new aspects of this film. With the colonization of the Philippines by the United States in the early part of the twentieth century and the closely following St. Louis World's Fair of 1904 as its historical backdrop, this film tells the story of an Igorot native's coerced travel to the United States, where he was exhibited to the paying masses as an exotic spectacle in a zoo. Fuentes, himself a Philippine diasporic subject living in the United States, narrates these events as the grandson of this Indigenous man, Markod. His melancholy voice-over guides the viewer through vast archival materials given as evidence of a devastating colonial period in the Philippines. Pivotal to this narration are the ethnographic wax cylinder recordings of his grandfather's voice. Although we learn that these recordings were reproduced by the filmmaker, their indexical effect remains remarkably intact. But their taint of the false is also operational. Their reproduction stages new encounters with history and memory in an act of self-determination. Fuentes calls upon ethnographic methods to create his own autoethnography, what Françoise Lionnet refers to as "an allegory of the ethnographic project" that does not shy away from the employment of fiction as a means to evoke colonial ethnography's own vortex of fictions and falsehoods, in particular its salvage paradigm.[78] Indigenous cultures and languages have long been operatively perceived by ethnographers as near extinct. If ethnographic sound recordings were made under the directive that Indigenous languages must be preserved before they disappear, then the reproduction and remediation of these sound recordings as part of a self-narrative in this film counter this practice by playing with and effectively invalidating the detrimental claim of salvage ethnography.

The final chapter explores Adele Horne's *The Tailenders*. A documentary about the still-active evangelical missionary organization the Gospel Recordings Network (GRN), this film ushers the study's attention to oppressive listening regimes and audio recording directly into the present. Similarly tackling the ideological and conceptual underpinnings of the colonial sound archive, the film takes us to the private and theological US-based archive of the GRN. It demonstrates the continuity of colonial listening, which is not just a thing of the past but a process that casts its long shadow into the present. *The Tailenders* tracks how missionaries enlist speakers to read scripts of biblical stories translated into their native tongues. The voices of these speaking subjects are recorded for the threefold operational purpose of accretion into the (master) archive, replication, and dissemination to new converts. Recordings serve to reach different language speakers the world over and to recruit them as new converts to Christianity. The GRN comes into focus through Horne's film for its creative and technological approach to evangelizing. While missionary movements have long worked with local languages as a means of conveying their message through a familiar medium, the GRN raised the efficacy of this project through the absolute manifestation of what Horne refers to as "the syncretism of technology and Protestantism."[79] The film draws out and repurposes the audio recordings of the GRN and many of its strange but fascinating ultra-low-tech devices designed to play the recordings anywhere in the world, even in the absence of electricity and batteries. I call these sonic objects "weird machines" and explore how the film's attunement to these weird machines as playful gadgetry ultimately subverts their intended purpose of spreading the word of God. Without our paying heed to their didactic messages, the presence and operation of these machines beckon us (and the filmmaker) to contemplate the power of the disembodied voice they emit. The balance of the final chapter takes up the haunting and reflexive question of the disembodied voice and its instrumentalization, through both evangelism and the documentary film medium itself. How does the disembodied voice of the remediated recordings compare to the "voice-of-God" narration of the filmmaker? Unequal power relations continue to assert their presence in the afterlives of unmoored voices. The question of the disembodied voice sneaks throughout this book and finally comes to form in this final chapter. Here I close with a more comprehensive discussion of the documentary film medium, its history, and the significance of the voice in its emergence and singularity.

Finally, in a brief conclusion, I return to the impulses set forth in this introduction and followed through in the course of this book. Raising the main points, challenges, and insights of investigating colonial listening, I reiterate the aims of advancing the Lautarchiv and the RPPC collection as a "paradigmatic entity," to borrow Mike Featherstone's expression, and how this entity is taken up in direct and indirect ways in the films.[80] This conclusion also seeks to synthesize the scholarly gains of *A Decolonizing Ear* in particular for film and sound studies. A coda concludes the book with an ultimate turn towards some of the installation work of sound artist Lawrence Abu Hamdan. Distinct from film but still unassailably audiovisual, Abu Hamdan's creative interrogation of the instrument of "Language Analysis for the Determination of Origin" (LADO) used in asylum cases signals the continuity of colonial listening in our contemporary world as a sinister afterlife that keeps on living.

Chapter One

Colonial Listening and the Making of a Sound Archive

Colonial listening challenges popular perceptions of listening as an activity or method that opens up radical empathy and understanding. Listening to each other, we are often told, provisions an encounter that nurtures true communication insofar as it places speakers and listeners on a plane of equality. Perhaps more than any other contemporary thinker, Jean-Luc Nancy perceived listening (in the French, *écouter* as opposed to *entendre*, meaning both to hear and to understand) as an unbounded gesture and embrace of immersion, sharing, and sincerity. With his methexic approach of community, borrowed from Greek theatre, Nancy even goes so far as to propose that in the act of listening subject and object positions collapse and among their wreckage a shared place of resonance and experience between speaker and listener emerges.[1] In Nancy's account, the listener strains towards a relation, and in that relation a possible meaning. Compelling as this post-phenomenological reading of listening may seem, it does not account for the power relations embedded in Western histories of listening. Not only does colonial listening reinforce subject and object positions, it also does so in an unexpected way. No longer is the speaker in a position of authority, but rather the listener. The one who speaks, whose voice is seized by the listener, is rendered object, subjugated to the designs of the listener, who already possesses a distinctive knowledge set and a conditioned sense of perception. In this configuration, listening is by no means a passive or objective sense of perception.

Colonial listening, like most colonial pursuits, is shaped by appropriation and driven by the desire for knowledge and the power it provides, what some documentary film theorists call "epistephilia" (a variation of fiction film's "scopophilia"), a fetishizing of knowledge acquisition.[2] We might add another variation here and call this "acoustophilia."[3] In the context of settler colonialism, Dylan Robinson calls this phenomenon "hungry listening." Derived and translated from "two Halq'eméylem words: shxwelítemelh (the adjective for settler or white person's methods/things) and xwélalà:m (the word for listening)," hungry listening signals for Robinson a form of perception that aptly characterizes colonial listening.[4] It is a type of listening that rapaciously devours auditory information. To be clear, however, colonial listening is not uneducated or untrained listening. It often simply serves to reinforce preconceived knowledge about culture and race. Much of the colonial listening addressed in this book materializes in ethnographic sound recording facilitated at the turn of the twentieth century by the phonograph. However, the notion of colonial listening as an act that upholds unequal power relations in the context of empire has an even longer history. Conceptually and historically thick, the term "listening" as opposed to "audio recording" invites the possibility to dramatically rethink the conditioning of our sense of sound and the systems of knowledge it shapes and is shaped by.

What concerns the present chapter is the ways in which listening serves the colonial enterprise, broadly interpreted. Although not unique to the German context, colonial listening is a concept I develop over an extended period of German history and by means of disparate events. In its more specific focus on the Royal Prussian Phonographic Commission (RPPC), this chapter amplifies colonial listening as a mode of listening inextricably linked to acts of observation, accrual, classification, and finally archivization at a time of both of colonial rule and world war. But more importantly, as this chapter demonstrates, these were acts rooted in Eurocentric ideologies that held to the superiority of Western languages, sounds, and cultures over all others, ideologies that extended over a much longer period than Germany's brief colonial rule.

Nascent efforts of ethnographic sound recording relied on pencil and paper and trace back to the birth of the discipline of ethnographic fieldwork and pioneering figures such as John Wesley Powell and Franz Boas in the United States and Bronisław Malinowski slightly later in Europe. But recording with pencil and paper was an onerous task that took time and was decidedly interpretative. As Boas indicated, ethnographers struggled with what he termed "sound-blindness," or what one might rephrase in contemporary parlance as "tone-deafness." This betrayed the inability to register the peculiarities of certain sounds in certain contexts. More specifically, Euro-American ethnographers struggled to hear and transcribe the sounds produced through non-European language and music. Such cultural amusia gravely inhibited the capacity to record through listening (with the naked ear) and writing alone.[5] The invention of the phonograph offered a solution: a more objective recording that could both "capture and preserve the auditory dimensions of language and culture in full."[6] After some initial scepticism, the phonograph was adopted as one of the ethnographer's most valuable instruments. The first audio-recording device to also play back sound, the phonograph, the pioneering 1877 invention of Thomas Edison, quickly became critical to ethnographic fieldwork of linguists and especially cultural anthropologists.[7] Long before the Edison Standard Phonograph was put on the market in 1898, Jesse Walter Fewkes became the first ethnologist worldwide to use the phonograph for such work when he recorded the language and music of the Passamaquoddy tribe in Calais, Maine, in 1890.[8] He was convinced of the benefits of phonographic recording for the study and demonstration of Indigenous languages, whose "inflections, gutturals, accents, and sounds" often elude the anthropologist at first listen.[9] Many followed his lead, and by the mid-1890s this was the preferred method of recording by American ethnologists.

Though the first to employ the phonograph for the purpose of ethnographic recording of language and music, American ethnographers were not immediately concerned with the preservation and archivization of these physical recordings. Even Edison himself identified his new invention as a textual device intended chiefly for taking dictation.[10] There are notable exceptions. The American Library of Congress does house many of those first recordings made by Fewkes in the Passamquoddy community, which are now also digitalized. But Fewkes's contemporary Frank Hamilton Cushing, who likewise employed the phonograph to study Zuni language and culture, was apparently concerned that the phonograph could undercut his credibility.[11] As Erika Brady affirms in the US-American context of early ethnography, the wax cylinder recordings of the phonograph were frequently discarded once written transcriptions were made.

> Wax cylinder records themselves were valued only as a means to derive written transcriptions in phonetic orthography, English textual translations, or musical transcriptions in standard notation more easily from the collected material ... It was theses "derived texts," not the cylinders themselves, that represented the primary basis for descriptive and analytical work in folklore and anthropology. Consequently, the wax cylinders containing recordings of songs and narratives seem to have been considered hardly more important than steno pads once a letter has been typed in its final form. The cylinders were often discarded; the texts derived from them were subject to modification according to the needs, taste, ideology, or whim of the transcriber.[12]

Despite the fact that the Bureau of American Ethnology supported the use of the phonograph and, as Brady indicates further, "thousands of cylinder recordings were made under the agency's auspices," there is no evidence of these holdings in its inventories.[13] Indicative of this early tendency towards disposal, we learn in chapter 4 in the context of Marlon Fuentes's *Bontoc Eulogy* that finding sound recordings in the American archives of Philippine subjects at the turn of the twentieth century presents a challenge to the filmmaker.[14] The preservationist ethos influential in early sound recording, which I discuss at great length in subsequent chapters, did not explicitly extend to the physical products of recording.

In search of historical examples of early sound archives, we must turn to Europe. The first sound archives were established not in the United States but in Vienna in 1899 and Berlin in 1900.[15] These were the Phonogrammarchiv der österreichischen Akademie der Wissenschaften (Phonogram Archive of the Austrian Academy of Sciences) founded by Sigmund von Exner and the Berliner Phonogramm-Archiv (Berlin Phonogram Archive) founded by Carl Stumpf.[16] At the turn of the century, the German-speaking world had a monopoly on sound archives.[17] According to Eric Ames, the Austrian archive became a collection of European languages, music, and the voices of famous personalities, while its German counterpart in Berlin specialized in non-European music.[18] But the Berlin sound archive quickly overcame the Viennese one in size and scope. By the end of the First World War, it had become the world's largest phonographic collection with over ten thousand recordings.

At first established under the auspices of the Institute for Psychology at the Friedrich Wilhelm University (later, Humboldt University), in the 1930s the Phonogramm-Archiv came under the mantle of the Ethnological Museum in Berlin, where it settled. Presently, the archive holds about 16,700 wax cylinder recordings made between 1893 and 1954 from all over the world.[19] Some of the earliest recordings in this collection were made by Stumpf and Erich Moritz von Hornbostel right in the German capital through live performances by international groups – backyard "ethnomusicological fieldwork avant la lettre."[20] By the turn of the twentieth century and with establishment of German colonial rule on the African continent and in the South Seas, the archive's cofounders began amassing recordings seized in the German colonies as well. Indeed, the majority of the recordings in today's collection were captured during the overlapping period of the archive's establishment and the latter stage of Germany's colonial rule, and hail from the country's colonies.[21] Evidently, Stumpf viewed the establishment of a sound archive and colonialism as more than just a conveniently pragmatic historical encounter. In his words, "Phonographic records should not be lacking … Such an [archive] is a necessary corollary of our colonial aspirations in the highest sense."[22] As Ames clarifies, Stumpf perceived the collection and preservation of sound as a direct service to Germany's imperial power.[23]

Although travel abroad abated with the start of the First World War, the colonial aspirations of recording the languages and music of different cultural and linguistic groups and the stocking of the archive did not cease. Some scholars even claim that German colonial audio recording reached its pinnacle during this period through the project of the Royal Prussian Phonographic Commission (RPPC). The collection resulting from the RPPC eventually came to form a distinct sound archive, the Lautarchiv of the Humboldt University in Berlin. However, the overlap in motivations, ideologies, and contributors (Stumpf was the official director of the project) between the Phonogramm-Archiv and the Lautarchiv underscores a compelling continuity and expansion of the colonial enterprise. If anything, the project of the RPPC introduced a new dimension to the colonial stakes driving previous ethnographic recording: militarism. In many ways, the war facilitated this work in its intensification of the unequal power relations between speaking subject and listening ethnographer. Indeed, during the war the work moved relatively quickly and efficiently and produced unprecedented results. As Jürgen K. Mahrenholz declares of the RPPC, "This collection is the earliest and most comprehensive systematic sound archive created for documentary and scientific purposes."[24] Thus, it is here where I set about filling in the historical and epistemological concept of the sound archive through this important case study of systematic colonial listening and its afterlife.

By focusing on Berlin and the project of the RPPC I do not intend to read one archive (here, specifically the Lautarchiv) as an absolute model for all archives and therefore to stamp out the epistemological complexities and local nuances of singular institutions. Instead, I seek to understand the sound archive more broadly as part of the system and production of colonial listening. I am aware that the historical particularity of the national in the formation of early European archives as repositories for history, memory, and legitimation for the nation threaten to draw us into a geographical and cultural corner. However, as we have learned from Michel Foucault and Jacques Derrida, two thinkers I return to in the final section of this chapter, we must shift our thinking about the archive as an institutional bulwark of centralized knowledge and truth in the service of a nation. My treatment of the Lautarchiv and the RPPC collection provides a paradigmatic example of the formation of a colonial sound archive and thus as the basis for this book's more concerted emphasis in later chapters on decolonizing listening through film. The Lautarchiv presents a kind of Ur-archive for this study. Its history offers a concrete and comprehensive case of the colonial power relations that have historically shaped the way we listen. With this archetype, we may also begin to think more generally of how to reverse colonial listening, as taken up in subsequent chapters. Although chapters 4 and 5 do not directly engage with the Lautarchiv and the RPPC collection, conducting studies of those distinctive archives has proven challenging. In the case of *Bontoc Eulogy*, the filmmaker's extensive work in several national archives did not lead to the discovery of sound recordings, and in the case of *The Tailenders* the private, evangelical archive of the GRN is inaccessible to the public. But a focus on the Lautarchiv is not simply motivated by dead ends. It instead opens up new and rich possibilities for thinking about *Bontoc Eulogy* and *The Tailenders*, whose own archival returns within the US-American context respond to similar ideological and epistemological structures as those which so emblematically took shape in Germany in the early years of the twentieth century.

The Royal Prussian Phonographic Commission

As the First World War was raging, in December 1915 one of the first major sound collection projects was initiated in Germany. With Edison wax cylinder phonographs and Berliner record graphophones in hand, groups of anthropologists, linguists, language specialists, and musicologists descended upon 70 prisoner-of-war camps in Germany (there were a total of 175 spread throughout the country) to measure, photograph, and, most importantly, record the voices of the captives.[25] Especially targeted for study were the many colonial soldiers who had been forcibly enlisted by their colonializing powers and sent to continental Europe to battle the German Empire and its allies. With the possibility to collect ethnographic material and data internationally halted due to the war, many German and Austrian scholars saw this as the perfect opportunity to continue the pursuit of research without the challenges of actually having to travel to far-off lands. One of the principal research missions was the RPPC, initiated and championed by Wilhelm Doegen (1877–1967) and under the auspices of the Oriental Seminar of what was then the Friedrich Wilhelm University in Berlin and the Prussian Cultural Ministry. A mere secondary school teacher of English by profession, Doegen was nevertheless long a visionary of phonographic pedagogy for language learning, what he called *"der lebendige*

Sprachunterricht" (living language teaching).[26] In 1909 he even invented his own recording device, the Doegen-Lautapparat (sound apparatus), which he showcased at the Brussels International Exhibition one year later. At that time Doegen also began performing sound recordings. His principal goal was to create a sound archive comprising samples of different languages from around the world. With the onslaught of the First World War, his aspiration would be realized.

With a greater focus on spoken language, the project of the RPPC sought to add an altogether new dimension to the existing Phonogramm-Archiv. Notwithstanding Doegen's prominent role as the driving force behind the RPPC, he did not officially lead it, for, as Judith Kaplan reveals, his lack of academic title took him out of the running. Instead, the chairship went to Stumpf, who was both founder of the Phonogramm-Archiv and a professor of psychology in Berlin.[27] The RPPC consisted of a team of fifty experts divided into seven groups, including anthropologists, linguists, musicologists, and various language experts. Between 1915 and 1918, they performed field work in war camps and collected data through brief interviews, photography, and, most importantly, recordings on wax-coated cardboard cylinders and shellac records. In his second monograph-length published report on the work of the RPPC, *Unter fremden Völkern: Eine neue Völkerkunde* (Among foreign peoples: A new ethnology, 1925), Doegen declares that 1,650 recordings of prisoners' voices were made.[28] Among them, samples of 215 different languages and dialects from around the world were captured.[29] These were preliminarily incorporated into the Phonogramm-Archiv and then amassed into Doegen's Lautabteilung (sound department) at the National Library in Berlin in 1920, and finally in 1931, the library's sound department was taken over by the Humboldt University, where it remains.[30] Today the Berlin Lautarchiv comprises a collection of roughly 7,500 shellac records, but the crux of the collection is still the recordings made by the RPPC, containing the voices of colonial prisoners as they recite standard texts, biblical parables, fairy tales, and personal narratives or sing folk songs in their native tongues.[31]

What does it mean to record the voices of prisoners of war? Doegen and his supporters were convinced of both the national importance and even goodwill of the project of the RPPC. In nationalist propaganda, Germany asserted itself as at once the victim of brutally inhumane "primitive" colonial soldiers and the more benevolent captor (of colonial prisoners of war) compared to its enemies who forced colonial soldiers to go to war in the first place.[32] In the preface to *Kreigsgefangene Völker* (Prisoner-of-war peoples), a book originally designed to be distributed as propaganda material to "troops and authorities," Doegen unapologetically declares Germany's overall laudatory position in this regard as a country that not only did not deploy colonial soldiers in its own armies but also cultivated relationships with colonial soldiers from the British, French, and Russian armies through apparent cultural inquiry rather than militaristic might.[33] To paraphrase Doegen, German scientists used the war to carry out thoroughly peaceful and humane work as a means to bring about a unique cultural project.[34] Agnostic detractors have referred to the project as simply opportunistic. But how do we disengage opportunism from the indelibly linked power relations of war, imprisonment, and colonialism that are unshakeably part of this collection? And how do we account for the epistemic violence inherent in the undertaking of archivization? Indeed, does not Achille Mbembe classify archivization as nothing less than "a process of despoilment and dispossession?"[35] The project of the RPPC may have been unique in scale, efficiency, and in its consolidation of the matrices of colonialism, war, and technology, but in many ways it sets forth the products of a long history of a particular mode of listening.

The Longue *Durée* of the (German) Colonial Ear

Within contemporary sounds studies, Ana María Ochoa Gautier's monograph on aurality in nineteenth-century Colombia alerts us to the listening texts by Alexander von Humboldt in his unedited, untranslated, and still largely unexplored travel diaries of what was then New Granada. Ochoa Gautier begins her study with an analysis of Humboldt's auditory impressions of the *bogas*, the boat rowers of the Magdalena River, whose "bellowing ruckus" he apparently found intolerable.[36] This strikingly emotive verbal description offers one of the first instances of colonial listening in the German context in its demonstration of an excessively patronizing attitude towards an auditory experience that serves to not only Other (even dehumanize) the speaker but also underscores the sound-blindness of the European listener:

> Aber am lästigsten ist das barbarische, unzüchtige, krächzende, wüthige, bald stöhnende, bald aufjauchzende, bald in langen Formeln fluchende Geschrei … So treiben die bogas, je stärker sie arbeiten, ein desto wüthigeres Geschrei, in dem die Laune aber oft die Cadence mangeln läßt. Sie heben mit einem zischenden Haß, Haß, Haß an und hören mit weitläufigen Schimpfreden auf. Besonders wird jeder Strauch am Ufer, den sie mit Palanke erreichen können, aufs unhöflichste begrüßt, aber bald geht das "Haß" in ein blöquendes Juchen, Schwören … über. Das Getöse, welches man bis S[anta] Fe 35 Tage lang ununterbrochen hört, ist ebenso

lästig als das Trampeln der Ruderer auf dem Toldo, welche so mächtig auftreten, daß sie oft durchzubrechen drohen. Unsere Hunde konnten sich viele Tage nicht an dies ungeschlachte Gelerm gewöhnen. Ihr Gebell und Geheul vermehrte das Unwesen.[37]

The most upsetting thing is the barbarous, lustful, ululating, and angry shouting, which is sometimes like a lament and sometimes joyful; at other times full of blasphemous expressions ... Thus, the heavier the work, the more angry the screaming of the *bogas*, among whom the cadence will be affected frequently by caprice. They begin with a sibilating "has has has" and end with exacerbated insults. Especially, each bush from the shore that they can reach with the pole is saluted in the most improper fashion, the "has" rapidly turns into a bellowing ruckus, into a blasphemy ... The racket you hear uninterruptedly [35 days long] until you reach Santa Fé (Bogotá) is as bothersome as the steps of the *bogas* on the roof of the champán, over which they stomp so loudly that frequently there is a threat of it collapsing. Our dogs needed many days to get used to this unbearable racket. Their barks and howling increased the scandal.[38]

Nearly a century before Thomas Edison screeched his momentous "Hullo!" followed by the nursery rhyme "Mary Had a Little Lamb" into the telephone mouthpiece of what was to become the first replayable sound-recording device in history, the phonograph, in July 1877, Humboldt had embarked on his five-year journey through the Americas (1799–1804).[39] Though he was certainly not the first German explorer to take to the seas, similar to Georg Forster (1754–94), Humboldt's travels are nevertheless among the most notable. Besides his study of animals, geological structures, and especially vegetation, Humboldt also peripherally observed the sounds of the people he encountered. Without the assistance of a recording apparatus, he had to mediate his auditory experiences with pen and paper. As Ochoa Gautier indicates, citing Julio Ramos, the challenge the "acoustic release" of the *bogas* presented to Humboldt's sense-making "scientific observation" was apparent in "his repeated use of negative adjectives of excess – barbarous, lustful, angry" to describe the voices he heard.[40] Unable to control his own grumbling, Humboldt's words lapse into a litany of complaints uncharacteristic of his "enlightened vitalist" approach and otherwise well-nigh idealist portrayals of his travel experiences.[41]

Humboldt's prejudiced description of the *bogas* is not simply an anomaly of auditory experience, one that did not fit into the ocular-centricism of modern perception and epistemology, and therefore only renderable with almost irascible disdain. Rather, his verbal description of the *bogas* offers a precursor of the colonial ear. Although Humboldt's travels were not in the capacity of a de jure colonizer, for Germany did not seize colonies until the late nineteenth century, Susanne Zantop reminds us that Humboldt was hailed as a "predecessor" to late nineteenth-century German colonialists, a kind of German Christopher Columbus, and was praised by the *Deutsche Kolonialgesellschaft* (DKG, German Colonial Society [1887–1936]).[42] Humboldt's travels and explorations of the Americas became an impetus for fantasies of what Sara Friedrichsmeyer, Sara Lennox, and Susanne Zantop refer to as an "imaginary conquest of new terrains." In this colonial fantasy of a "Second Discovery," Humboldt as "a visionary heroic male figure 'discovers,' explores, and takes possession of virgin territories."[43] At its most basic, the colonial ear implies discursive formation through the mediation of certain auditory experiences in the context of unequal power relations. This can, in Ochoa Gautier's words, "creat[e] and mobiliz[e] an acoustic regime of truths, a power-knowledge nexus in which some modes of perception, description, and inscription of sound are more valid than others."[44] For, as Ochoa Gautier notes further, the *bogas* were certainly not disturbed by their own sounds. According to Ronald Radano and Tejumola Olaniyan, European travelogues from over four centuries are replete with such "noise" afflictions. "Tonality brought into audible form a naturalized, iconic civility, which in turn, rendered that which sounded different as many calamities of noise in need of discipline, muting, silence."[45]

A similar story unfolds nearly a century later when Carl Stumpf visits Carl Hagenbeck's ethnographic exhibition of Indigenous performers of the Bella Coola tribe in Halle, Germany, in 1885. This was his first documented attempt to transcribe non-European music with pencil and paper, which fails miserably. Indeed, he too apparently hears only an incomprehensible howl (*"ein unfaßliches Geheul"*).[46] For Stumpf, an expert of psychoacoustics, this presented a significant occupational challenge that needed to be overcome. An ostensibly more objective approach to listening that relinquished the cultural conditioning of the European ear was necessary.[47] At first sceptical of the use of a mechanized recording device, eventually Stumpf found his solution in the phonograph: through the phonograph we now have the opportunity to gain wholly accurate impressions of exotic music devoid of any subjective conception. This is why extensive collections of phonographic recordings are a necessity.[48] There was widespread optimism that the phonograph could provide a more objective mode of mediation, or even an unmediated medium, what German physicist Otto Wiener referred to simply as "the extension of our senses," that could eschew the inscriptive imperative of the written word.[49] Even Friedrich Kittler maintained that the phonograph presented an important unfiltered mode of hearing what the ear could not.[50] Certainly, in the context of ethnography, the conceit that the phonograph imparted a sense of authenticity as an almost live medium capable of capturing and preserving "real" voices and languages long endured.[51] Finally, Theodor W. Adorno mused that the phonograph and its recordings were the first instances of technology emancipated from human influence and dominance – autonomous art inventions.[52] But this new technology did not disavow the conditioning of the European ear. If anything, it further facilitated and accelerated colonial listening practices. With the aid of the phonograph sound material could be adjusted and even manipulated for easier acquisition and dissection; it could be slowed down, sped up, paused, and repeated. The written descriptions and classifications accompanying the recordings also provided another element of mediation, or at least mediated framing. Classifying became another means of appropriating. The colonial ear takes us to different sites of mediation. From Humboldt's listening texts to Doegen's wax cylinders and shellac records, we can trace a history of the colonial ear that shifts with the invention of new technology and the development of new media but maintains a listening regime underpinned by power and the pursuit of knowledge against a backdrop of asymmetrical subject positioning.

The historical context of the RPPC was highly charged. Not only was this a period of war, in which Germany was the aggressor, but it was also during the short-lived and particularly aggressive era of German colonialism on the African continent, in northeastern Papua New Guinea and a number of surrounding islands, as well as in Kiautschou in China (1885–1918). Finally, this was a critical moment of transition in which the popularity of social Darwinism and eventually eugenics began to take hold of both academe and society. Germany's period of colonialism, and the height of European colonialism in the late nineteenth and early twentieth centuries, was shaped by an era of intense measurement and classification. With the publication of Charles Darwin's *On the Origin of Species* in 1859 and its increased currency in the late nineteenth and early twentieth centuries, this period ushered in an age of evolutionary theory with its attendant methods of rabid data collection and taxonomy. This transition was perhaps most alarmingly evident in the area of anthropology, which was not an academic discipline strictly confined to the ivory tower but also a field with enormous popular interest. As Andrew D. Evans contends, "World War I played a crucial role in the transformation of German anthropology from the decidedly liberal discipline of the late nineteenth century into the racist and nationalist race science of the 1920s."[53] Imperialism, what Angela Zimmerman calls the "sine qua non of anthropology," served the discipline both in its endeavours abroad and at home.[54] Such figures as the Austrian Felix von Luschan, an outspoken supporter of "scientific colonialism" but still not wholly invested in eugenics, represented this gradual shift and were also instrumental in the efforts of the RPPC.[55] At the same time, a certain historical continuity vis-à-vis the methods of anthropological and linguistic study is perceptible.

While there exists an entire discourse on German Orientalism that troubles Edward Said's erstwhile claim that Germany's "protracted sustained *national* interest in the Orient was made the subject of lyrics, fantasies, and even novels,"[56] rather than the pursuit of colonial rule, Germany was indeed a latecomer to the imperial pursuits abroad long carried out by its European counterparts and thus gained a reputation for colonial armchair fantasies. German scientists, scholars, and artists did not seem to mind practising colonial endeavours from the safety and comfort of European cities.[57] As Joseph Errington puts it, "It is interesting that German-speaking intellectuals were just those Europeans who were developing dominant ideas about language, history, and identity which served their nation-building project at home, rather than a project of colonial power abroad."[58] Although the early 1900s ushered in some ethnographic fieldwork to the German colonies, this was brief and, as Evans indicates, not particularly desirable due to the hardships of travel and the risk of disease.[59] Instead, scholars often waited for global cultures to come to them, and at the turn of the century this did not require much patience. Zimmerman confirms that "the majority of encounters between anthropologists and the people they studied occurred in Germany, in circuses, panopticons, and zoos."[60] So-called ethnographic exhibitions or *Völkerschauen* (human zoos), a phenomenon pioneered as early as 1874 by Carl Hagenbeck, in reality an animal importer and zookeeper by profession, became vastly popular and widespread at the height of the imperial age in Europe and the United States. There is even extensive footage of a scene of the Carl Hagenbeck animal exhibit in *Bontoc Eulogy*. Fatimah Tobing Rony describes these exhibitions as "new popular science entertainments visualizing the 'ethnographic.'"[61] They consisted of displays of individuals and troupes from non-Western countries who typically performed Indigenous customs, dances, music, and other practices from their country of origin for European audiences.[62] The intent was to offer European audiences the thrill of the "exotic" without the strain of travel or the unpleasurable sense of alienation. In David Kim's words, "Their [*Völkerschauen*] success depended on balancing foreignness with familiarity, exoticism with authenticity so that visitors were amazed, not alienated, by what they saw and heard."[63] Anthropological work was underpinned by voyeurism. But the existence and success of these exhibitions were just as dependent on the anthropologists as the anthropologists were on them. This was a mutually beneficial set of circumstances. The professional interest of the anthropologists attested to the authenticity of these popular shows and offered a certain legitimacy.[64]

It was in this established spirit of domestic adventure and pursuit of the opportunities presented by war and the colonialism of other nations that the members of the RPPC also embarked on their backyard fieldwork. Doegen prefaces his report on the RPPC, *Unter fremden Völkern*, with the opening declaration: "Nicht die Schilderung einer Forschungsreise zu fremden Nationen der Erde ist es, die hier geboten wird, sondern eben das, was der Titel ankündigt: ein großes Erleben unter fremden Völkern in Deutschland im Weltkriege"[65] (This is not the description of a research trip to foreign countries of the world, but precisely what the title announces: a great and vast experience among foreign peoples in Germany during the World War). From Humboldt's more privately penned grumblings about the ostensibly animalistic sounds of the *bogas* to the RPPC's officially sanctioned (indeed, assented to and financially supported by Emperor Wilhelm II himself) and local phonographic recording, the colonial ear developed and modified in its media practices apparent scientific neutrality, and efficacy, qualities I will explore further in subsequent sections. Humboldt's listening texts may have established the paradigm of colonial listening, but the shape it took over a century later in Germany was altogether distinct. If "Humboldtian Science," originally a coinage intended to foreground the positive and the scientific over the vitalist and the Romantic, still resonated with this selfsame tension, then the science of the RPPC followed more reductive approaches.[66] The principal goals of the RPPC were to record, collect, and classify.

Listening with a Phonograph

On the one hand, listening with a phonograph presented a possible objective auditory practice. In Kittler's articulation, "The phonograph does not hear as do ears that have been trained immediately to filter voices, words, and sounds out of noise; it registers acoustic events as such."[67] But, on the other hand, listening with a recording device is purposeful. For indeed, the phonograph both recorded and played back its recordings. Erich Moritz von Hornbostel described listening with a phonograph as something akin to surgery, a violent dissection of the internal organs of a sound recording.[68] What is meant here by listening with a phonograph is listening as recording. Colonial listening is not an act of documentary listening; it is a highly contrived and ideological mode of audition. Visits to the camps were typically brief, spanning less than a day or two. Members of the RPPC did not move around the prisoner-of-war camps, phonograph in tow, and simply record the soundscape. Such a project would have no doubt yielded an overall more authentic and insightful aural portrait of life in the camps. This would have also been technologically untenable at the time. Rather, the phonograph was set up indoors, typically in smaller rooms in which outside noise or echoes would not distract, with a large funnel. As Monique Scheer indicates, the room was often one associated with cultural programming for the prisoners, such as a reading room or a chapel.[69] Doegen would visit the camp in advance of the team to select and prepare the space for the recordings.[70] Prisoners were gathered in small groups, if possible, by language, in order to participate and take their turns speaking into the funnel. Given the limited recording ability of the shellac records and especially the wax cylinders, roughly three to four minutes, each oral session was accordingly brief. It is unclear how willingly prisoners participated. Some speculate that prisoners received small bribes, such as cigarettes, sweets, or extra blankets, or they simply welcomed the reprieve from perpetual boredom or forced labour and displayed curiosity about the recordings and the technology of the phonograph, but most scholars agree that the unequal power relations between scientists and their subjects in the camps meant that access to prisoners was not limited.[71] Doegen claimed that he never forced prisoners to participate, and even literally underlined this in a statement closing his unpublished, typewritten report.[72] Some prisoners demonstrated reluctance to speak into the funnel for fear of losing their voices to the machine. Photos documenting the sound recordings reveal that military guards were almost always present and if prisoners resisted or became unruly, scientists could defer to this power. Subjects could not run away. Further, maintaining silence or deviating from the instructions or texts set forth by the scientists met with vexation.[73] The coercive, even violent, nature of this context is evident and significant. While camp life varied depending on the commander, as Evans notes, "the POWs were under the martial law of the German army and subject to a battery of rules … the prisoners' movements and behavior were always supervised and monitored: a camp schedule determined the prisoners' daily routine, mail was censored, escape attempts were punished."[74] Heather Jones observes that unsanctioned violence against prisoners was frequent in German camps, especially during the early years of war.[75] Overall,

German camps had a bad reputation due to severe conditions, including disease, hard labour, lack of hygiene, abuse, and food crises.[76] This was a brutally repressive regime of imprisonment whose conditions proved ideal for the scientists insofar as they provided them with accessible and submissive subjects.

The same way that one might at once mechanically and voyeuristically gaze with the aid of the camera, one also listens with a phonograph. The scientist is not exceptionally interested in the subject but more concerned with the process, the science, and the product of technology in practice. A comparison can be drawn with observations made by Victor Serge about his own experiences as a subject of anthropometry in prison in France between 1912 and 1917:

> The clerks, attentive but with perfect professional indifference, measure the prisoner's skull, foot, hand, forearm; note the scars and the tiniest marks on his body; examine and record the exact color of his eyes, the folds of his ear, the cut of his lips, the shape of his nose; gently take fingerprints. I observe these automatons, noting that they are free men occupied in compiling an exact scientific description of the prisoner: me. They don't notice me at all. They ignore me. For this man who, with three rapid, deft movements, stretches my forearm out on a kind of short measuring rod, I don't exist. There is nothing in front of him but a forearm, so many inches long, bearing this or that peculiarity. Two numbers, ciphers to be entered, always in the same place, on a file card. Each day, the man enters these numbers several hundred times. He has no inclination to look at faces.[77]

This passage brings into relief the absolute objectification of the prisoner as a body to be measured and inspected, which bears out in the cold, meticulous indifference of anthropometric pursuits. These were part of a system of identification pioneered by police officer and biometrics researcher Alphonse Bertillon in the late 1800s and instituted in parts of Europe and the United States. For Avery F. Gordon, Serge's account directly evokes the historical reality of prisons at the time, what she refers to as "open laboratories for the scientists and bureaucrats to test their theories and systematically to advance their own interests."[78] Similarly, Britta Lange characterizes the German prisoner-of-war camp as a colonial laboratory.[79]

How would an account of a prisoner of war coerced to speak into the phonograph at the behest of the scientists and technicians of the RPPC compare to that of Serge in front of the anthropometric gaze of the camera? The linguists and their assistants might have physically led the man to the phonograph, adjusted his head and lifted his chin, so that his mouth was directly positioned before the cavernous opening of the phonograph's funnel. They may have given him a cue to begin to speak and then employed hand gestures to make him stop, slow down, speed up, or to speak louder or more softly. Tempo and volume would have been carefully controlled. His name and language, dialect, country and region, education, profession, and religion all would have been noted with precision. But these identity markers did not serve to communicate with or understand this man so much as inscribe the recording. Subjectivity here too is revoked. Voice and language become severed from the man. He becomes a mere living specimen of language production with an assigned number. Listening in the prisoner-of-war camps directly contradicts the idea, maintained by many, that to "'hear' a person is to recognize their subjectivity."[80] Subject and object positions of scientist and prisoner are instead brutally reinforced. Doegen perceived the research objectives of the RPPC as opportunistic, but it is evident that these also buttressed military efforts and colonial practices and ideologies.[81] In his writings about the RPPC collection, Doegen even asserts, similar to Stumpf, that it ought to serve colonial interests and goals.[82]

Some images of this scene of listening with the phonograph exist in the archives (figures 1.1 and 1.2). In the first black-and-white photograph from 1916, a crowded room comes into focus. One group of men cluster against a wood-panelled wall, some sit, others stand. With minor exception, their gazes are cast in the direction of the camera. They appear bored, uncomfortable, possibly annoyed. In any case, they are not meant to make themselves comfortable in this space. They all don outdoor clothing, including hats. These are Nepalese (Gurkha) prisoners in the Halfmoon prisoner-of-war camp in Wünsdorf, near Berlin, designed specifically for colonial soldiers. (This camp is the subject of greater scrutiny in subsequent chapters.) Deeper into the space of the room, yet centrally positioned in the image, is another group of men. The two groups are spatially divided by a wood stove and its chimney pipe. In the latter group, these men appear oblivious to the camera and are engaged in the labour of recording. Another prisoner, whose back faces the camera, stands erect with his head tilted upward. Directly in front of him is the phonographic funnel. He is flanked by three men, two scientists and a technician identifiable by dress and gesture. One of these men, Doegen himself, stands in extreme proximity to the prisoner, with his left hand clutching the prisoner's left shoulder not in affection but what appears to be in stiff coercion. The prisoner must maintain a certain position in relation to the funnel. In the scientist's right hand, he holds a piece of white paper likely containing a text to be read aloud by the prisoner in his native tongue.

Figure 1.1. Wilhelm Doegen and Heinrich Lüders during voice recordings of Nepalese prisoners of war during the First World War, probably in the prisoner-of-war camp in Wünsdorf, Brandenburg, Germany, 1916. © bpk Bildagentur/photographer unknown/Berlin-Brandenburgische Akademie der Wissenschaften (BBAW), Germany/Art Resource, NY.

The other two men in this group occupy themselves with some task or other, one to the left of the prisoner, Heinrich Lüders, a professor of ancient Indian languages and literature, and the other, a technician, positioned behind the makeshift partition that separates the prisoner from the phonograph itself. To the right of the image, leaning against a table, is a soldier dressed in uniform and carrying a sword. His gaze is turned to the operation in front of the phonograph. The presence of the soldier is not overtly ominous; his body language suggests that he is relaxed. He is nevertheless a reminder of the military violence of this context and the inequality of power sanctioned in this scene. From the vigorous grasp of the scientist to the military man listening and looking on, this image of phonographic recording vivifies the enterprise of colonial listening. One of the most circulated visual records of the work of the RPPC, this image was first published in 1930.[83] The composition of the second image (figure 1.2) bears many of the same qualities as the

Figure 1.2. Wilhelm Doegen during voice recordings with English prisoners of war in the Wahn prisoner-of-war camp, 1915–18. © bpk Bildagentur/ photographer unknown/Deutsches Historisches Museum, Berlin, Germany/ Art Resource, NY.

first, but it appears less posed, as no one seems to notice the camera. Moreover, the subjects presented here are not colonial soldiers; they are captured British soldiers. War does not so much reconcile racialized differences as it remaps power positions. As this example demonstrates, colonial listening as a practice concerns itself first and foremost with linguistic difference. In this photograph, a British prisoner interned at the Wahn prison camp is shown speaking into the phonograph funnel. Here again, the prisoner as subject is flanked by two scientists and a technician, including Doegen, whose grip now appears around the neck of the subject and suggests even greater physical compulsion, and Alois Brandl, a professor of English philology. Notable is also the more central position of military authority in the figure of the camp commander, who stands in close proximity to the prisoner and appears to listen. Indeed, the inscription included with the image describes him as *"Zuhörer"* (listener). The categorization of the military prisoner guard as "listener" reveals much about the nature of colonial listening and its assertion of violence, power, and oppression.

These visually recorded "scenes of listening" give us pause. Are they not also scenes of speaking? They certainly recall the ethnographic images of the European myth of first encounter of the Othered subject and Western technology explored in the introduction of this book. This is particularly noteworthy in the composition of the first image, which follows an aesthetic informed by scientific and voyeuristic objectivity. Here yet another colonial prisoner, barely visible behind the frame of the window, appears to gaze on the scene from outside with clandestine interest and curiosity. He displays the marvel at the technology absent from the expressions of the men inside the room. But we risk straying too far into the experience of the visual here. As photographic documentation of the RPPC's process, these images do offer some insight (staged for the camera or not) into the practice and experience of colonial listening, which extends of course to those orchestrating the scene. Let us consider this more conceptually.

What is the experience of the listener as scientist or technician? Does he (in this case) even listen to the language projected into the funnel at that moment, or is he too concerned with the success of the recording? Pierre Schaeffer would respond in the negative, because one whose perception of sound is based solely on analytical reasoning is no longer a listener, but an analyst of a written text, et cetera.[84] I suggest that this also applies to the scientist or technician whose primary interest at the time of recording is technical precision. Does listening thus come later in mediated form when the cylinders or records are checked and properly labelled? This is also unclear. Each playback of the wax cylinders reduced their sound quality. While the shellac records were more durable, the tasks of collection and preservation appear to prevail. In general, it seems that members of the RPPC were not overly concerned with the content of the recordings so long as the recording process itself was successful.[85] Some early comparative linguistic analysis did result from this collection and archivization project but is wholly insignificant when compared to the data accrued.

More attentive listening to the recordings has transpired only in recent decades through the postcolonial work of scholars and artists. These later listeners have taken up the task of deciphering the messages contained within these recordings beyond typological concerns. Contemporary listening brings the alternative narratives, subjective experiences, and thoughts of the prisoners to the fore.[86] This is something I explore in greater depth in chapter 2. Colonial listening is not concerned with any of that. Such a lack of interest in this direction is indicative of what Anette Hoffmann describes as the selective deafness of the colonial production of knowledge.[87] For the purposes of contextualization, this was a mode of listening that might be located somewhere between what Michel Chion calls "semantic listening" and Schaeffer's "reduced listening." The first refers to listening to codes or language to interpret information and the second to listening to sound itself distinct from both cause and meaning.[88] Thus, listening becomes a mechanical act: it is semantic in its attention to language and linguistic properties, but it is reduced in terms of its scant interest in meaning. One might call it a kind of reductive semantic listening. Mechanical is never just mechanical, however. It oppresses in its systematic treatment of oral language through linguistic properties moored to national and racialized stereotypes.

If the archival photographs provide a somewhat more complex perspective of the scene of colonial listening in the prisoner-of-war camps, Doegen's own report on the work of the RPPC reveals not only deep ethnocentrism in its categorizations and uncritical descriptions: it is quintessentially taxonomic and absent of any speculative analysis. As he declares in the preface in bold: "Auf Lautplatten also die lebendige Sprache, in der die Volksseele sich am deutlichsten offenbart, und als Erläuterung dazu in dem vorliegenden Werk die Schilderung dieser Volksindividualitäten in Sitte und Gebrauch, in Geschichte und Herkommen, nach Typus und Abstammung!"[89] Through a dubious confluence of popular Darwinian methods of (mis)measurement and more traditional nationalist notions of "*Volk*" identity, Doegen and the RPPC found in spoken language another means of studying race. Language becomes a narrow and even parochial determinant of identity and belonging. His descriptions of each language group further illuminate this through his exuberant application of biased labels throughout: "*pflichtbewußte Iren*" (dutiful Irish), "*von dem belgischen Volke heißblütige*" (the hot-blooded of the Belgian people), "*muntere französische Kreolen*" (talkative French Creoles), "*sangeslustige Italiener*" (singing Italians), "*die rassigen, sentimentalen Serben*" (the fiery, sentimental Serbs), "*schwerfälligen, gutmütigen Großrussen und Weißrussen*" (dull, good-natured Russians and Belarussians), "*eckig muskulöse Litauer*" (angular muscular Lithuanians), "*leicht reizbare Tunesier*" (irascible Tunisians), "*kaffeebraune, intelligente Berber*" (coffee-brown, intelligent Berbers); the list continues in this fashion for several pages.[90] The assignment of innate characteristics to these groups reflects the Othering, racializing, and even stigmatizing that subtends the entire project of the RPPC. Later sections of the report focus on individual language or regional groups and are authored by linguists, who formed part of the RPPC. These do contain transcribed and translated samples of the recordings and occasionally some linguistic analysis. However, the narratives are likewise riddled with colonial rhetoric of ethnocentrism and denigration. For decades, Doegen's report was the sole comprehensive work on the project of the RPPC. Even Doegen's originally envisioned pedagogical language project for the recordings was never carried out on a large scale. Further work on and with the recordings beyond transcription and translation was evidently not thorough.

The overall role the project of the RPPC played in this transitional period of language research from historical philology to more structural linguistics remains debatable. Joseph Errington contends that comparative philology, in many ways a discipline developed within the German tradition from Johann Gottfried von Herder, the Schlegel brothers, and Wilhelm von Humboldt to Franz Bopp, Jakob Grimm, and August Schleicher, was not only pivotal to nationalism but also later participated in social Darwinism as a means of, in Errington's words, "demonstrat[ing] the underlying dynamics of civilizational progress, from industrialization to imperialism, in the world at large."[91] Certainly, the context of colonialism, war, and imprisonment rendered the captive subjects fungible property for scientific experimentation, but the propaganda politics of the RPPC further supported the nativist imperative of war shored up by evolutionary theory. Enemy armies could also be declared both inferior and hypocritical for their deployment of colonial soldiers in a mission to defend civilization in Europe.[92] This site of colonial listening in a prisoner-of-war camp becomes nothing less than an echo chamber in which existing perceptions of language difference and identity are simply reinforced and documented. In this context, listening with the phonograph becomes tantamount to colonial listening. It serves to marginalize subjugated persons, their voices, and their histories through an anchoring in ethnocentric ontologies and epistemologies.

With one final example, I conclude this section. In *Unter fremden Völkern*, the content and grammar sampling of transcriptions of speech acts and especially songs recorded appear to directly implicate the prisoners further as non-modern, Orientalist fantasy subjects. Doegen declares that the Maghrebi prisoners sing songs of love and war full of melancholy. The Japanese and Koreans sing sentimental songs of nationalism.

The northern Indians offer melodies about the divination of the caste system. The Roma (referred to with pejorative *"Zigeuner"* in Doegen's text) sing about nature. Colonial listeners seek auditory authentication for their fantasies and derive satisfaction from these fulfilments. Listening for illicit satisfaction is nothing short of eavesdropping – not in the form of surveillance here but instead as a kind of voyeurism in the form of surreptitious listening entangled in a panoply of power at once dictated by and in support of imperialism. That these recordings swiftly became the inventory of an archive would appear to further dispossess and historicize acts of listening. This is all part of the strategy of colonial listening as it crystalizes in this period at the beginning of the twentieth century.

A mode of listening that is reinforced by unequal power relations is the broad basis of what is at stake in colonial listening and begins to show itself in the German space in the private writings of Alexander von Humboldt, one of Germany's first "explorers." But it is nearly a century later that we witness the full development of the colonial ear with its technological apparatuses and conveniently proximate subjects. The massive project of recording conducted by the RPPC during the First World War synthesizes the myriad sinister dimensions of colonial listening and serves as a paradigmatic example of what this does and means.

What's (in) a Colonial Sound Archive?

Reflecting on the paradigm of the Lautarchiv and the RPPC, this final section moves from the narrow to the broad and invites us to think more generally and theoretically about the archive, the knowledge it produces, and the authority it sanctions. The massive scale of collection that occurred under the aegis of the RPPC within just three years is unwieldy. Britta Lange compares the recording operation to assembly-line work; on average fifteen recordings were produced each day at a camp.[93] Sheer quantity and the quantifiability of scientific work carried much significance. While both phonograph and graphophone were used, some sources suggest that preference was given to the phonograph because the apparatus itself was easy to transport – the mere size and weight of a typewriter, it was also crank driven and less expensive than the more fashionable graphophone.[94] But this meant that to perform the recording, one required an abundant number of wax cylinders, which were more cumbersome than graphophone records. Sources indicate that in the context of the RPPC the linguists used graphophones and the musicologists used phonographs.[95] Other sources, however, suggest that most fieldwork at the time was performed using a special phonograph, the "Archivphonograph," fashioned by Fritz Hauser and Ludwig Castagna. This phonograph still employed the Edison stylus arrangement but utilized wax discs instead of wax cylinders.[96] Whether shellac records or wax cylinders, here accretion was key. Doegen made no secret of his motivation and ultimate goal – to create an archive of voices.

The archive Doegen no doubt had in mind summoned the tradition of the institution established in mid-nineteenth-century Europe as "a symbol of truth, plausibility, and authenticity."[97] Certainly, archives have existed much longer – indeed, the term originates from the ancient Greeks – but it was not until this later period that documents and records became centralized as part of a repository for a synthesized "national history and national memory."[98] The rule of the nineteenth-century archive prescribed an empirical, objective, and positivist approach to the past through documentation, classification, and authorization of facts. French sociologist Auguste Comte, as the founder of positivism, is typically named in connection with the birth of this archival science, but Germany was in fact also at the forefront of this new discipline of history under the influence of source-based historian Leopold von Ranke, an influence that prevailed until well after the Second World War.[99] Its dismantling unravelled in a radical scholarly turn most notably contributed to by Michel Foucault in the early 1970s and continues in different forms today.

Challenging the (national and colonial) archive is a well-travelled path. But while most would agree that the "archival turn" that marked this opposition was already well underway when Jacques Derrida delivered his famous 1994 lecture (first in French and then in English) entitled "Archive Fever: A Freudian Impression," he introduced a new and important conceptual shift to this direction of research that offered a theoretical fillip.[100] As a means of approaching the topic of the colonial sound archive, I will reproduce the basic premise of his argument here. According to Derrida, archive fever is at once characterized by the dogged drive of the historian to get to the truth of things, that inception and origin of a matter, and the challenge of accomplishing this task. This challenge is due both to the unwieldy accretion of information, data, and material that comprises the archive and the systematic exclusion that is the consequence – and also often the intent – of collecting, classifying, and taxonomizing. Certain information, evidence, and narratives will always fall through the cracks of the archive, consciously or not. Derrida's invocation of Freudian psychoanalysis in this context is illuminating. The archive, Derrida suggests, is not unlike the human mind; there are memories and bits of information that rest in consciousness, and there are those that are unconscious and buried in the depths of the psyche. The archive is constituted much like human consciousness. Derived from the Greek term *arkhē*, meaning both "commencement" and "commandment," to begin and to rule, the archive, Derrida reminds us, has a "nomological principle."[101] It shores up information and knowledge in line with ruling powers and presents these as history and truth. There is an underlying violence of repression in the constitution of the archive that is not dissimilar to the Oedipal drama of bourgeois subjectivity for Freud. But just as the *Verdrängung* (repression) at work in human consciousness by way of the reality principle works against itself in the form of the death drive, according to Freud, so too does Derrida perceive the nomological principle of the archive as undercut by archive fever, that which also incites amnesia, and with it the destruction of the archive's accumulation and capitalization of memory.[102] The subjugated knowledges and memories, what Derrida calls the "specters" and what Foucault, to whom I will return, refers to as "the silent monuments" or "the inert traces," haunt every archive.[103] For the moment, these ghosts must continue to tarry in the cracks of history.

But how does the sound archive fit in to this schema with its echoes of voices and "noisy monuments"? In the remainder of this chapter, I want to think about the sound archive and its discursively distinct history and epistemology. As much as the ear has not been fully scrutinized with regard to its role in imperial epistemes the way the eye has, scholarship on the sound archive as an institution shaped by nomology is growing but still inchoate. Scholarship within the broader discipline of sound studies (especially from the North American perspective) tends to focus on settler-colonial projects of phonographic sound capture and preservation. If the German and Austrian contexts are mentioned at all, the colonial history of their emergence is often skirted. Jonathan Sterne's *The Audible Past*, the authoritative history of sound, offers an example. His analysis of turn-of-the-twentieth-century sound recordings and collections concludes with critical recognition of the devastating paradox of what he calls the "preservationist ethos" of the sound archive that sought to preserve the very cultures and languages that it helped to eradicate through genocidal policies towards Indigenous North Americans. He only briefly discusses the European sound archives, and principally as important spaces of preservation. "Recordings for the future generations needed archives," he writes, for "the speaking dead needed a cemetery for their resonant tombs."[104] Disregarding the specific history of these European archives, the Berlin sound archives in particular founded on ideas of empire and grandly supplied by recordings collected from human zoos (*Völkerschauen*), the colonies, and colonial prisoner-of-war camps, Sterne also elides all mention of the matrices of power that provided the conditions for such an archive to emerge in the first place.[105]

The archival turn established that archives are not simply storage spaces or accounts of records and of what happened but subjects of study in their own right, which warrant careful scrutiny.[106] The epistemic practices that prevailed at the turn of the twentieth century at the height of European colonial power were not only recorded into the archive but also gave it shape. As Foucault has taught us, "The archive is not that which … safeguards the event of the statement, and preserves, for future memories"; it is instead at the root of what is knowable and utterable insofar as it is the site of power relations, which determine the very conditions for knowledge. The archive is the very "law of what can be said."[107] This law has long been perceived as entrenched in colonial and imperial politics. The sound archive is no different. Although the ostensible and material intent of the sound archive as a multimedia archive has been informed by designs of preservation, the discursive principle of the archive and its grounding in colonial politics cannot escape attention. As Ann Laura Stoler provocatively declares, "What constitutes the archive, what form it takes, and what systems of classification signal at specific times are the very substance of colonial politics."[108] If, in the case of the early sound archives, the goal was to serve scientific research, documentation qua preservation, and cultural memory, as Lange indicates, then one must take note of the scientific and cultural context of this period and the politics and ideologies that gave it form.[109]

Monique Scheer invites us to consider the colonial project of the sound archive from a slightly different perspective: through its utility and materiality. In the early years of the phonograph, particularly in the fieldwork of American ethnologists, recordings were made in lieu of note-taking and served merely as a source for later written transcriptions, after which they were discarded. When the phonograph reached Europe soon after, scientists opted to preserve the recordings, but this presented a challenge. The wax cylinders commonly used could not be efficiently deployed for study later on due to their unsustainable sound quality. Not only did the technology of the phonograph alter the way fieldwork was carried out and analysed, it also altered the drive to preserve and archive sounds.[110] While the transfer of the recordings to more durable and current technology has taken place over the decades, the lag in this reproduction meant that scientists could not easily work with the recordings. Thus, at its origin the sound archive was an altogether self-serving, insular pursuit, which was possibly even a burden on linguistic fieldwork because scientists were still reliant on their notes and additionally obligated to record. Ultimately, Scheer's assessment of the inutility of the sound archive reinforces Foucault's thesis that the archive is not a mere library or repository of documents to be (re)used and circulated. Yet her attention to the material reality of the sound archive opens up another point of entry for thinking about the singularity of the sound archive.

The curious ontology of an archive that does not in truth endure, or endures only insofar as it exists as an archive, is tautological. If, according to Diana Taylor, the archive is an enduring body and source of information and knowledge, immune to the tides of time and change, then the sound archive as a multimedia archive is distinct.[111] To begin with, if the phonographic sound recording is, as Otto Wiener claimed, "an extension of our senses" and far closer to the live than the written document or text, then would it not make more sense to speak of a repertoire of voices than an archive? This categorical distinction has, however, been troubled, Taylor's definition of the repertoire as ephemeral "embodied practice/knowledge," consisting of "spoken language, dance, sports, ritual," does resonate with the qualities of the voice recording.[112] Reading the sound archive more like a repertoire aligns with Lange's claim that the voice recordings of the RPPC constitute an archive of "oral history" and are as such immaterial.[113] But while Lange's argument also seeks to expose the power structures of colonialism that underpin this archive as metaphorically "immaterial" in their obscure methods, the real materiality, albeit impermanent, of the sound archive and its analogue media objects is a quality also relevant to its ontology and status. The aporia of the material archive as at once permanent and perishable is not unique to the sound archive, but perhaps it is amplified. Documents, which could not be subsequently investigated and returned to for reasons of preservation, out of concern for the acceleration of inevitable archival entropy, were gathered and produced in order to institutionalize a history through an archive of representation.[114]

While the yields of the RPPC did not immediately give rise to a unique archive, the constitution of the archive was crucial to the project and this collection. Even before embarking on the work, Doegen declared this to be his goal. The archive imparts status and power to its objects. By the same token, the regime of the colonial ear is maintained through the imperial regime of the archive.[115] "With each new archive," Ariella Aïsha Azoulay declares, "imperialism is regenerated as the only possible political species, even though many others necessarily exist."[116]

The archive of languishing records (quite literally) of the voices of colonial prisoners did not serve language-learning purposes or practices of cultural empathy; rather, it demonstrated German scientific mastery through acquisition and inventory at a time of imperialism and war. According to Richard Thomas, the imperial archive was pivotal in "the supplanting of power by the force of knowledge" in the twentieth century.[117] Indeed, the sustained establishment of the sound archive coincided with the conclusion of Germany's short-lived colonial rule abroad, which ended with the nation's defeat in the First World War. If, as Thomas suggests, "an empire is partly fiction," then Germany's longer "colonial" history had always relied on the work of fiction and imagination.[118] Susanne Zantop has drawn our attention to the extended precolonial period of "colonial fantasies" from the late eighteenth to the late nineteenth century, which anticipated actual colonial rule.[119] This was directly reflected in the literature and philosophy of this period as it shaped and was shaped by Orientalist epistemes. Therefore, the shift Thomas notes into the twentieth century from imperialism through diplomacy or military force to knowledge and the archive was not altogether new for Germany, but instead a return to a honed, or at least familiar, modus operandi of historiography from afar.

Carolyn Steedman alerts us to what is lost in the English translation of Derrida's "archive fever" from the original title *"mal d'archive."*[120] Whereas "fever" means "illness" or "obsession," and is tinged with a tenor of silliness, the French *"mal"* also means "evil" and "wrong." In the French-language edition, there is an insert about the Freud Museum conference, during which Derrida first presented his lecture on the archive. In this insert, Derrida also discusses the *"les archives du mal"* (the archives of evil), which hide, repress, and even destroy: *"les désastres qui marquent cette fin de milléniaire"* (the disasters that mark the end of the millennium).[121] Archives frequently engage in the toil of revisionism in their fashioning of certain histories. Practically speaking, the rabid data recording, collecting, classification, and inventorying that came to characterize both scientific inquiry and colonialism of the late nineteenth century of course needed a domicile. The colonial archive did not usher in the end of colonialism; instead, it introduced a new phase of colonialism, one that worked on its alibi through its coffers of accreted objects and information. Many would argue that we are still in the throes of this phase. Azoulay even provocatively proposes ceasing work on the archive until colonialism no longer conditions the world; in her words, "Going on strike until this knowledge is no longer denied would mean going on strike until imperial politics is abolished together with the kind of history used for its legitimization."[122]

In 2020, the contents of both the Phonogramm-Archiv and the Lautarchiv were scheduled to be moved to the Humboldt Forum housed in the newly constructed Stadtschloss (City Palace), designed to replicate the fifteenth-century palace (the Prussian and later the imperial residency) that was destroyed during the Second World War. There has been much controversy surrounding the erection of this building and its opening. Founded in 2013, the activist group "No Humboldt 21!" formed in order to bring visibility to the highly fraught history and future objectives of the Humboldt Forum, which recasts a relic from Germany's colonial period. At the height of its pomp, the City Palace exhibited tens of thousands of artifacts from the African continent and elsewhere, stolen and otherwise procured by dubious means. Within this collection were even the remains of Herero people murdered in the genocide perpetrated by Germans in Namibia between 1904 and 1907. As Fatima El-Tayeb clarifies, the rebuilding of this edifice and its museum serves to re-establish "German normalcy, away from the memory of national socialism, war, and holocaust towards an unburdened future in the tradition of enlightened Prussianness."[123] But, of course, as she further explains, this is highly problematic because it offers a revisionist, internalist narrative that whitewashes Germany's colonial history.[124] That these sound archives would also be subsumed under this broader institutional narrative and historiography precipitates the possibility of a recolonization of the collection and the voices of prisoners of war.[125]

Significant to the debates surrounding the Humboldt Forum have been demands for restitution of the artifacts to their countries of origin, and therefore their rightful owners. To a limited extent, restitution processes have occurred and continue. Contemporary scholarship on the sound collections has contributed to this broader discourse about restitution and the importance of the return of what Mèhèza Kalibani refers to as captured "immaterial heritage."[126] No national ambitions to return these recordings to their families or communities have been announced, however.

Comprehensive explorations of the Lautarchiv beyond Doegen's circumstantial, not to mention ethnocentric, reports have been slow to follow. In 1981, there was even discussion about disposing of the Lautarchiv entirely.[127] As Lange writes, it was not until the 1990s that scholars and archivists rediscovered the collection and in the following decades began to digitalize and catalog its objects, an endeavour that was not completed until 2015.[128] But much work still remains. As the sound archive's website states, efforts are still needed to "decolonize" the inscriptions accompanying the materials. While the archive has attracted the attention of some scholars and artists, not least Philip

Scheffner, whose documentary *The Halfmoon Files* (2007) I will explore in chapter 3, a wide-ranging study only appeared in 2019 with Britta Lange's tome *Gefangene Stimmen: Tonaufnahmen von Kriegsgefangenen aus dem Lautarchiv 1915–1918*. The volume is the product of over a decade of work and combing through the archive. It engages in what Lange calls close listening and begins the critical counterarchival toil of raising Derrida's spectres and Foucault's inert traces.[129] Most importantly, it asks what the prisoners said when they were asked or coerced to speak into the phonograph funnel. It brings forward those voices, captured (*gefangen*) on so many levels.

The conceptual grounding that this chapter advances through the example of the Berlin sound archives and the RPPC collection as a paradigm and site of colonial listening to be destabilized and ultimately decolonized guides the balance of this study. The following chapter will explore how a more profound sonic investigation of these rediscovered voices can reveal unexpected, even emancipatory, historiographies, which in turn challenge the locus of authority, so long firmly planted in the authoritative ground of the colonial archive. As part of this pursuit, it also turns its ear to other sites and draws on explicitly North American examples of colonial and decolonial listening. What drives this study of the colonial ear is not, however, what these voices can tell us if we listen closely enough, since it is often what they do not tell us – that is, what they refuse to tell or say – that is most important. Following Lange's example, I ask the broader question of methods of decolonizing the sound archive, as well as listening practices. The following chapter looks to decolonial studies as well as media studies and media archaeology. What can we do with the phonograph? That it was quickly put into the service of ethnographic study seems to speak volumes about the colonial history of the medium. Is it reclaimable? What would this mean for media in toto?

Chapter Two

Decolonizing Listening: A Methodology in Three Parts

To propose the decolonization of listening inevitably raises questions about common perceptions of audition itself within Western thought and culture, in particular with regard to its relationship to vision. In the postcolonial age, much attention has been paid to the hegemonic gaze and the critical work of its undoing. From philosophy and cultural studies to media and film theories, vision has been interpreted as central to modernity and Western hegemony.[1] Sustained efforts to counter the "ocularcentric" approach have sought, inter alia, a turn to that neglected "second sense": audition. Jacques Attali was one of the first to promote this "auditory turn" with the rousing declaration: "For twenty-five centuries, Western knowledge has tried to look upon the world. It has failed to understand that the world is not for the beholding. It is for hearing. It is not legible, but audible."[2] But much has changed in scholarship since the late 1970s, and Jonathan Sterne's much-cited "audiovisual litany" has more recently cautioned against the opposition of vision and audition as two contrary modes of perception.[3] In the context of the present study, we might also ask the more subtle question: "But what of the ethnographic ear?" As Veit Erlmann has made clear in his address of James Clifford's striking yet enigmatically posed question, "a countermonopoly of the ear" deserves equal challenging.[4] Sound, listening, and the various forms of audio technology have likewise, albeit with greater stealth, intensely shaped processes of modernity and coloniality. Indeed, is not the epitome of the modern, enlightened man, according to Theodor W. Adorno and Max Horkheimer, embodied in the myth of Odysseus, who was determined to listen to the fatal call of the Sirens on his own terms? Filling his oarsmen's ears with wax and having himself shackled to the mast of his ship, he experienced the sublime beauty and seduction of this music without succumbing to the mortal danger it typically posed to the listener.[5] In brief, he had mastered sound. What if

Odysseus had had access to a recording device, such as a phonograph, to record the seductive cries of the Sirens?[6] Surely this would have facilitated his auditory adventure, not to mention permitted a reliving of the experience through repeated playbacks. Is the absence of an extractive recording device in this myth what stops Adorno and Horkheimer short of identifying Odysseus as the original colonial listener?

While the phonograph was certainly not a condition of colonialism, or colonial listening for that matter, its invention with Thomas Edison's 1877 prototype is historically significant. Not only did the introduction of the phonograph coincide with both a period of broad colonial expansion, otherwise known as New Imperialism, and the development of the disciplines of anthropology and ethnology, its "mechanized inscription" of speech and music was also quickly put in service of the ethnographic practices ratified by colonialism and settler colonialism. Colonial encounter becomes a scene of technological reproduction.[7] If, according to Tina M. Campt, the camera served as a "pernicious instrument for knowledge production," then the phonograph was was its mate.[8] Popular iconography from the period even calls out the imbrication of the phonograph and colonial ethnography.[9] For, as Michael Taussig observes, Westerners have long been riveted by the mise-en-scène of "primitives" marvelling at the phonograph.[10] As a technological invention that rather quickly evolved beyond itself, the phonograph presents an obsolete museum piece condemned to the historical period of its emergence and rather short use. Despite efforts to reconfigure the history of the phonograph's tremendous influence on the development of media, not least cinema, it did not evolve the same way, for instance, that the camera did, at least not in terms of collective perception and name.[11] If according to Friedrich Kittler, following Michel Foucault, the history of all media is nonlinear, discrete in their influences and effects, and separated by gaps and discontinuities, I would argue that the phonograph follows this archaeological model more manifestly than others.[12] It remains condemned to this colonial epoch and its imaginary.[13] Many audio-recording and playback devices would follow in its wake, but the phonograph set an important precedent.

With the phonograph and its mechanized means of inscription, listening became an act of recording for the purposes of transmission and even dissemination. Ethnographic fieldwork now produced inscribed mechanical devices that could not only be played back but also stored for future use. Like the machine itself, the accrual of the phonograph's sonic yields in the form of wax cylinders and shellac records amounts to nothing less than the aggregate of its colonial entanglements. In the case of the Berlin sound archives, both the Phonogramm-Archiv and the Lautarchiv, and especially the prisoner-of-war collection produced by the Royal Prussian Phonographic Commission (RPPC), the stakes of recording were particularly ominous in their intense context of uneven power relations: colonialism, war, imprisonment. As demonstrated in chapter 1, this was a coercive and systematic seizure of the voice for the sake of scientific collection, what Tanja Seider patently calls stealing.[14] Britta Lange also reminds us that similar to so much colonial appropriation, the prisoners of war were not in a position to decide or negotiate the scientific terms and social afterlives of the recording of their voices.[15] While the history of its collection may be unique, its ideology and its structural relationship with the colonial ear are nothing if not paradigmatic.

How is it possible then to decolonize (phonographic) listening, or its corollary the sound archive? On the basis of extensive work in the sound archive, Lange and Anette Hoffmann advance the practice of close listening as a critical tool of decolonization. For both scholars, close listening entails listening well beyond the purpose of identifying a specific language or dialect – that is, beyond an ethnolinguistic approach. It seeks to understand the meaning within the speech act or the song performed; semantic extractions of the recordings strain towards an understanding of their messages and provenance. This mode of listening treats the speaker as more than just a "native informant" but rather as a person with an identity and a story. Close listening furthermore strives to pay heed to all of the sounds produced by the recording. These include as well as exceed the target object of the recording. When we listen closely we can hear the machinic sounds and background noise, as well as the non-verbal expressions such as pauses, sighs, coughs, laughter, and so forth. Close listening is also attuned to the (in)voluntary utterances and noises, which may be read as possible moments of dissent and rupture.[16] Even beyond a firm acknowledgment of the colonial matrix of power within which the sound recordings were taken, close listening opens up the possibility to hear the deliberate albeit subtle ways in which informants sought to undermine the efforts of ethnographers, who for the most part attempted to turn a deaf ear to these sounds as annoyances and distractions to be avoided and, when that was not possible, ignored.[17]

I am sceptical of the rhetorical imperative of close listening as a method of decolonial listening more broadly, however. Does listening more closely decolonize what Carl Stumpf referred to as the "European ear," or does it simply serve to discipline sound itself?[18] Indeed, Erich Moritz von Hornbostel's proposed method of dissection of non-European sound in pursuit of a "more objective" analysis (facilitated by the phonograph) was also indicative of a certain mode of close listening.[19] As Kittler puts it, Hornbostel proposed a possible fix to "the chaos of exotic music assailing European ears by first interpolating a phonograph, which is able to record this chaos in real time and then replay it in slow motion."[20] This new close and measured listening exemplified a perpetuation of coloniality's epistemic violence. The concept of close listening thus becomes burdened by divergent historical motives. Without simply reproducing Hoffmann and Lange's approach to the sound archive or dismissing it, I would like to explore it further within a thick dialogue of sound, listening practices, and recording media technologies, the phonograph in particular.

This chapter follows up from the previous one with its explicit survey of a paradigmatic colonial sound recording project to begin to ask how we might reclaim the recordings. Following Rey Chow and James Steintrager, I contemplate these recordings and their found "sound objects" (with an equal nod to Pierre Schaeffer), amassed under conditions of colonial rule and the epistemic violence it sanctioned.[21] To begin, this chapter lends a close ear to the colonial sound archive. No longer immediately concerned with the emergence of the archive, here we instead listen along. Yet listening along, or listening closely, to this historical soundscape takes us only so far. The broader question of decolonization and the challenges and possibilities of decolonizing listening are thus taken up in the following section via direct examples of reclaiming and remediating the sounds captured on turn-of-the-century recordings. Thoughts on media and what resonates in their ruptures and their integrations bring this chapter to a close. As we return to the phonograph through a media-archaeological rubric of plumbing the ear-splitting depths of noise, new knowledge reverberates.

Found/Sound Objects: "Close Listening" to the Archive

The irony of this section's title is that "found objects" and "sound objects," despite their felicitous rhyming, are conceptually mutually exclusive. Sound objects cannot be found. This is a paradox we can trace back to Pierre Schaeffer. The sound object is not, as one might expect, the source of sound, such as an instrument, nor is it the object, wax cylinder, shellac record, magnetic tape, or compact disc, that recreates a recorded sound.[22] It is in fact no material object at all. The sound object exists as an intermediary between the source of sound and the listener; that is, between two subjects, but detached from the site of production and perception. In Schaeffer's words, *"The sound object is the coming together of an acoustic action and a listening intention."*[23] James Steintrager and Rey

Chow similarly read Schaefferian sound objects as "discrete and multifaceted phenomena rather than as carriers of meaning or as effects bound to sources and causes."[24] As a result, acousmatic listening, or listening without seeing the source of the sound, a topic taken up with greater scope in chapter 5, frequently shapes our reception of the sound object. Listening to a sound object is not referential; rather, it demands a new type of awareness.[25] Historically contingent, Schaeffer's sound object is a concept that defies recording; meanwhile, it is keyed into new forms of recording technology. Steintrager and Chow acknowledge this aporia. "The sound object," they write, "was thus neither found nor captured. It was in part machine-made; in part, a construct of iterative perception."[26] While this is certainly true for the inevitable noise of the machine, something I explore in a later section, I offer a variation to their account of Schaeffer's sound object as a direct product of mechanized inscription.[27] Instead, the concept of the sound object might also be contingent upon recording. This opens up something akin to Walter Benjamin's aura or Phillip Auslander's later notion of liveness, both of which characterize at once the loss of ephemeral experience and its emergence as a concept plumb at the site of its disappearance through mass art and mediatization, respectively.[28] In other words, the aura and liveness only came into existence as concepts when the qualities they represent ceased to exist. Similarly, the sound object was conceptualized with the rise of sound recording. When recorded, the sound object does not come into existence nor does it cease to exist, according to Schaeffer; instead, it becomes flattened, so that it is always perceived in the same way by all listeners – across space, time, and experience.[29]

Thus, to speak of sound objects in the colonial archive might seem counterproductive, if not altogether inaccurate. I evoke the genealogy of this concept as a means to think about sound that, while recorded, still perplexes in its intentionality and its source. These are sounds dismissed by the scientists as irrelevant and insignificant to the objective of the study. They are kinds of hiccups and glitches in the recording. Although I later move beyond Lange and Hoffmann's method of close listening to the archive, it provides an indispensable starting place. Lange listens closely as a means to achieve an understanding of what the informants in the prisoner-of-war camps throughout the German empire during the First World War said when they were not simply given a predetermined text to read or recite. In her archival work, she predominantly engages in semantic listening and works with first-language speakers to transcribe, then translate, the songs, poems, and stories originally captured on record or cylinder. She wants to learn more about these prisoners of war, as people – their thoughts, desires, fears. But it is her additional close listening to potential sound objects that I would like to examine further and draw out here. These are the breaths, pauses, throat clearings, coughs, chuckles, inadvertent repetition, or even commentary, all the sounds that to the dismay of the scientists could not be cut from the recording. Lange writes: *"All dieses Andere, das nicht zum Ziel oder Interesse der Wissenschaftler gehörte, verstehe ich nicht als Abfall, sondern als wertvolle Information"*[30] (I do not perceive all the rest, that which did not belong to the goals and interests of the scientists, as waste, rather as invaluable information). What if these hiccups were indeed acts of subversion intended to trick or disrupt the recording?

I return once more, with a different passage, to Victor Serge's first-hand account about prisoners reduced to objects of anthropometric study in his tremendous memoir about prison life in turn-of-the-century France, *Men in Prison*. Here he discusses the ways in which prisoners had learned how to manipulate the tools of scientific capture, such as the camera.

> Experienced prisoners have explained to me the way to fight the camera, to fool it. Some men stubbornly close their eyes, make faces, screw up their features. These are soon made to submit; and not by friendly persuasion … The clever ones know how to distort their features in advance, how to put on an abnormal expression, make it seem calm and natural, hold it as long as necessary. The stiffness of the pose, the fixed stare of the eyes, the dishevelment of the clothes, all add to the effect: the image they leave on the photographer's plate differs enough from their normal appearance to deceive an unpracticed eye.[31]

Just as prisoners learned how to fight the camera through honed, surreptitiously skewed facial gestures, some of the recordings in the archive reveal similarly tell-tale sonic disturbances. Since these are disruptions of speech, they serve as indirect examples of seizing the right to be silent – of not speaking when told to speak, of not satisfying the colonial ear by providing optimal linguistic matter. Both the anechoic dictate of silence, or at least non-speech, and its frequent placeholder – noise – here in the form of clearing one's throat, coughing, or even chuckling, what Michel Chion calls that "shapeless zone,"[32] frustrates and disorients the listener, or worse. Despite R. Murray Schafer's sustained efforts to bring order to that otherwise shapeless surplus of sound called noise in *The Soundscape* (1977), it continues to disturb on many levels. David Novak reminds us that "noise" etymologically originates from the ancient Greek meaning "nausea" or "seasickness."[33] According to media archaeology, noise is thus marked by irregular movement, interception, and accident.[34] In this particular instance, with its possible link to illness and even retching, there is a certain satisfaction to be drawn from the thought, speculative as it may be, that the scientists were subject to confusion and even nausea when they listened to the "noise" occasionally produced by the prisoners.

The first instance of close listening described in Lange's study *Gefangene Stimmen: Tonaufnahmen aus dem Lautarchiv 1915–1918* begins by listening to a recording of the singing voice of Jasbahadur Rai.[35] According to the record card that accompanies the recording, Rai was a colonial soldier from the northeast region of the Indian subcontinent, what is now Nepal. He was a Gurkha and spoke Gorkhali, an antecedent of modern-day Nepali. He was interned at the prisoner-of-war camp in Wünsdorf, referred to as the Halfmoon camp. The name "Halfmoon camp" referenced the large number of Muslim prisoners imprisoned there. While estimates vary, the vast majority of the recordings of the RPPC were made at this camp, roughly one third.[36] Could Rai be the man in front of the phonograph funnel in the image discussed in chapter 1? This is a possibility but at the same time also pure speculation. Unlike the scientists, the prisoners in the images remain nameless. Rai's recording is especially noteworthy here because it is full of irregularities.

Before singing into the funnel, Rai, as Lange notes, draws breath ("*Luft holt*"), starts ("*absetzt*") and stops ("*stockt*"), loses his concentration ("*den Faden verliert*"), begins the song again ("*das Lied wiederaufnimmt*").[37] Near the end, his song is interrupted. The recording stops. It continues on a second record. Perhaps Rai took too much time to start, or his song went over the designated time. This would have likely annoyed the scientists, as they would have had to make him repeat the song and then begin recording on a second record where the first left off. So that the reader may listen along and directly experience the recorded sounds, Lange's book includes a CD with Rai's recording as well as others. The first part of the recording opens the CD; the second half ends it. In the second half of the recording, the disruptions are audibly evident. There are several brief pauses and instances of repetition. When the song seems to conclude, the recording continues in a stream of abrasive crackling and humming. A voice returns and there is muffled, barely audible speech. This is followed by another drawn-out pause, then a coughing fit, and then another pause. It is unclear why the recording continues once the song appears to have finished. Could the technician simply not turn off the phonograph or graphophone quickly enough? Or was Rai supposed to say more but could not muster up the vocal energy after his song and its multiple takes? In any case, no speech follows on the recording. The silence (although the sound of the record is always present) and the bouts of noise in the form of incomprehensible background speech and coughing do confuse the listener. Even now and via multiple rerecordings and remediations, the bodily in the voice is brought forth in these "glitches." With reference to Roland Barthes, one might call this "the grain of the voice," which he defines as "something which is directly the cantor's body, brought to your ears in one and the same movement from deep down in the cavities, the muscles, the membranes, the cartilages, and from deep down in the Slavonic language, as though a single skin lined the inner flesh of the performer and the music he sings."[38] With this concept Barthes wilfully turns away from philosophy's metaphysical tradition of the voice and the linguistic dimension of speech in order to embrace the corporeal qualities of the voice.

In the case of Rai's recording, the voice is inhibited by exhaustion or bodily uncertainty. It responds to a dryness or a tickle, which the body attempts to expel. The result is far from the effect desired by the objectifying measures of the scientists. Instead, as Lange and filmmaker Philip Scheffner put it, "every stutter, every stumble, every gasp makes it possible to experience the physical presence of the person sitting in front of the funnel."[39] Barthes's concept of the grain of the voice, or what Lange and Scheffner call the physical presence of the speaker or singer, encourages a different kind of listening that is also a mode of close listening but opens up the senses beyond hearing. This more synesthetic approach to perception has been widely discussed in film studies (in particular through the writings of Vivian Sobchack and Laura Marks). Irina Leimbacher takes it up for sound studies (in the context of documentary) with the concept of "haptic listening," by way of which the listener becomes attuned not only to the contents of the speech or song but also to the "melodies, tonalities, timbres, and rhythms" of the voice.[40] When we listen to Rai stumble on his words, muffle speech, and cough into the funnel, we cannot help but be reminded of the grain of the voice that betrays the flesh-and-blood person on the other end of our listening – a person also with a unique story and history. Lange evocatively brings this into relief as she details the identity of Rai in a manner that reaches well beyond the brief and systematic notes jotted onto the original identity card completed by a member of the RPPC.

What strikes one most about Rai's second recording are the disruptions to the recording. In the ears of the scientists, this is unusable audio material. The trouble with the phonograph or graphophone was that it recorded everything, including the noisiness of the body. Following Kittler, Jussi Parikka contends that "the gramophone picks up not only the meaning inherent in human speech, but just as effectively, the whispers, the noises of the body, the 'extras' of communication, so to speak, that come with every opening of the mouth."[41] While wax cylinders were relatively cheap and easy to procure, shellac records were not. Every "mistake" or prolongation would have placed a burden on the work of the scientists, in terms of both time and expense. We can only speculate that these interruptions to the mimetic flow might have been intentional – that is, a means of tricking the phonograph, the way the prisoners in Serge's account subtly tricked the camera with their cunning facial gestures. A semantic close listening to the content of the prisoners' speech acts and songs offers an important alternative to colonial listening, but the silences and noise already embedded in the recordings take things further. They obstructed colonial listening from the start. There are multiple such emancipatory moments of dissent in the archive. The recordings are riddled with pauses of silence, coughing, clearing of the throat, false starts, and repetitions. These ruptures are critical in their defiance, even resistance – strategic or not – to colonial listening.

Lange's method of close listening is informed by Ann Laura Stoler's notion of reading along the archival grain, an orientation that does not simply position itself contra the colonial archive in a more conventional "against the grain" reading but instead is one that attempts to achieve a more comprehensive perspective of the archive. It delves into both the materials that underwrite history and colonial power as well as those previously ignored. She writes: "Some would argue that the grand narratives of colonialism have been amply and excessively told. On this argument, students of colonialisms often turn quickly and confidently to read 'against the grain' of colonial conventions. One fundamental premise of this book is a commitment to a less assured and perhaps more humble stance – to explore the grain with care and read along it first."[42] Reading along the archival grain allows us to take heed of the unexpected occurrences and ruptures that resist.[43] Metaphorically speaking, it "draws our attention to the archive's granular rather than seamless texture, to the rough surface that mottles its hue and shapes its form."[44] Before one may resist the archive itself, one must discern the disturbances and resistance already present. If we may also read the grain (of the voice) in Barthesian terms, we are invited to think about reading "along the archival grain" as a reading for materiality, for signs of the body, for signs of life. Lange's close listening and Stoler's reading along the archival grain do not decolonize the archive nor listening practices per se; however, they are significant, even foundational, as an antecedent to the project of the decolonizing ear.

Towards a Decolonization of Listening

Many critical voices have given shape to the discursive project of decoloniality. Earliest and most resonant is the voice of Frantz Fanon, who radically declared in his indispensable *The Wretched of the Earth* that decolonization "sets out to change the order of the world, [and] is clearly an agenda for total disorder."[45] The revolutionary spirit of Fanon's words calls for an upheaval on all levels. This spirit continues to underpin subsequent theories put forth by decolonial thinkers in various forms. As a theoretical frame, decoloniality has developed most fully through the scholarship of Latin American scholars and theorists, beginning most notably with Aníbal Quijano's conceptualization of decoloniality as "epistemological decolonization." For Quijano, coloniality is deeply connected to the European paradigm of modernity and rationality, which conditions knowledge systems. Decolonization is thus epistemological reconstitution.[46] According to Quijano, we need "to clear the way for new intercultural communication, for an interchange of experiences and meanings, as the basis of another rationality which may legitimately pretend to some universality."[47] Quijano was one of the first thinkers to theorize coloniality beyond political and economic spheres to propose that it even governs the very way that knowledge is produced and circulated.[48] The accent on the epistemological tangle of coloniality that must be unravelled has influenced further thought. Walter Mignolo and Catherine Walsh have taken up Quijano's argument and extended its possibilities. Mignolo's notion of delinking from the colonial matrix of power propounds a critical thinking from outside, what has been referred to as border thinking.[49] As he indicates, Western foundations of knowledge are both inescapable and detrimental in their limited scope.[50] Delinking therefore promotes a total abandonment of Western thinking and its foundations in Cartesian logocentrism that views ontology as epistemology.[51] It encourages, instead, the embrace of other knowledge sets and cosmologies within, for instance, Indigenous or Islamic traditions not as different or lesser ontologies but as critical alternatives to ontology informed by binary and objectified thinking, in favour of relationality.[52]

Within Indigenous studies, decolonial scholarship is frequently inspired by activist efforts for reparation and especially to reclaim stewardship over land.[53] Fanon, too, famously remarked on the priority of land. "For a colonized people, the most essential value, because it is the most meaningful, is first and foremost the land: the land, which must provide bread and, naturally, dignity."[54] The more recent writing of Eve Tuck and K. Wayne Yang has been particularly influential in this regard. For them, decolonization should not simply be used as a metaphor for all civil and human rights-based social justice projects. Rather, "decolonization specifically requires the repatriation of Indigenous land and life."[55] Tuck and Yang return to Fanon's revolutionary call for total change in the world order with the assertion that no minor shift in the current state of things is commensurable with the task of decolonization. Incommensurability is the acknowledgment of this truth.[56] Following Tuck and Yang's example, to propose a decolonization of listening and the sound archive might seem premature, even misguided. Yet colonial listening is also a form of dispossession, not of land but of language and culture, which are stolen and distorted according to the logic of the colonial production of knowledge.[57] Scholars and artists in Indigenous sound studies have taken up these questions of dispossession tout court, and it is among their work where I find the most illuminating responses. Dylan Robinson's monograph *Hungry Listening: Resonant Theory for Indigenous Sound Studies* (2020) is especially germane here. He explores alternatives to settler-colonial listening positionalities that, in his words, "counter normative listening practices" and foreground "resurgent listening practices based in forms of Indigenous sensory engagement and ontologies."[58]

If we take Robinson's argument as a model, decolonizing listening practices appear distinct from Lange and Hoffmann's approach of close listening, insofar as the former propound an "against" rather than an "along," to cite Stoler's play with prepositions. "Listening along" becomes a tricky positioning because it implies a denial of the ethic of incommensurability. Rhetorically, to listen along proposes a listening *with* settler colonialism and therefore also *with* the colonial ethnographers. That being said, close listening certainly does not have to mean commensurability; it can also infer a kind of deep listening that opens one's ears to the possibilities of the unknown. In conversation with fellow scholars at the close of his book, Robinson evokes the concept of "deep listening" as proposed by American composer Pauline Oliveros in her study *Deep Listening: A Composer's Sound Practice* (2005). For Oliveros, deep listening is a kind of radical attentiveness, "a practice that is intended to heighten and expand consciousness of sound in as many dimensions of awareness and attentional dynamics as humanly possible."[59] Deep listening, like close listening, presents itself as an important starting place for decolonial listening practices. But strategies of decolonial listening must take things further. We cannot simply adjust the way we listen – listen more closely, more deeply. We must also question listening itself. For listening (not unlike vision) is a perception indelibly shaped by colonial discourse of self or Other and its ambitions of acquisition, power, and mastery.

In Mladen Dolar's words, "To be the master is to be the master over sound and its emission."[60] The myth of Odysseus and the Sirenic voices as put forth by Adorno and Horkheimer might be noted again here. What would it mean then not to be master over sound and its emission? What would listening without mastery entail? Julietta Singh reminds us that the critique of mastery is intrinsic to decolonial practices. "Perhaps embedded within the knotty contradictions of decolonizing discourse lies the very possibility of unmasterful styles of being."[61] Dolar's illustration of the relinquishment of mastery via Franz Kafka's unfinished short story "Der Bau" ("The Burrow"), about a badger driven to anguish because it is unable to detect the source of an omnipresent whistling in its burrow, directly evokes the experience of listening without mastery as listening to acousmatic sound. The latter identifies a listening situation in which the cause of the sound is not seen and might also be unknown. Since Pierre Schaeffer first conceptualized the phenomenon of acousmatic sound in his groundbreaking *Traité des objets musicaux* (*Treatise on Musical Objects: An Essay across Disciplines*, [1966] 2017) via the Pythagorean paradigm of the disembodied voice – namely, the teacher hidden behind the curtain – the topic has been intensely explored in various disciplines from philosophy and sound studies to film and literature. I hesitate to raise this notion of "sound unseen" here, for Schaeffer has compared the concealing apparatus of the curtain to modern methods of reproduction, and Brian Kane has explicitly paired phonographic listening with acousmatic listening.[62] Involving the visual as an anchoring for sound and sound mastery slides into what Jonathan Sterne deplores as the "audiovisual litany." According to Sterne, audition is so often idealized as this pure sense perception untouched by cultural influence and ideology, whereas vision is portrayed as the postlapsarian sense that is always perspectival and shaped by ideology.[63] Acoustic regimes of capture are just as sinister as visual regimes of capture. Eliminating the visual from the acoustic will not magically disentangle the latter from colonial epistemologies; acousmatic listening is not equivalent to decolonial listening. To be fair, though, as an example of listening without knowledge of the source of the sound and therefore without a certain mastery, acousmatic sound does take us in an important direction.[64] What might be drawn from the concept for this context is the loss of referentiality in the experience of acousmatic listening that demands a new relationship to sound, a new awareness.

The challenging yet pivotal question of what it could mean to decolonize listening is perhaps most intuitively answered by way of an example. While this book will offer further expanded examples of decolonizing listening through remediation and documentary film in subsequent chapters, I will begin here with a brief illustration that will keep us rooted in the insights of Indigenous approaches to decoloniality and offers an important frame for thinking about how colonial sound recordings can be repurposed, reappropriated, and remediated through new forms of media. An important figure in Indigenous music, and what has been referred to as the "Indigenous Renaissance" in Canada, Jeremy Dutcher is a classically trained Wolastoqi composer, pianist, singer, musicologist, and activist, and member of the Tobique First Nation. His first album *Wolastoqiyik Lintuwakonawa* (2018), translated as "Our Wolastoq (or Meliseet) Songs," was recorded in his ancestral language of Wolastoq and a reworked collection of traditional songs. The album is a culmination of intensive archival work at the Canadian Museum of Civilization in Gatineau near Ottawa. The museum holds the nation's largest collection of wax cylinder recordings, numbering 3,312. Half of these hold Indigenous voices and were recorded by ethnographers such as Marius Barbeau and William H. Mechling in the early part of the twentieth century. During the summer of 1911, Mechling made Wolastoq recordings in what is now the maritime province of New Brunswick.[65]

Mechling's work was shaped by the colonial salvage paradigm and the aporia of destruction and preservation that it embodied. James Clifford most notably critiqued this problematic ethnographic model of the salvage paradigm as a "relentless placement of others in a present-becoming-past."[66] It is nothing more than a paradox of convenience by way of which colonial destruction and preservation go hand in glove. Indeed, through the Indian Act introduced in 1876, a culmination of separate pieces of colonial legislation ostensibly enacted to assimilate Indigenous communities into the newly founded Confederation, the Canadian government legitimized and violently concretized the "cultural genocide" underway since the start of settler colonialism.[67] This Act decreed the suppression of Indigenous language usage and cultural practices and ceremonies. It also implemented the establishment of so-called Indian Residential Schools, boarding schools and work camps for Indigenous children. Here Indigenous children of all ages were not only separated from their families and forced to assimilate into the Christian-dominant culture and languages (either English or French) of the Confederation, but were also often subject to unspeakable physical and sexual violence at the hands of the schools' staff (administered by Christian churches). It is estimated that 30 per cent of all Indigenous children in Canada were forced into residential schools, the last of which closed as late as the 1990s.[68] The systematic decimation of Indigenous culture, language, and lives for well over a century continues in the form of systemic racism, police mistreatment, and poverty as well as intergenerational trauma.

In interviews, Dutcher describes his perception of Mechling as "complicated." He indicates the "heavily mediated" nature of Mechling's recordings of Wolastoq as a "dying" language as well as his complete neglect of the voices of women in the communities.[69] The project of *Wolastoqiyik Lintuwakonawa* thus sought to reclaim these stolen voices and liberate them from a history of repression. After closely listening to and carefully transcribing the songs of his ancestors, Dutcher composed new work based on these traditional Indigenous melodies. He sings these songs anew, fusing traditional music with classical cross-over influences. But what is perhaps most intriguing about this project is its remediation of the phonographic recordings in this collaborative composition. As Alexa Woloshyn describes it, "Dutcher welcomes another singer out of the misty texture: a voice emerges (Jim Paul), with the recognisable grain of the turn-of-the-century phonographic recording."[70] Digitally integrating some of the original recordings of song, some speech, and instrumental interludes into nearly all of his songs, Dutcher brings alive the voices of his ancestors captured over a century ago in the grooves of wax cylinders. Remediation here is not only conceptual but also technologically real in its application of a new digital medium to refashion an analogue one. A term famously applied by Jay David Bolter and Richard Grusin, "remediation" bears a double logic. In their words, "Our culture wants both to multiply its media and to erase all traces of mediation: ideally, it wants to erase its media in the very act of multiplying it."[71] The aporia of remediation permits a reading of the aspired proximity between Dutcher (and the present) and Jim Paul (and the past) that opens up the possibility for a rich transhistorical dialogue in Dutcher's music.

Legally speaking, as long as the use of the archival materials is "transformative," that is, "altering the original with new expression, meaning, or message," it constitutes fair use according to a 1994 US court ruling.[72] The endorsement of reusing materials with the intention of differently signifying them, or signifying with new and different intentions, becomes a crucial part of this process. The act of repurposing at work in these examples might be more informatively elucidated through Catherine Russell's concept of archiveology. A type of repurposing, Russell characterizes archiveology as "a means of returning to the images of the past that were produced to entertain, or produced for more serious purposes of documentary recording, and reviewing them for new ways of making history come alive in new forms."[73] While Russell focuses on images, archiveology might also encompass the reappropriation of sound recordings. Dutcher relistens to (and remediates) these sound recordings to make "history come alive in new forms." Decolonizing listening extracts products of ethnographic capture and collection, or in Beverley Diamond's words, "aural regimes of coloniality,"[74] and reclaims them for contemporary creations in a manner that bears witness to their historical entanglement and by the same token subverts this condemnation of pastness, encapsulated in the "salvage paradigm" or "preservationist ethos." The songs Dutcher sings should not merely be remembered but also immediately experienced in the present.

If the project of remediation (or archiveology, for that matter) of the album itself were not enough, Dutcher also offers bold visual signals of decoloniality. Designed by Dutcher and Cree visual artist Kent Monkman, the images that adorn the album's front and back covers feature Dutcher with a phonograph. On the front cover (figure 2.1), Dutcher is seated in front of the phonograph apparently mimicking the mise-en-scène of a widely circulated series of images featuring Mountain Chief (Ninna-Stako in Blackfoot), chief of Montana Blackfeet, during recording sessions with ethnologist Frances Densmore in 1916 (figure 2.2). These images also echo the scene of Rudolf Pöch's short film *Buschmann spricht in den Phonographen* (Bushman speaking into the phonograph) that opens this book. A visual riff, Dutcher's image cover provides a subversive act of imitation that calls to mind Homi Bhabha's notable theory of postcolonial mimicry as at once a mode of appropriation of colonial discourse and strategic disavowal.[75] Dutcher positions himself stiffly and deferentially as ethnographic informant at the funnel of the phonograph. Unlike Mountain Chief, he is not wearing a feathered headdress and buckskin, but he does don a jacket embroidered with Wolastoqi design. He incites settler-colonial expectations in order to resist them. Missing from Dutcher and Monkman's image is the white ethnographer. This lends the message of self-determination via an act of self-recording – *I* decide the conditions under which my voice will be recorded; *I* choose its afterlife. The absence of the ethnographer in the composition of the image further clears the view of the background, which in Dutcher and Monkman's version opens onto Monkman's 2012 landscape painting *Teaching the Lost*. Here Monkman's alter ego "Miss Chief Eagle Testicle," a queer trickster figure featured in much of the artist's work, lectures to a stray gaggle of Cubist figures against a Romantic majestic Canadian landscape. The painting serves likewise as a playful gesture at Dutcher's own self-identification as two-spirit and his refusal to submit to Western norms of gender binarism. Flipping

Figure 2.1. Album cover image of Jeremy Dutcher's *Wolastoqiyik Lintuwakonawa* (2018). © Courtesy of Jeremy Dutcher and Valeo Arts Management.

over the album cover to the reverse image visually inverses the message of the front. Here Dutcher, now all in black and in a relaxed position, has placed himself on the ethnographer's stool. His hands on the phonograph seize control of the machine. That the funnel appears to project the titles of the songs inserted onto the image makes the composition of the artwork – that is, image and graphics – appear as though Dutcher himself is now in control and making the phonograph sing again. Is he also reclaiming the instrument? Wrenching it from its colonial heritage? This is something to be discussed further.

Figure 2.2. Piegan Tribe member Mountain Chief listening to a recording with ethnologist Frances Densmore, 1916. Rights holder unknown. Courtesy of the Library of Congress LC-F81-3332.

Other similar projects of decolonizing listening by reclaiming and remediating phonographic recordings made at the turn of the twentieth century are worth mentioning here as well. Predating Dutcher's work but still ongoing is the project Language Keepers, a digital media project developed by Ben Levine and Robert M. Levitt that combines documentary video and descriptive linguistics as a means of reviving the use of Indigenous languages among heritage speakers. Based in what is now Maine, much of its focus has been on Passamaquoddy-Maliseet communities, whose language and music were captured on wax cylinders during that first phonographic trip made by ethnographer Jesse Walter Fewkes to Calais. The project has sought to reconnect heritage speakers with their language traditions and the possible resources in the phonographic collections. The Jesse Walter Fewkes Collection of Passamaquoddy Cylinder Recordings at the Library of Congress in Washington, DC, is one example. Language Keepers have also engaged with Dutcher's community of Tobique First Nation further up the coast in New Brunswick. The short documentary videos, which continue to be available online, feature heritage speakers discussing their relationship to the language, sharing songs, and teaching these skills to new speakers.

In the postscript to his study *Savage Preservation: The Ethnographic Origins of Modern Media Technology* (2014), Brian Hochman draws our attention to a 2010 video made by Language Keepers entitled *Let's All Sing*, which features the elder, mentor, and song keeper Maggie Paul.[76] The video is short, just under four minutes, and its cinematography is ostensibly non-professional. The image is shaky and skewed. It feels more like a home video and therefore also very personal. Filmed in the Passamaquoddy language with a few English-language words and phrases thrown in, the video also contains no subtitles. Instead, a transcript of the conversation accompanies the video. A group of seven middle-aged members of Passamaquoddy-Maliseet nation appear to sit comfortably in a semicircle of friends (or at least acquaintances) in what appears to be the living room of someone's house. To begin, they briefly and casually chat about language. Paul then sings and drums "Esunomawotultine." The presence of Paul is significant in this context because she is also the person who advised Dutcher to visit the archives in Ottawa to listen to the recordings of the Wolastoq songs. In the video her captivated audience listens on. When Paul completes the song, the group members ask about the provenance of this song, which is at once familiar and unfamiliar to them. Paul explains that it was rediscovered through the "wax tapes of Wechling or Mechling." Someone offscreen corrects her: "Wax cylinders." Yes, "wax cylinders," she agrees. Another inquires if the wax cylinders are at the Smithsonian, but Paul does not know.[77] She of course also means William H. Mechling.

Unlike Dutcher's album, the premise of Language Keepers runs the risk of perpetuating a preservationist ethos, or what Hochman calls "a new brand of salvage ethnography for the digital age," with its emphasis on the endangered status of many of the Indigenous languages and their communities featured in its videos.[78] However, Hochman ultimately rejects such a reading. Instead, he counters that the digital archive "functions as a creative platform for the persistence of Passamaquoddy culture rather than as a technological memorial to its expected extinction."[79] The Language Keepers' video archive is interactive, creative, and widely accessible. It is an archive that works not against or along but perhaps in spite of the colonial phonographic archive. Paul's approach to the archive is notable here. After performing the song, she explains how she repeatedly listened to the song's recording until she could make it out. She engaged in a close listening that culminated in an auditory revelation: "But finally, we could make it out," she says. Yet despite this close listening to the recording, she demonstrates scant knowledge and concern for the archive. Perhaps this is decolonizing listening: attentive listening to the recording without deference to the ethnographer or the archive where it was stored for nearly a century.

What is critical to these related examples of decolonial listening, of returning to the sound archive and reclaiming its objects, is their remediated nature. These are not simply cases of digitalizing analogue recordings but of reworking and recontextualizing sound recordings in a way that begins to delink them (to recontextualize Mignolo's term) from the colonial epistemes that conditioned their mechanized inscription. The version of decolonial listening I pursue both in this chapter and in the larger project of the book is one shaped by the possibilities of media to scramble and split its objects in creative derangement of its motives and messages.

Sounding Media Archaeology

At this juncture, I turn to media archaeology not so much as a road map but as means of thinking through a theory of decolonial listening that intersects with the ontologies and histories of media, not to mention what Jussi Parikka calls the "epistemic thresholds" within which they operate.[80] Are media determined by dominant epistemes at the site of their emergence? Are the sense perceptions they highlight and shape likewise conditioned in this way? Or is it perhaps the other way around, as media determinists would suggest: are we formed by media technologies? Can we learn to listen differently? Can new and digital media help us to do so? These questions drive the following section as it ushers us into several significant examples of decolonial listening developed through the medium of film.

Media archaeology might seem like an unlikely place to turn in the discussion of decolonization. It is a field dominated by European thinkers that draws its influence from poststructuralism and especially the work of Michel Foucault, whose own disregard for the epistemic violence of coloniality has been criticized by postcolonial thinkers, especially Gayatri Chakravorty Spivak.[81] Further, to stay with the influence of Foucault, media archaeology is inherently interested in the present.[82] It looks to the past to ask what it can tell us about where we are now, what Foucault famously calls the history of the present. To be clear, this study tracks new approaches and remediations of sound recordings as entry points to the (neglected) past. Finally, the influence of German media theory has promoted an agnostic approach to media, maintained by key thinkers of the "Berlin School" such as Friedrich Kittler and Wolfgang Ernst, referred to as the "cold gaze" of media archaeology that focuses on the machine itself and not the historical and cultural context within which the machine was developed and put into operation.[83] However, as Parikka declares in his essential *What Is Media Archaeology?* (2012), one elemental question of media archaeology is: "What are the conditions of existence of this thing, of that statement, of these discourses and multiple media(ted) practices with which we live?"[84] I want to suggest, therefore, that this field of study can also offer insight into historical conditions and practices of media, specifically the emergence of the phonograph within the matrices of modernity and coloniality. This follows and builds on the productive thesis put forth by Rakesh Sengupta in his proposal for a decolonial media archaeology. He writes: "If media archaeology reveals the various epistemological conditions that have historically privileged certain media forms and practices at the expense of others, I argue that a decolonial media archaeology would investigate how coloniality/modernity may have informed many of those epistemological conditions."[85] Although Sengupta applies this postulation to the history of screenwriting in India, it articulates possibilities for the study of different historical media practices, including listening with the phonograph at the turn of the twentieth century.

If colonial listening can be characterized by pursuits of recording, acquisition, and collection in the service of empire, then decolonial listening must not only perform the opposite but also aspire to an undoing of colonial listening. Decolonizing listening through remediation, as we have seen in the examples of *Wolastoqiyik Lintuwakonawa* and to some degree through the videos of Language Keepers and, as I will demonstrate, in subsequent chapters through documentary and archive-based film, requires a twofold methodology. It demands both a return to the sound archive and a mediatic excavation. Media archaeology allows us to account for both: it brings the archive into relief as a challenge to and not bulwark of a historiographical law; it furthermore draws attention to the materiality as well as the colonial vectors of the now obsolete phonograph and its entropic output. Siegfried Zielinski's early definition of media archaeology provides an account that resonates with the task at hand. "Archaeology (of media or audiovision) would, then," he writes, "be a method of foregrounding the resistant local discursivities and the expressions and conceptualizations of technologically based imaginings and worldviews that are at work within our largely linear and chronologically constructed history."[86] In Zielinski's description, media archaeology brings forth the discrete insurgent moments of the past that defy the straight lines of historiography, moments that leave a technological trace. Present as they may be, these traces are often left unmarked in the archives.

Although there exist multiple approaches to media archaeology, the return to the archive is a well-travelled path. Thomas Elsaesser reminds us that *archaeology* and the *archive* are imbricated by more than just the ancient Greek prefix indicating "origin," "*arkhē*." He writes, "What the extraordinary interest in the archive signifies is that media archaeology is thus also a symptom of a general distrust in history, of impatience with linear narrative, and of changes in our concept of causality."[87] Drawing on Foucault as well as Sigmund Freud via Jacques Derrida's archive fever, Elsaesser aligns media archaeology and the archive. The two connect through crisis. To this crisis coalition, he of course also adds cinema, but that is another matter. For a return to the archive is typically borne of scepticism and the aspiration to rewrite the past or at least to trouble the histories we are told. In Elsaesser's words, "The archive now shapes our view of the past more decisively than history, since the archive allows us at all times to revisit and thus to rewrite the past, to reverse engineer our present, and thus to fashion out of the archive also a different future."[88] Although counterarchivists might argue that the archive can also serve as an assurance of historical thinking and processing in the wake of crisis, certainly since Foucault we approach the archive as the domain of discursive practices and not an inscription of an unbroken linearity in what he calls "the mythical book of history."[89] Following Elsaesser, media archaeology similarly reflects a wariness of history and of its continuity between past and present.[90] Media archaeology's rejection of linearity and positivism becomes replaced by a preoccupation with stochastic processes. History turns into machine memory. Approaching the sound archive – indeed, most multimedia archives – media archaeology attends to the remarkable elements of materiality, technology, recording, and memory storage, which independent of historical or cultural sense-making tell their own stories.

Wolfgang Ernst's radically materialist-driven method exemplifies this media-archaeological cold gaze upon the archive disengaged from social life. But his attention to sonic media offers a specificity that is particularly relevant and insightful. As Parikka puts it, Ernst's approach may be characterized more aptly as that of the "dispassionate ear."[91] Not to be mistaken broadly for a synonym of the colonial ear, the dispassionate ear bears out Ernst's preference for the "sonic" over the "acoustic" and consequently the displacement, or decentring, of the listening human subject in his work in favour of the machine. Here the implicit influence of Gilles Deleuze and Félix Guattari comes to the fore.[92] Yet Ernst's dispassionate ear does resonate with the machinations of the colonial ear in its purposeful mode of listening. The ear of the media archaeologist is attuned to the machines that mark the passage of time. This ear stimulates reflection on the materiality of machines and especially their noises. In Ernst's formulation, "There is something like the 'media-archaeological ear' that listens to the sound of material tradition, in fact the technically mediated *sonic* processuality of what is otherwise called history, an alternative to the cultural emphasis on listening to musical semantics."[93] While I disagree with Ernst's strict separation between the material and the cultural, the corollary of his argument that we need to listen before we mount judgment or interpretation is altogether critical to the project of decolonizing listening.[94] Further, listening to the sounds of material and technological tradition alerts us to the noisiness of history's inventions. The noises of the sound machine and the entropy of its recorded objects manifest the challenges and irony of sound capture, whose unwieldy nature occasions possibilities for subversion.

Hardly dispassionate in his perception and judgment of the mechanized reproduction of sound and its effect on music, Theodor W. Adorno was very alert to the phenomenon of "noise" that accompanied, even ushered in, the sounding message of the record or cylinder. He recounts, "When you place the needle upon the revolving phonograph record first a noise appears. As soon as the music begins, this noise recedes to the background. But it constantly accompanies the musical event. Non-musical people who are not able clearly to realize this main event, always complain about the noise. The slight, continual noise is a sort of acoustic stripe."[95] Tendering a wry critique of the phonograph and its "main event," noise, Adorno observes that the sound of the machine formed a critical new dimension of the whole of the listening experience. The voices written into the deep relief of the Edison wax cylinders at the turn of the century are overwhelmed by static and scratching, which due to the limited lifespan of the wax cylinder have gradually taken over the voice and its message. As preoccupied as Adorno was with mechanized recording, he was no media archaeologist. Media archaeology is keenly interested in noise. Preserving the message also means preserving the sonic residue of the medium itself. A transfer of sound recordings to digital files serves to store the noise of the wax cylinder rotating with the stylus as well. Connecting Kittler's application of the term "noise" as one of the defining factors of the discourse network of the 1900s, Ernst considers this the (inevitable) storage of *media-archaeological information* and not *discursive information.*[96]

As we listen to Jeremy Dutcher's music, the inserts of archival recordings are immediately perceptible. The crackling transitions usher in a new voice, or rather, a detectably *old* voice, recorded on a media artifact at the turn of the century. For the ethnographer or the musicologist, this noise is a nuisance; it gets in the way of the voice's message. For the media archaeologist, the noise *is* the message. But what does this brand of noise, that Chionian shapeless zone, tell us? In his study of world music, Michael Denning makes a compelling argument for the revolutionary potency of noise, beyond the evidence of technological processes of audio recording to minoritized and racialized music, such as calypso, rumba, tango, and jazz, historically classified as "noise."[97] Indeed, what of the fact that many would call certain types of music noise? Recall Erich Moritz von Hornbostel's assailed ears at the apparently noisy "chaos of exotic music." Listening is not only subjective; it is most certainly culturally conditioned. Following Tony Schwartz, Jennifer Lynne Stoever maintains that the perception of noise is in the ear of the beholder.[98]

Insofar as media archaeology listens beyond cultural semantics, it becomes an exercise in listening differently. As Parikka intones, "For media archaeology, epistemic thresholds can be used as heuristic devices."[99] Thus, media archaeology facilitates; it is a kind of newfangled hearing aid. The crackling and scratching not only become materially perceptible, they also attune the listener to an era in the past. By lending an ear to noise, media archaeology listens for discrete blocks of signals, removed from any semantic meaning.[100] But given that the static and hum of sound machines such as the phonograph do not lie beyond the threshold of human perception, they challenge an altogether heuristic listening experience. Working within media archaeology, I loosen these microphysical parameters here just a little to pursue an attunement to alternative temporalities beyond those inscribed in history books, beyond those dominant narratives of preservation and salvage. The noise in the sound archive reverberates as a haunting static that refuses to become the ambient "white noise" of concealment and suppression discussed by Robinson.[101]

Through an unfurling of the vast reaches of the field of media archaeology, the pursuit of the sonic takes us to what Steven Feld calls "acoustemology." The portmanteau of "acoustics" and "epistemology," acoustemology theorizes sound as a way of knowing. It asks what is knowable and how things become known.[102] More importantly, as Feld indicates, "Acoustemology prioritizes histories of listening and sounding and their reflexive productions of feedback."[103] In this sense, acoustemology moves away from the Foucauldian postulation underpinning media archaeology, which does not ask how the discourse came into existence as much as it acknowledges its presence. Feld's concept might therefore seem more of a piece with Marxian theory in its interest in the histories of relations and productions. However, I do not view media archaeology and acoustemology at odds. If media archaeology teaches us to listen to the sonic refuse of sound histories – that is, to the noise of its machines – then acoustemology guides us to an understanding of what we are listening to. Sound becomes a chest of knowledge, and listening to that sound unlocks this knowledge. Critical to acoustemology is a distancing and delinking from ethnographic listening and its disciplinary paradigms deeply entrenched in the colonial tempor(e)ality (to borrow one of Ernst's neologisms). Contrary to ethnographic listening, which was more concerned with "propagation than perception," and therefore acquisition over understanding, acoustemology provides a means of inquiry into knowing in and through sounding that is, in Feld's words, "always experiential, contextual, fallible, changeable, contingent, emergent, opportune, subjective, constructed, selective."[104] Emerging from a reflexive turn in anthropology and ethnomusicology, the acoustemological approach carries with it an important recognition of the archaeology of sound recording and the rise in importance of the phonograph as an instrument of ethnography and colonialism. It is also a recognition of the Benjaminian sort, namely, that "there is no document of culture which is not at the same time a document of barbarism."[105]

I began this chapter in the spirit of Jonathan Sterne and his warning against strict binary approaches to the categories of the audio and the visual. As much as vision-centred paradigms have shaped modernity, so too has audio. The colonial gaze has been extensively troubled, especially through film. Visual materials in the form of archival ethnographic footage and photographs are not uncommonly remediated through film, most famously in works such as Vincent Monnikendam's 1995 compilation film *Mother Dao, the Turtlelike*, containing found footage from documentaries and propaganda films shot by Dutch ethnographers between 1912 and 1932 in the former colony of Indonesia. Another example is Marlon Fuentes's 1995 docudrama *Bontoc Eulogy*, which visually and acoustically traces the colonial regimes of the Philippines through a very personal story (see chapter 4). If we can trouble the colonial gaze by turning it back on itself, can we not do the same with the ear? To turn the funnel of the ethnographic phonograph back on itself, as it were, might be understood as methodologically analogous to the metaphor of turning the lens of the ethnographic camera back on itself in the establishment of what Fatimah Tobing Rony has called the third eye.[106] The third ear, or the decolonizing ear, listens to the machine and machinations of ethnographic listening. Decolonial listening must always be reflexive listening. In this way a praxis-oriented approach to decolonial listening, as I have discussed here, is brought forth through remediation and Russell's concept of archiveology. Dutcher remediates century-old wax cylinders through digital sound. But it is ultimately my aim to explore the recycling, reconfiguring, and recodifying of colonial sound recordings through the audiovisual medium of film. This pursuit forms the balance of the book.

As a medium capable of challenging positivist conceptions of time and therefore memory and history, film offers a significant mode of counterarchival or, as I will discuss in the following chapter, of anarchival representation.[107] Much has been written on the topic of colonial and decolonial imaging in film, but there still exists scant scrutiny of decolonial audition in this context. Not least is ideological precedence of the visual vis-à-vis the audiovisual medium of film an attribute of this dearth in scholarship. The first case study is a film that turns a decolonizing ear to the Lautarchiv. Philip Scheffner's 2007 *The Halfmoon Files*, and its 2005 short precursor *From Here to Here* codirected by Scheffner and Madhusree Dutta, offers continuity to the geographical focus of this broader study and therefore provides a fitting transition to the balance of the book and its attention to the hums of film's "re-presencing" (a term I borrow from Vivian Sobchack) of the recordings accreted in the sound archive.[108] Beyond this continuity, *The Halfmoon Files* directly grapples with the pervasive question of how to make a film that turns our attention to sound and the conditioning of its emergence. But Scheffner does not stop there. Both films prick a formidable ear to the heady slips of noise in the sound archive and all of their resounding possibilities.

Chapter Three

The Noise of Decolonial Listening: *From Here to Here* and *The Halfmoon Files*

Perhaps more than any other filmmaker, Philip Scheffner consistently alerts us to the challenges and promises of listening in documentary film. Beginning with his early compilation short *a/c* (2003), based on a seven-track sound project recorded between Berlin and Mumbai, all the way to his more recent documentary *Havarie* (2016), Scheffner's films have more than amplified sound matters. His audience is moved to listen in startling new ways and through unexpected modes. But his accent on audio is not borne of a wariness of the image and the conviction of sound's candour, as one might surmise, for he duly puts pressure on the latter – its sources and the ways in which it is construed. Taking up political topics, such as the colonial archive, militarization, systemic racism, and migration, Scheffner's films are likewise polemical in form through their resistance to the hierarchies of both image and sound. Under his direction, the film as medium is pulled apart. In this way, Scheffner's work lucidly and instructively opens up possibilities for decolonizing listening through film.

Versed in the techniques of sound effects and mixing, Scheffner frequently performs the sound design for his own films. Evident is his penchant for repurposing and remediating audio, occasioning more than a few instances of asynchronous and even acousmatic sound. In interviews, Scheffner has stated that his career began with experimental sound and not image, first as part of the independent film and television production collective dogfilm (1991–99) and later with pong, his collaborative and multimedia production company, founded with long-time collaborator Merle Kröger in 2001. As the latter states on its website, "pong stands for the production of creative documentaries on the border to the arts – films in which the filmmakers' aesthetic and/or political positions are formed and expressed."[1] It was under the aegis of pong that Scheffner began directing his own films and honing his style of documentary filmmaking. Some might find other film genres more fitting in a description of Scheffner's work, for instance "essay film" or "compilation film." In its more capacious definition and its established scrutiny of social issues, the category of documentary offers an apt, and perhaps slightly less prescriptive, grouping.[2] That being said, I reserve the right to return to other modes and genres as points of comparison and cross-over at various junctures.

Madhusree Dutta, the co-director of the first film I consider in this chapter, *From Here to Here*, is an Indian filmmaker, curator, and author based in Mumbai and Cologne. She is also the co-founder of *Majlis*, an interdisciplinary arts institute in Mumbai dedicated to the rights of women, and artistic director of the Akademie der Künste (Academy of Arts) in Cologne. Dutta's documentary shorts are frequently oriented towards the political, activist, and pedagogical. Her directorial contributions in *From Here to Here* provide a fascinating temporal, geographical, and personal balance to the film. With a focus on contemporary India, she develops a series of interviews with a community of German women who immigrated to the country in the years following the Second World War with their Indian husbands. These interviews crisscross with Scheffner's parts in Germany. However, since this chapter directs its attention specifically to the film's material return to the colonial archive in Germany as witnessed in both *From Here to Here* and *The Halfmoon Files*, I do not reference Dutta's work as frequently as that of Scheffner.

The Halfmoon Files (2007) was Scheffner's first full-length film and will form the central focus of this chapter. More than any other work by Scheffner, this film directly grapples with the question of what it means to engage in decolonial listening. Returning its audience to the site of the Halfmoon prisoner-of-war camp in Wünsdorf in operation during the First World War, *The Halfmoon Files* is an audiovisual excavation of the past. But this is not a history of the camp. Instead, Scheffner explores the traces left in the archives, specifically the yields of the Royal Prussian Phonographic Commission (RPPC) between 1915 and 1918. As a camp designed specifically for captured colonial soldiers from Asia and Africa forced into war by Belgian, British, French, and Russian imperial powers, the Halfmoon camp was of particular interest to the pursuits of the RPPC. Of the 1,650 sound recordings produced in the camps, the vast majority were made at the Halfmoon camp.[3] It was not until the 1990s that scholars began to explore this history of the camp as part of a broader discursive turn towards social-historical narratives in research of the period, which had hitherto been dominated by a military focus.[4] This turn precipitated a return to the Lautarchiv at the

Humboldt University in Berlin after decades of neglect.[5] As I discussed in chapter 2, a return to the archive is always marked by the drive to at once resist the archive in its official role of upholding uncontested histories and to probe it further. Scheffner's own extensive research, both with *The Halfmoon Files* and *From Here to Here*, follows in this spirit of return.

Garnering significant attention from scholars across fields, *The Halfmoon Files* has been instrumental in bringing attention both to its filmmaker and to its topic. My own research has been and continues to be indebted to the scholarship of Britta Lange, Avery F. Gordon, Nicole Wolf, Tanja Seider, Priyanka Basu, and surely others to come, whose investigations of *The Halfmoon Files* have contributed to unlocking some of the complexities of this profound film and will provide reference at various points throughout this chapter.[6] But *The Halfmoon Files* is not even the sum of all its parts, as it were. It was preceded two years earlier by the aforementioned sixty-minute film *From Here to Here*, dubbed "video scribbles," and co-directed with Madhusree Dutta. This film explores similar themes and material. Subsequently, *The Halfmoon Files* was followed up by an exhibition in the form of a text montage entitled "Making of ..." in late 2007 to early 2008 at the Kunstraum Kreuzberg/Bethanien in Berlin.[7] The latter was a collaborative project between Lange and Scheffner. For this chapter, I will focus my attention on the films that developed from this research topic. A growing area of scholarship exists on *The Halfmoon Files* and its outgrowths, but no scholarship to date has examined it together with *From Here to Here*.

Originally, I set out to write a chapter that would focus on *The Halfmoon Files* and address *From Here to Here* solely for the purpose of thinking about the breadth of the topic of the colonial sound archive in Scheffner's oeuvre. I quickly came to realize, however, that this earlier video demands its own analysis. Not only do both projects directly return to and interrogate the archive, they also pursue a decolonial mode of listening realized through the repurposing and remediation of its colonial artifacts in the form of analogue audio recordings. The audience is not permitted to consume these objects without a reverberating reminder of their social-historical emergence and legacy. But Scheffner's documentary work is not merely a project of uncovering and problematizing a history of colonial violence. Nor is its decolonial commitment a straightforward pursuit of alternative narratives that return the subject stripped by the indifferent instrumentalization of the scientists of the RPPC to the scene of colonial empirical encounter and technological capture. Indeed, such a project does not require the medium of film.

Instead, *From Here to Here* and *The Halfmoon Files* present two highly mediatized documentaries that expose the audience to noise.

But what do we do with noise? Is it not that "shapeless zone," that "chaotic din," that nausea-inducing phenomenon that disturbs and eludes intention?[8] R. Murray Schafer suggests that the definition of noise has evolved with its increase in the modern world. He rejects the commonly advanced etymology of noise with the Latin "nausea" and draws our attention instead to the evolution of the definition of sound from the general to the more specific as well as from the analogue to the more digital (or from the more natural to the mediated). He orders these definitions as follows: "unwanted sound," "unmusical sound," "any loud sound," and "disturbance in any signaling system."[9] In this ascending order, noise assumes a definition of wholly mediated sound. This is instructive in the context of recorded sound and its remediation through film. If we turn our attention to Schafer's fourth definition, it is evident that noise does not occur in isolation or without consequence. Both Michael Serres and Jacques Attali have argued for the radically creative and even revolutionary power of noise. It is, succinctly according to Serres, "the opening."[10] Or, in Attali's proclamation, "nothing essential happens in the absence of noise."[11] For Attali, noise has the power to rupture networks and destroy social order, all the while creating something new.[12] Noise may remain that offensive and defiant acoustic phenomenon, but we must learn to pay it heed and to listen for its traces to tell us stories off the grid.

This chapter examines noise as the elusive but still tangible trace of mediated pasts. For noise is, to borrow José Esteban Muñoz's term, a form of "ephemera." Just as ephemera are, following Muñoz, "a kind of evidence of what has transpired but certainly not the thing itself" that "does not rest on epistemological foundations but is instead interested in following traces, glimmers, residues, and specks of things," so too, I propose, is noise.[13] Not the artifact itself, noise is the trace of how the artifact came to be. Distinct from Muñozian "queer ephemera," though, noise in this case is not in and of itself reparative. It does not access a critical dimension of art, affect, and lived experience. Yet in its resistance to interpretation, its illegibility, noise likewise surpasses epistemology and thus opens up an unchartered realm of experience. Listening to noise can invoke irritation, confusion, even motion sickness. That's the point. But I am less interested in the listening subject than in how digitally remediated noise draws out new auditory practices. Not a smooth connection, listening to noise does not equate to a direct problematizing of the colonial past and its instrumentalization of technology. Through noise, signals of different relations, transmissions, and processes emerge. Taking away our well-honed epistemological tools, listening to noise makes us pause, stumble, question, and constantly rewind. Moving forward along that decolonial and reparative force is slow but sure.

Noisy Archival Scribbles: *From Here to Here*

As a precursor and lesser-known work, *From Here to Here* is a fascinating and worthy entry point into a study of *The Halfmoon Files*. For a more exhaustive consideration of Scheffner's sustained preoccupation with transnational dialogues between Germany and India, one could begin even further back with the 2003 short *a/c*, but thematically this would take us in a very different direction. *From Here to Here* introduces Scheffner's work in the Berlin sound archive and his developing focus on the phonographic recordings made at the Halfmoon camp. The premise of this earlier film is, however, remarkable; it tracks personal histories of emigration and immigration to and from Germany and India. Beginning with a group of German-born women who in the post–Second World War years followed their Indian husbands to India where they settled, the video in its balance then tracks the stories of immigrants and descendants from India who have made a life in Germany. Composed with personal accounts, a rich transnational dialogue unravels. *From Here to Here*, so named in its attentiveness to multidirectionality and in its resistance to the common binary positioning of "here and there," feels like a much more intimate film than *The Halfmoon Files* and one that stands on its own as a different approach to the topic of German-Indian migrations. Yet there is noteworthy overlap between the two works vis-à-vis remediations of material from the colonial archive. These "video scribbles" sketch blueprints of things to come; they work out kinks of remediated transpositions of sound into the audiovisual realm.

First hints of the Halfmoon camp and its legacy appear in the form of the typed word "Wünsdorf" on the back of a postcard presented in a close-up shot of several loosely piled postcards featuring landscape images of colonized India. This close-up is part of a series of similar shots of postcards that are first displayed in a clutter and then individually, set off in a montage series of black-framed shots. The final postcard displayed bears an image of the striped mosque erected at the site of the Halfmoon camp for Muslim prisoners as part of a strategic military project, here shot in black and white but garishly colourized in shades of fuchsia and turquoise.[14] (The original colours of the mosque were in fact red and blue.) To the top left of the image is a smaller embedded one of a group of so-called Mohammedaner (so the caption reads, employing an archaic and derogatory word for Muslims), robed in traditional, utterly Orientalized costume, likewise garishly colourized in bright yellows, reds, and blues. A mediated spectacle of the Other unlike any other in the film, this postcard demonstrates an erstwhile fetishized attraction consumed, shared, and collected via modern technology. But the film rejects a re-aestheticization or nostalgic sensibility of the image through its pairing with an uncomfortable listening experience. The soundtrack during this brief interval is striking and even earsplitting. Bridging from an earlier scene, the extradiegetic music is a contemporary electronic music composition that conjures a strange, almost otherworldly effect with sonic analogies of data transfers and Geiger counters. Gradually, a noise remarkably similar to that of a jet engine about to take off overwhelms the soundtrack. The thundering sound crescendos and then abruptly cuts with the image of the final postcard, succeeded by a voice-over and the rhetorical question "*Ist das Indien?*" (Is that India?). With potential sonic signals of travel and jet-setting, the soundtrack is perhaps not excessively at odds with the overall content but still forceful in its assertion of noise that is meant to disturb us, if not give us pause.

If the preceding sequence offers visual hints of what is to come in *The Halfmoon Files*, then the following montage sequence is an unambiguous audiovisual scramble through the colonial archive, which firmly ushers in more to come. It begins with shots of Wünsdorf in winter: a large puddle against a dismal landscape of a parking lot and a deeper-situated dilapidated building, another puddle from closer up, a blurry shallow focus shot of brush encrusted in a layer of sleet. The shot focus is racked to reveal a deteriorated shack set back among the overgrowth (part of the old barracks of the Halfmoon camp). All the while the faint crackling sound of static tickles the listener's ears. Is this the residual noise of the camera? Acoustic confusion is amplified in the following montage sequence of short shots, sharp cuts, and fast-tracking; imagine a horizontal newsreel effect. For faint crackling turns to the loud clacking of what sounds like 35 mm projection noise as intercut shots of the ruins of the Halfmoon barracks, aisles of filing cabinets, and silent black-and-white archival footage of the camp and its soldiers flash by. This old footage would have been captured on a 35 mm reel, commonly employed for early ethnographic filming. That Scheffner in his sound editing employs, rather than edits out, the noise of the projector as part of this remediated audiovisual experience brings the might of the analogue technological realm into play. We are not only taking in Dutta and Scheffner's contemporary film but also the anonymous footage from the Bundesarchiv (Federal Archive) made nearly a century earlier in the camp. The noise accompanying this montage brings this temporal variance into perception.

Jussi Parikka surmises that "noise becomes an index of archival logic."[15] With this he indicates, following Michel Duchamp, that the archive is not simply a collection of historical materials and facts but an utterance of the very condition for their uncovering. The noise of the 35 mm projector signals the archive and the technological stamp imprinted in its material stockpiles. Reels clacking as they madly turn in the machine, the instruments of archival creation allow themselves to be heard. There is an element of immediacy, that sense of being present to the original recording, that resonates with Jay David Bolter and Richard Grusin's double logic of remediation. According to Bolter and Grusin, the paradox of the hypermedial technique of remediation in our digital world is that it actually strives to achieve its opposite – greater immediacy.[16] Scheffner takes his audience into the archive not with an explanation in voice-over or direct visual cues but via the noise of the apparatus.

This nearly minute-long accelerated montage concludes with a return to silence and the present-day Wünsdorf parking lot. There is a dissolve to another close-up image of a row of black filing cabinets; a person approaches and opens a drawer. Brown folders stamped with the letters "PK" and a number are revealed. We have entered the Lautarchiv and the "PK" stands for Phonographische Kommission (Phonographic Commission), for these are the shellac records containing the sound recordings made by the RPPC. The same person, the archivist, fishes out a folder labelled PK 619, carefully opens the folder, and inspects the record. The film offers a close-up of the record's brief, handwritten label indicating the contents of the record; it appears that the record contains two voice recordings, the first belonging to Mall Singh. Carried to a nearby desk, the record is then placed on a turntable. Up to this point only the synchronous sounds of the actions undertaken by the archivist may be heard: the padding of his footsteps on the floor, the filing cabinet being opened and closed, the shuffling through files. Once the archivist has placed the record on the platter of the turntable, he flicks a tuning fork, which reverberates in a piercing hum. The film then cuts to a close-up of the stylus being placed on the record; the hum mutates into a scratching and then a signal sound with increasing pitch. This sequence of sounds is specific but also not likely detectable to the untrained ear. The tuning fork helps the archivist find the correct rotation speed for the turntable appropriate for this record, which is critical when working with a more advanced, variable-speed turntable, especially if the record requires a specific rotation speed. The tuning fork is A-440, and it seems like the signal at the start of the record is also a constant A-440. A siren-like sound emerges, and we can make out the variable pitch as the archivist adjusts the speed of the turntable so that the tone matches the tuning fork.[17] The visual close-up introduces a possible acoustic close-up. While Béla Balázs contends that the acoustic close-up, not unlike the visual close-up, offers a humanly impossible sense of perception – that is, sounds barely audible to the naked human ear can be heard – I propose that the amplification and isolation of sounds may also serve as variations of the acoustic close-up. In this scene, the visual close-up already plays with our perceptions.[18] At such proximity to the record stylus, we can anticipate the intense scope of sound.

In the Lautarchiv amid the collection of phonographic recordings made by the RPPC at the prisoner-of-war camps between 1915 and 1918, we listen to the recording of Mall Singh, a Sikh prisoner once interned at the Halfmoon camp. This particular recording becomes the impetus for Scheffner's film *The Halfmoon Files*, which involves a search for further traces of the person who left his acoustic fingerprint behind.[19] As we will discover, the search for the identity of Mall Singh entails an audiovisual project of significant political and social proportions. Excavating this archive of war and empire, Scheffner asks what it would mean to listen beyond the conditioning of the colonial ear that gave shape to these recordings. If *From Here to Here* is the prototype and test run for this later project, it is also the rough notes, the scribbles, by way of which ideas are worked out, and in some cases later discarded. In this first playing of Mall Singh's recording, there is a cut from close-up images of the stylus and then the turning spindle to archival footage of what appears to be a group of Sikh prisoners lined up against a wooden structure. The camera moves in a pan and slightly out of focus along the structure. More men appear. Could the voice belong to one of these men? The audiovisual composition in *From Here to Here* seems to suggest that this recording is not unique but rather representative of many voices of Indian prisoners of war interned in Germany. Indeed, Singh's recording is just as general as it is particular. It could be the story of any one of the men pictured here. The original recording was made in Punjabi, with a smattering of Hindi words. Here it is in English translation provided by Santanu Das:

There was once a man who would have butter back in India
He would also have two sers of milk
He served for the British
He joined the European war
He was captured by the Germans

> He wants to go back to India
> If he goes back to India then he will get the same food
> Three years have already passed
> There's no news as to when there will be peace
> Only if he goes back to India will he get that food
> If he stays here for two more years then he will die
> By God's grace, if they declare peace then we'll go back.[20]

This recording was labelled PK 619 and eventually placed for preservation in the Lautarchiv, where it can still be found today on a shellac record. The film does not directly comment on the semantic or rhetorical content of the recording. As a personal account of war and imprisonment, the recording is distinctive. I will return to these aspects briefly in my discussion of *The Halfmoon Files*.

Contrary to *The Halfmoon Files*, *From Here to Here* enfolds the history of the Halfmoon camp and its colonial prisoners into a broader narrative of migration (both voluntary and forced) throughout the twentieth century, as opposed to a narrative of turn-of-the-century colonialism and the concomitance of the First World War. Thus, in this earlier video Mall Singh's recording becomes another testimony of the experience of travel and homesickness. Later, Scheffner will forsake the arbitrary pairing of sound and image and isolate the archival media artifacts more explicitly. We learn that despite much searching, Scheffner does not find any images of Mall Singh in the archive. His identity begins as and remains a mystery to the filmmaker. *From Here to Here* gives rise to the significance of sound, and particularly noise, in a probing of the archive. Once the recording of Mall Singh comes to an end, there is a cut to the close-up image of the identity card that accompanies the recording. It contains a printed set of questions about the recording and the identity of the so-called informant and handwritten responses. Moving from left to right, the camera eye appears to read the card. As an accompaniment, the noise of the static and signal hum of the variable pitch of the record that preceded Mall Singh's narration has returned and now fills the soundtrack. The machine refuses to be silenced. If, according to Parikka, noise is the index for archival logic, then that is because it is, in Greg Hainge's words, "the trace and index of a relation."[21] But the noise of machines of the past made audible by the machines presented in *From Here to Here* do not simply point us back to the physical archive from which they were drawn; this indexicality is not tautological. Instead, it invites us to contemplate a new archival logic that destabilizes the knowledge that may have once found validation by way of the archive, especially the colonial archive. Such logic re-presents itself in *The Halfmoon Files*, which scrambles things further as it calls forth the ghosts of the archive.

The Noise of Ghosts in *The Halfmoon Files*

The same year *From Here to Here* appeared and just two years prior to the release of Philip Scheffner's *The Halfmoon Files*, the American horror-thriller *White Noise* (Geoffrey Sax, 2005) hit the theatres. Although it was a critical flop, the premise of the film nonetheless offers food for thought. A man's wife gets in a terrible accident and eventually dies. He discovers that he can still communicate with her ghost via electronic sound recordings, or electronic voice phenomenon. She speaks through the "white noise" of static. Staying true to its genre, *White Noise* reveals the horror that can take place when you attempt to communicate with the dead – that is, if you listen too closely to the noise. Not only do you become obsessed to the point of all abandon, you might also begin to hear threatening voices. Eventually, listening to these voices becomes the man's downfall. Raising spectres is a dangerous game. Following a stock narrative of horror, this film nonetheless rings novel in its warning against the potential menace of digital noise and the inundation of technological recording in our contemporary world. The film even seeks legitimacy in historical invention and opens with a 1928 quote from Thomas Edison himself: "Nobody knows whether our personalities pass on to another existence or sphere, but if we can evolve an instrument so delicate as to be manipulated by our personality as it survives in the next life such an instrument ought to record something." The instrument in question was of course the phonograph. There was great promise and wonder attached to the original invention of the phonograph and its ability to "let the dead speak." Notwithstanding the significant political connotations of *white* noise, as precisely those inundating, majoritarian sounds that attempt to drown out minoritized voices, the notion that noise produced by signal processing might contain muffled voices and reveal hidden truths fires our attention and our imagination.[22]

Scheffner's 2007 documentary *The Halfmoon Files* is also a ghost story. It too listens for spectres within the static and hum of history's recording machines not at the site of their capture but at the site of their storage – the sound archive. Treading on the plane of horror, this film furthermore uncovers the traces of a sinister history of violence – of colonialism and militarism. But this rendering is incomplete. Exploring the period of the First World War in Germany nearly a century later, the film uncovers events carefully tucked away and overshadowed by others during the country's long twentieth century.[23] These events are mapped onto a network of minor and major, which loosely coalesce but foreground four occurrences: the birth of Mall Singh in 1892, Thomas Edison's invention of the phonograph in 1877, the birth of Wilhelm Doegen also in 1877, and the recording of Mall Singh's voice in the Halfmoon camp by Doegen with the Edison phonograph in 1916. With this proposed cartography, Scheffner does not aim to provide a new historicism of causal connections nor a new overarching narrative but nodal points for new relationalities. This is a set of relations Scheffner seeks to trace with an eye and especially an ear to the future it became.

Developing beyond the so-called scribbles of *From Here to Here*, *The Halfmoon Files* explicitly takes as its object the German colonial archive, and the Lautarchiv in particular. Such a focus places it conceptually in the company of many other archive-based films, a list of which is too long to include here but some of which I examine throughout this book. There is also no dearth of scholarship on the archive-based documentary and its upheaval of indexical logic. Let us consider some of these arguments. According to Paula Amad, film in its genealogical concern for the fragments of the historical present, as opposed to the historical past, has always posed a challenge to the archive, its positivism, "its sacred myths of order, exhaustiveness, and objective reality."[24] Through Jaimie Baron's concept of "the archive effect" in film, she notably argues for "an *experience of reception* rather than an indication of official sanction or storage location."[25] Further, Catherine Russell uses the term "archiveology" to describe the process of filmmaking that "return[s] to the images of the past that were produced to entertain, or produced for more serious purposes of documentary recording, and review[s] them for new ways of making history come alive in new forms."[26] In direct dialogue with *The Halfmoon Files*, Priyanka Basu describes Scheffner's archival approach as a project of "undo[ing] the original scientific and colonial intentions of its archival elements, loosening sounds and images from their official contexts and standardised formats in order to make them available for interpretation and so they may impact viewers and listeners bodily and cerebrally."[27] She importantly adds, "Instead of an immersive, fictionalised reproduction of the past, smoothing over of lacunae, or authoritative use of documents as evidence, the film foregrounds mediation, accident, and partial truths."[28] What underpins all of these methods is the conviction of film's anarchival potential. But to conceive of film as in and of itself a radical medium is a flawed line of thought. Archive-based films, especially colonial archive-based films, must reflect on the challenge of representing archival material without reinforcing the very structures of taxonomy and representation that informed the archival practices in place at the time of their collection.[29]

The Halfmoon Files begins with what turns out to be the first in a series of futile meetings between the filmmaker and the vice ambassador of the Indian embassy in Berlin, Amit Dasgupta, in which the impulse for the film is given full expression by way of a request: the desire to shoot a ghost story in India. Taken aback by the request, the ambassador appears confused, uneasy even, and already alludes to the trouble that will ensue in granting permission. Indeed, Scheffner never receives permission to film in India, but his ghost story still comes to life. What emerges instead is a film in spite of itself. Ostensibly performing preliminary research for this film-to-be, Scheffner goes to the archive and listens. There he discovers that the ghosts of his story are actually geographically much closer to home than first presumed. But to construct a ghost story involves much more than a flight of fancy. One must take the evidence seriously and be prepared to reach out to the other side of what is representationally possible. On the subject of piecing together ghost stories, Avery F. Gordon insightfully writes:

> Following the ghosts is about making contact that changes you and refashions the social relations in which you are located. It is about putting life back in where only a vague memory or bare trace was visible to those who bothered to look. It is sometimes about writing ghost stories, stories that not only repair representational mistakes, but also strive to understand the conditions under which a memory was produced in the first place, toward a countermemory, for the future.[30]

Writing about the haunting residues of unfinished histories of, for instance, American slavery and *los desparecidos* during Argentina's Dirty War, Gordon describes the ghost story as not only an alternative narrative but also a reparative one that counters those in place and looks towards the future. Her formulation befits *The Halfmoon Files* and what I emphasize as its project of decolonizing listening. Scheffner's microphone and camera bother to listen and look. The acts of listening and looking for both Gordon and Scheffner do not simply amount to an exposure of hidden violences of history, what Eve Kosofsky Sedgwick has referred to as the "paranoid" impulse of New Historicist inquiry.[31] Instead, they offer the ghosts that haunt (the sound archive), dismissed by history, a new lease on life. This means that beyond replaying old recordings and letting the voices of the dead resonate, the film exhorts its audience to listen to the noise – the traces, the ephemera – that saturates the archival artifacts and their remediation.

Ontologically speaking, noise may be nothing at all but, as Greg Hainge maintains, it echoes "the relational process through which the world and its objects express themselves."[32] By listening to noise, we begin to perceive these relations. To propose as Jean-Luc Nancy does that listening is an act that opens up our perceptions and attunes us to the phenomenological relations that shape our world, ourselves, and others, seems metaphysically circumscribed.[33] It neglects the history of listening I have charted in earlier chapters as entangled in the colonial matrix of power that reinforces subject and object positions. Thus, listening alone, whether with understanding or not, cannot upset or delink the binaries underpinned by Western thinking. Listening to that uncontrollable, uncontainable, and oppositional phenomenon of noise, however, gets us closer to this promise.[34] Insofar as noise resists meaning and understanding, it has the capacity to disturb dominant epistemologies. Listening to noise in *The Halfmoon Files* raises the spectres of colonialism in a manner that shunts direct consumption (what Dylan Robinson calls hungry listening) and unsettles one's position as listener in the first place.[35]

The opening scene that follows the film's prologue in the office of the Indian ambassador is indeed a chimerical filmic orchestration of all the elements of a ghost story that orally and visually plunges into an oblique moment in history. In this scene, a thick layer of fog blurs the objects within the frame; the image appears milky white. As the atmosphere clears, a static narrow river flanked by marshy overgrowth comes into view. In a reverse tracking shot from an invisible source and perspective, the viewer's gaze is pulled back along this patch of water as though on a ghost ride. This mobile retreat visually vivifies the historical passage of the film, a regressive moving away while facing forward. One hears the faint chirping of birds and the swishing of water, coupled with an almost inaudible extradiegetic chorus of bells. As the film's title shimmers across the screen, the static of a record is audible, and then a voice. According to the subtitles, this voice belongs to a prisoner of war from India, Bhawan Singh. The voice sings what sounds like a Punjabi folk song, marked by steady tempo and repeating melody. The placement of the song at the opening of the film and its affective attunement are significant. Folk music traditionally has a storytelling function that relies wholly on oral transmission and often cannot be traced back to its source. The noise of what sounds like digital scrambling begins to fill the soundtrack. The crackle of analogue static follows. As the song continues, so too does the hum of static. The camera stops and the song turns to speech in a curious introduction about storytelling that concludes with the heady words "This is a true story." Settling on this landscape, the lingering crackle of static of the recording grows in intensity and continues on after the voice has faded. With another cut to black, the noise briefly bridges and then new noise begins. This is one of 765 recordings made at the Halfmoon camp and the neighbouring Weinberg camp, which make up a third of the RPPC collection in the Lautarchiv.[36] Bhawan Singh's voice is just one of many colonial prisoners' voices remediated throughout the film. If the film's prelude in the ambassador's office frames *The Halfmoon Files* as a story told otherwise, then this opening scene ushers in a "truthful" tale through the piercing drone of noise.

A shift to the Lautarchiv in the following scene offers grounding in more ways than one. Not only does it return the film to a more identifiable and realistic setting, the turn to the archive lends an air of authority and historical legitimacy to *The Halfmoon Files* and its premise. More than just a dusty storehouse for historical artifacts, as Michel Foucault maintained, the archive sets the rules for what can be said or written, or – now I am extrapolating – what can even be filmed. The archive is *"the general system of formation and transformation of statements"*; in other words, it is the site that determines all possible enunciations.[37] In a similar vein, Jacques Derrida reminds us that "archivization produces as much as it records the event."[38] Their respective arguments are of course not founded a priori on the ideology of the authority of the archive and the history it has come to tell, but on their understanding of how discourses form and historical "truths" have come to be. But as excavation site and construction site, as Catherine Russell contends following Walter Benjamin, the power of the archive is by no means immutable. As Foucault would have it, as well as Derrida, the archive bears unspoken dialectical potential.[39] Scheffner's own take on the archive reflects this mix of deference and scepticism. In voice-over he matter-of-factly begins to describe the physical properties of the sound archive but allows his voice to be cut off by the extradiegetic voice of the archivist, who comments on his own personal experience of working alone in an archive where one is never really alone in the presence of the thousands of voice recordings on shellac records (7,500, we are told). Even Scheffner's description of the archive cannot escape the enunciative conditions set by the archive itself, and therefore becomes suspicious, too. His voice wanes into the background.

That the voice-over of the filmmaker, traditionally perceived as the authoritative voice of God common to expository documentary, should be truncated by another voice demonstrates the reflexive quality of Scheffner's approach. Reflexive modes of voicing in documentary are of course nothing new. Since the post-war years, documentaries have moved away from their early antecedents with the didactic films of

John Grierson and Robert J. Flaherty, to name the most prominent, and consequently away from authoritarian modes of direct address and voice-of-God narration. Bill Nichols has referred to this as the "evolution" of the four phases of documentary film: the Griersonian mode of direct address, cinema verité, direct address or interview style, and finally self-reflexive (what Nichols would later refer to as expository, observational, participatory, and reflexive).[40] But a number of scholars have also criticized this linear approach. Whereas Nichols proposes a move away from the voice-over altogether in favour of a multiplicity of voices (consider for instance the documentary films of Trinh T. Minh-ha), documentary scholars counter that the device of the voice-over is not the problem, but its early mode of use. For, as Pooja Rangan has more recently argued, the use of a reflexive first-person voice-over can also be "transgressive," and this voice-over "not only grapples with who has the right to speak in documentary but also who dismantles cultural preconceptions with respect to the so-called voice or worldview of a given documentary film."[41] In interviews, Scheffner has expressed his own challenges with voice-over narration. Subtle as it may seem, what is perhaps most exceptional about the reflexivity of Scheffner's voice-over in *The Halfmoon Files* is its pairing with his reflexive approach to the archive. He refuses to allow the ideological authority of the documentary voice to stand in as a metaphor for the selfsame authority of archive. Instead, he recognizes the need to scramble the logic of both.

We might call this film's approach anarchival. A compound used first fleetingly by Derrida, "anarchive" not only presents a state of archive-less-ness, it moreover gives expression to the absolute self-effacing death drive of the archive that subtends "the violence of forgetting."[42] Subsequently taken up and drawn out by scholars, the anarchive has been theorized with greater nuance as not the destruction and loss inherent in the archive but as something productive and reparative, what Benjamin Hutchens calls "counter-memory," Siegfried Zielinski "an effective alternative to the archive" that "necessarily challenge[s], indeed provoke[s], the archive," and Brian Massumi *a repertory of traces*."[43] Broadly conceived, since Derrida the anarchive has been reconceptualized as a different, counterarchive. Hutchens's notion of countermemory is particularly instructive to this study and felicitously ties back to Gordon's description of the ghost story as a countermemory for the future. Hutchens writes: "Now, counter-memory can arise at this nexus whenever a forgotten memory becomes remembered in direct opposition to the normative and canonical ('official') tradition in which it was forgotten. In other words, counter-memory is anti-archival in the sense that it seeks to remember what has been consigned there (or deemed unworthy of consignation); but it also composes a counter-archive which, in opposing the 'official' tradition, constitutes an alternative thread of discursive connectivity."[44] For Hutchens the anarchival impulse does not seek to destroy the archive but to glimpse under its dusty piles and in its cobwebbed corners of neglect. It attends to the fissures and gaps. Out of these overlooked crevices, different traces of events emerge. Recognizing how these traces evidence other, less canonical narratives is the ambition of the anarchivist (indeed, the orthographic proximity to "anarchist" is duly noted). Countermemory runs counter, not parallel, to dominant narratives of history. It is memory whose repression is mechanized by such narratives. The reality of the prisoner-of-war camps strewn across the German countryside during the First World War, and the fact that some of them became laboratories for colonial ethnography, have not been part of Germany's rehearsed narrative of the war.[45] The anarchivist instrumentalizes the emergence of this countermemory.

If *The Halfmoon Files* transfigures the colonial sound archive into an anarchive, then this is an *anarchive* of noise. This offers a twist on Mary Ann Doane's concept of the "*archive* of noise," which draws on Friedrich Kittler's observation about the storage of the excessive noise of the machine.[46] The consequence of the twentieth-century inventions of recording technology was the recording of their own noise. Thus, for better or for worse noise became the indexical element of the era of mechanical reproduction. For Doane, the concept of the archive of noise accrued from new technology, such as phonography and cinema, and its capacity to "record indiscriminately."[47] Doane focuses on the emergence of time and the possible recording of time through these media. For her, noise is rendered a measure of time. Most instructive about Doane's concept of the archive of noise, however, is its indication of the sound archive's indelible storage of excess, that immaterial materiality. Noise is excess. Noise is also ephemera. The concept of the archive of noise proves paradoxical. Does not noise resist the discursivity and epistemology of the archive? An anarchive of noise therefore seems fitting: an archive that is not really an archive. Wolfgang Ernst also recognized this paradox. He applies the designation "anarchive of sound" to convey the phenomenon of the technological storage of noise, which for him is always "opposed to the archival order of musical notation."[48] The physical place of the sound archive featured in *The Halfmoon Files* thus becomes a place of its own negation, or at least its undoing.

This first of four explicit visits to the sound archive in the film, which visually consists of nothing more than a static shot of a poorly lit room containing filing cabinets and desks, is cacophonous. A series of voices and machinic noises fill the soundtrack. The off-screen voices of Scheffner and the unnamed archivist are followed by that of the phonograph. Accompanied by the swell of mysterious music, the phonograph speaks through a recording. As the camera begins to lethargically move forward, another voice emerges. This one is tinny, machinelike. It is a promotional address for the phonograph that concludes with the words, "I am a genuine Edison Phonograph." The machine speaks. Then a fit of static inserts itself and the voice of Thomas Edison himself sounds: "This is … ah … Edison speaking." The visual track leaves the archive. There is another cut to black. Scheffner's voice returns: "In 1877, Thomas Edison invented the phonograph itself. He is the first man to listen to a recording of his own voice. I can hear him even though he died in 1931. Ever since Edison's invention, the dead can speak."[49] For Scheffner, this story begins not with the dawn of German colonial rule in 1885 or the ascent to power of Emperor Wilhelm II in 1888, which bore catastrophic consequences, but with the invention of the Edison phonograph. In Foucauldian fashion, Scheffner soberly identifies this moment as the discrete historical break that seems to have set everything else in motion. With one fell swoop, a new discursive point in time emanates through the realm of technological recording. From this moment forth, the ghosts of the dead could speak and the past itself acquired a new medium of return.

Ghosts are not just symbolically summoned in *The Halfmoon Files*. Throughout the film the speech of the prisoners of war assumes a self-reflexive mode and twice we hear stories about ghosts. "What is a ghost?" Bhawan Singh asks. He then continues: "How does it live? How many types of ghosts exist? How does one become a ghost? This is what I will tell you." Surfacing early in the film, questions posed by the recording offer a premise for the film itself. How felicitously these questions serve this story, so much so that their validity as part of a recording in the Lautarchiv seems almost too good to be true. Would this have been a text drawn up for the prisoner to read? Did he suggest the topic? How did the scientists respond? Recording-as-becoming-ghost adds another dimension to the salvage paradigm at the heart of ethnographic recording, what James Clifford has referred to as "present-becoming-past," discussed in the previous chapter and to be considered further in chapter 4.[50] At the site of recording, one becomes a ghost. Replayed, even remediated, the recording brings the ghost to life.

What Is the Noise that Precedes the Image?

Voice recording made it possible to listen to the dead. But not all early technology has had the capacity to connect us with the past in the same way. Consider the tacit old black-and-white photograph: it does not enliven so much as it embalms its subject. From André Bazin to Roland Barthes, photography has been defined as the medium that is frozen in time.[51] In his meditation on the essence of photography, Barthes goes so far as to link it with death. The cold mortification of the photograph is "the spectrum," in other words, its spectacle of death, he declares.[52] Photography's death mask contrasts with the analogue voice recording. (One wonders how Barthes would have responded to a voice recording of his dearly departed mother.) As drowned out as the latter might be by the noisy memory of the machine, the fiery crackle and hum still bear an enlivening quality. In *The Halfmoon Files*, even when the image itself ebbs, as it so often does, Nicole Wolf intones that "the crackling of a more than 90-year-old sound recording of a striking voice enlivens an image that is as black as a shellac record."[53] This image as black as a shellac record is nothing less than the black screen, a device repeatedly employed in the film. Typically rendered a sign of absence or negative space in cinema, the black screen can serve as a placeholder for what is missing, or it can convey the ethical and aesthetic limits of representation itself. In the context of death in documentary, Vivian Sobchack identifies the black screen as a "visual silence" that commemorates.[54] Perhaps a more intuitive reading of the black screen here returns us to the medium itself, to the cinematic apparatus. Drawing on Ágnes Pethő, Tanya Shilina-Conte describes the black screen as a cinematic mirror capable of reflecting the material properties of its medium.[55] Metaphors aside, the black screen is always a reminder that we are watching a film. Tremendously integral to the grammar of Scheffner's cinematic language in *The Halfmoon Files*, the lingering black screen cuts every scene, forging recursive ellipses in the visual logic of the film. But where vision splits, sound bridges. As Wolf remarks, "Tones, voices, crackling, and rustling – beside, with, behind, or without an image – open up spaces of resonance."[56] If nothing else, the black screen gives primacy to sound.

In voice-over, Scheffner informs us that "there are no images in the sound archive." While this observation is not entirely accurate – according to Jürgen Mahrenholz, of the 1,650 recordings made of prisoners of war, fifty photos did survive – it should be understood beyond mere quantitative reasoning.[57] By making this observation, Scheffner both points to a lacuna, of something missing that should be there, and makes a statement about the film. Some may be inclined to read this statement as the impetus for Scheffner's search to put a face and an identity to the voice of Mall Singh, for all intents and purposes the protagonist of this ghost story. Indeed, part of his fascination with Singh's recording stems from the mystery of his identity. I read Scheffner's statement as another kind of truth, however. This is not a film about the absence of images but about the presence of sound.

Listening again to the 1:20-long recording of Mall Singh's voice, first heard in *From Here to Here*, we discern a tragic story about a homesick man from India forced into war in Europe and surely to perish should the war persist. In this second listening, though, our eyes settle on a black screen. Unlike the speculatively representational footage of Sikh prisoners presented as visual referentiality to the content of Singh's recording in *From Here to Here*, which could be read as the troubling strategy of generalization so common to ethnographic film, *The Halfmoon Files* does not speculate or substitute.[58] The same close-up image of the stylus pricking the deep grooves of the shellac record drowned in a vibrating hum cuts to black, and only the white subtitles are visible for the duration of the recording. The black screen stands in for what is missing – an image in the archive – but it also demands our auditory attunement. The black screen is always situated at the threshold of impossibility as well as possibility.[59] We listen and treat Singh's words as a speech act with semantic weight. What is this story Mall Singh tells? How does he tell it? Scheffner notes twice during the film that the scientists at the Halfmoon camp were not interested in the personal stories of their study objects. By contrast, we are implicitly instructed to listen differently, to listen beyond the stratum of linguistic analysis. This recording is unique among the recordings in its status as a personal anecdote. This plaintive narrative about a prisoner of war from India is further striking due to Singh's use of the third person. Could this narrative refer to someone other than Singh, possibly one of the other nearly two thousand Indian prisoners of war at the Halfmoon camp? Or, as the vice ambassador Amit Dasgupta speculates during a direct reading of Mall Singh's recorded monologue on the occasion of the reinauguration of the war cemetery in Wünsdorf by the Commonwealth War Graves Commission, perhaps Singh had become so alienated from himself throughout the course of war that he could only refer to himself in the third person: "There was once a man ..." As a speech act of a colonial prisoner of war, Singh's words also form a testimony; he bears witness to the catastrophes of colonialism, war, and imprisonment in a foreign land. Giving testimony is a subjectivizing act. According to Giorgio Agamben, if the archive "presupposed the bracketing of the subject, who was reduced to a simple function or an empty position; it was founded on the subject's disappearance into the anonymous murmur of statements," then testimony is its opposite.[60] Testimony asserts the subject not simply through speech but through speech at the site of its impossibility. Agamben's example of course is testimony from

Auschwitz, so often mired in the province of unspeakability: how can one speak of such horrors? Without drawing historical comparisons, I think that a similar approach to testimony could be applied to Singh's speech act.

But speech, with its emphasis on meaning, distinguishes itself from sound, and noise in particular. *The Halfmoon Files* neither wishes to reduce Mall Singh's recording to linguistic analysis nor to submit it solely to Platonic logos. Instead, within its audiovisual realm, the film raises the question posed by Fred Moten: "How do sound and its reproduction allow and disturb the frame or boundary of the visual?"[61] Overall, Moten does not seek to replace the ocular with the aural and therefore lead us into the trap of the audiovisual divide. Rather, in his words, he "is interested in what the noise carries" as something other than what can be seen.[62] Against the black screen, the sounds emitting from the shellac record transcend the visual frame. Sound becomes irreducible to the image. This moves beyond Michel Chion's assertion that there is no auditory container commensurable with the visual frame in film.[63] Moten's question attends to the very metaphysics of sound as exteriority itself. What if we read Scheffner's "search" for the image as instead a "resistance" to the image? Without resisting the visual per se, I propose that *The Halfmoon Files* instead resists the structures and formations of identity and interpretation entangled in Western thought. Whereas Moten and Tina M. Campt after him ask "what sound precedes the image?" this film relies not on a linearity or teleology of sound and image but rather on the categorical absence of the image that forces us to listen and thus belies the possibility of sound as a mere precursor or animator of the image.[64]

Scheffner's recurring use of the black screen confirms this insight; it is not only about absence but also about presence – the presence of sound. The black screen is a penumbra of possibility. Exploring the cinematic technique of pairing sound and a black screen activates other possibilities. What happens to sound against the black screen? Certainly not acousmatic sound, Mall Singh's recording evidently issues from a record drawn from a filing cabinet in the Lautarchiv. Yet once the screen cuts from the turntable to black, the sound becomes extradiegetic, no longer anchored to the on-screen world. Localization and spatialization of the sound subsequently become a challenge. For this on-screen world briefly ceases to exist. Occupying a space outside the diegetic film world, the extradiegetic sound can directly address the audience. This is sound that moves beyond the frame and penetrates the space of the listener. A sense of proximity and even presence opens up. The choice to pair Singh's recording with a black screen may also serve to bring forth the man himself whose voice we hear. Contradictory as it may seem, the juxtaposition renders Singh as a tangible person and a concrete being – that is, as much more than just a voice labelled with the register number "PK 619." Scheffner describes this experience of listening in the following way: "Every stutter, every stumble, every gasp makes it possible to experience the physical presence of the person sitting in front of the funnel."[65] Suggestive of what Barthes famously refers to as the grain of the voice, here Scheffner emphasizes the physicality of Singh's voice over and above speech and representation.[66] The identity card appended to the recording, apparently completed by Wilhelm Doegen himself, includes a brief description of Singh's voice: "*starke, helle Stimme mit guter Resonanz*" (strong, clear voice with good resonance). Yet, according to Santanu Das, the speech is "interrupted by awkward silences and sharp intakes of breath."[67] Mall Singh pauses, stutters, repeats words, and clears his throat twice during the recording. Further, his voice sounds toneless, as though he is performing solely for the sake of the phonograph with scant regard for the pathos reflecting the content of his speech. Why did Doegen not note any of these peculiarities? Scheffner indicates that the scientists would note any diversions or interruptions to the recording. He offers the examples of Baldeo Singh's parenthetic "*Guten Abend!*" (Good evening!) or Rajwali Khan's "*Salaam Aleikum!*" (Peace be upon you!) that may be heard in other recordings later in the film. Perhaps annotation did not extend to the grain or the noise of the voice of the so-called informant. Against the black screen, speech enveloped in the grain of the voice and the media archaeological grain of the humming phonograph resonates. As Das compellingly puts it, "A voice calls out from the phonograph, strains itself in the act of recording: the trepidation, the timbre, the laboured enunciation, the slight breathlessness seem to bridge the gap between technological reproduction and lived experience."[68] An admixture of man and machine equals a penetrating din.

The film demonstrates particular interest in not only the recordings that contain personal stories and anecdotes, such as those of Mall Singh or Bela Singh, who also narrates his own story of war and imprisonment for the RPPC, but also those with unforeseen, compromising noise, in the form of parenthetical statements or the resonant grain of the voice that pierces the mechanics of speech. Scheffner informs us in voice-over: "The unforeseen is not desired. It endangers scientific comparability and creates additional work." Yet it seems that the undesirable was inevitable. In another breath, Scheffner indicates that "the strictly standardized process of scientific data collection is prone to disruptions of all kinds." Through a sound montage of sundry recordings edited together in what strikes the ear as a collection of truncated self-introductions including name and place of birth, the listener is exposed to various errata that include slips of opinion, personal addresses, and information as well as background chatter. Most prominent are the multiple reverberating guffaws let loose by yet another prisoner, Chote Singh, and recorded by the RPPC. Catherine Russell describes this accidental intervention of reality as dissenting in its subversion of the unexpected subversion of ethnographic pursuits, which ultimately did not strive to achieve a realistic picture of a cultural experience but instead sought to reinforce its own preimagined conception. The almost accidental emergence of a trace of history – real people doing real things – is the obverse of the salvage paradigm, which tends to endow the historically and culturally specific with meanings well beyond the documented experience (meanings of primitivism, of anthropological humanism, of pastoral romanticism, and so on).[69] Scheffner allows this sound montage of minor resistances to the colonial rubric of scientific collection, analysis, and preservation to fill out over not a black screen but an overexposed white image of barely visible tree branches swaying in the breeze: an image unable to form. Looking upon history is a foreclosed privilege. The contrapunctual soundtrack is furthermore composed of voice recordings layered with electronic music, the noise of the fast-forwarding and rewinding of the digital files, and the natural sounds of the leaves in the trees. I am struck by the palimpsestic stylization of this later scene, distinct from the remediation of Mall Singh's singular recording against a black screen. Both sound and image appear layered and out of focus. J. Martin Daughtry's concept of the "acoustic palimpsest" deserves mention here. He describes this as "the multiple acts of erasure, effacement, occupation, displacement, collaboration, and reinscription that are embedded in music composition, performance, and recording, as well as in acoustic experience more broadly."[70] While remediation may threaten to erase or reinscribe the colonial context within which these recordings came to be, its resulting palimpsest, not unlike the anarchive, cannot shake the traces that impress on it in the form of noise.

Remediation in *The Halfmoon Files* does not simply acknowledge and proliferate the promise of a particular medium. It bespeaks all of its media traces with the lapidary insight of media archaeology. The sound recordings of Mall Singh and other prisoners of war rendered on film engender a renewed sense of liveliness through contingency and proximity. At the same time, the percussive analogue static frame historicizes the voices of these prisoners. These are the paradoxical consequences of (auditory) remediation. Playing the sound recordings on digital film alters the semantic weight of both media, the one being cited and the one doing the citing. The same can be said for the panoply of medial artifacts in *From Here to Here* and *The Halfmoon Files*, from historical documents to photographic plates, images, and even footage. Just as audio citation is frequently accompanied by a lack of image in the film, black-and-white archival footage of the Halfmoon camp is also shown completely without sound, such as a lengthy sequence of camp life on the occasion of what appears to be the Muslim Festival of Sacrifice, Eid al-Adha. In these moving images, a series of spectacles are captured from a distance. Men march through the gate of the camp. Sheep are sacrificed and their carcasses strung up to drain. A large crowd of men sit on the ground and listen to a man orate from a platform, likely the imam offering the Eid service. Groups of squatting men gather in circles and eat. In a ritualistic dance performance, four men dressed in costume whirl to the beat of two drums. For over four minutes there is absolutely no audio. The effect is uncanny. Even in the case of a silent film, a musical score usually serves as accompaniment. Scheffner's relinquishing of a soundtrack is no doubt exemplary of the sweeping care he takes not to burden the archival materials with additional representational weight in *The Halfmoon Files*. What he shows is an example of documentary film from a century ago. In its remediation, one is struck by the flatness of these moving images and their silence. They seem to lose a dimension. Perhaps this missing dimension, where image and sound align, as they so seldom do in this film, is that missing space "between sound and image" that Scheffner seems to avidly seek but simultaneously resist – what Gordon refers to as the space of the ghost story.[71]

I propose that the space of the ghost story is invoked through remediation. This is where spectres come to life. When *The Halfmoon Files* cites the silent texts, images, and footage from the archive, the film does not (simply) infuse them with sound; it emphasizes their silence. In this regard, Rebecca Schneider's question about the relationality of media in the act of remediation is particularly to the point: "How can we account not only for the way differing media cite and incite each other but for the ways that the meaning of one form *takes place* in the response of another?"[72] Set against the digital media of Scheffner's film, this early, silent example of 35 mm film footage with sped-up frames (it was likely originally filmed at a lower speed) is a spectacle of the past made present, an undefined arena of becoming made to appear once more. This is not a matter of simply reliving history, as it were, for these moments and materials that Scheffner's film enlivens were never part of the archive of history, writ large. It is about bringing them forth in the anarchival project of *The Halfmoon Files*, which constitutes, inter alia, a repository of spectres. For as Achille Mbembe vividly writes, "The ghostly sphere is a stage where events unfold constantly but never congeal to the point of becoming history."[73]

Remediating found ethnographic material does not automatically delink it from the paradigms of modernity and colonialism. Citing such examples as Peter Kubelka's *Unsere Afrikareise* (Our trip to Africa, West Germany, 1966) and Chris Marker's *Sans Soleil* (France, 1983), Catherine Russell contends that found-footage films remain implicated in these selfsame paradigms despite ostensible attempts to revise their representations.[74] I tend to agree. The avant-garde poetics of these two named compilation films, and others, trouble audiovisual efforts towards decolonization of ethnographic materials, insofar as they offer no, or at most scant, contextualization. Generally speaking, this argumentation may also extend to found-sound recordings. *The Halfmoon Files* works against this. While formally experimental, it makes its sources and motivations abundantly evident and provides commentary on the filmmaking process along the way. If, as Russell indicates further, such compilation films also run the risk of perpetuating the ethos of loss and rescue, reminiscent of salvage ethnography, through the remediation of analogue media, then Scheffner's response is to unsettle possible nostalgia with noise.[75]

The ghostly sphere is the sphere of noise. Shapeless, resistant, interruptive, anarchival, palimpsestic, emetic, sinister noise haunts *The Halfmoon Files*. By galvanizing the forgotten media artifacts of the archive, the film not only remembers and re-presences, it also challenges our perceptive capacities and expectations. This is not an untravelled path. Experimental cinema has long weathered us to the disconnects of sound and image as well as to the reveals of the senescence of media, and certainly to noise. What is startlingly novel about both of the films analysed in this chapter is their return to the colonial sound archive in a direct treatment of ethnographic phonographic recordings. Both *From Here to Here* and *The Halfmoon Files* recognize the imperative to trouble audio history as part of their own genealogy as audiovisual media. Since its inception, film has been a self-reflexive *visual* medium, aware of its ideological entanglements vis-à-vis the image. However, the same cannot be said for sound. In the film work of Scheffner – and here one could point beyond these two earlier films to include later documentaries such as *Der Tag des Spatzen* (Day of the sparrow, 2010), *Revision* (2012), and *Havarie* (2016) – sound becomes reprioritized and resignified. Its perceptual legacy is shown to be equally underwritten by the ideological constitution of modernity and coloniality as that of vision. The decolonizing force of Scheffner's films bears witness to the complicity of the ear and ethnographic phonography in the horrors of colonialism. But it does not return to it with nostalgic longing. Attunement to the clamour of the unexpected and the once undesirable unearths a noisy narrative of resistance, as subtle and abstruse as it may seem.

The most recent and most categorical in this cadre of films to treat ethnographic audio recordings as a forebear of cinema, Scheffner's films open up this study. From here, things go in different directions. Subsequent chapters move away from the book's hitherto cultural and historical focus on Germany and chronologically back in cinematic history. A much more internationally renowned film, Marlon Fuentes's docudrama *Bontoc Eulogy* (US, 1995), will be the main object of the next chapter. Less explicitly about the phonographic recordings performed at the turn of the century, in its exploration of the colonization of the Philippines and the ethnographic and imperial spectacle of the infamous 1904 St. Louis World's Fair, the film conjures up the phonographic imaginary in its troubling of the collections amassed at the University of Pennsylvania Museum of Archaeology and Anthropology, the National Archives at the Library of Congress, and the Smithsonian Institution Archives together with the legacies they uphold through a personal narrative mode of memory and family trauma. Still perceptually abuzz in the following chapter, noise as a tool of the audiovisual decolonizing ear mingles with the self-empowering genre of autoethnography.

Chapter Four

(Re-)Sounding Autoethnography in Marlon Fuentes's *Bontoc Eulogy*

Marlon Fuentes's *Bontoc Eulogy* opens with a still black-and-white 16 mm shot of a crank phonograph positioned on a mat spread out over an uneven cobbled floor in the corner of an otherwise empty room. The walls of the room are concrete and bare. The setting of this medium shot evokes the stark aesthetics of a prison. A man enters the frame, seats himself in front of the phonograph funnel, winds the side crank, then places the needle of the stylus onto the record. The machine produces a noise. A static hum reverberates. Then the barely audible percussive sound of tribal drums emerges. There is a quick fade to a black screen and the soundtrack cuts too. A brief but perceptible interlude of silence and darkness interjects before the same image returns. The man repeats the actions, winding the crank of the phonograph and positioning the stylus onto the record. Again, noise and then an admixture of noise and percussive sounds issue from the machine. The man appears to listen intently and slightly longer this time. He sits cross-legged in front of the funnel of the phonograph with head bowed as though in prayer or meditation. Another cut to black follows with no sound bridge. A third time the image of a man in front of the phonograph funnel appears and the same procedure is performed once more. This time the machine emits speech. The words are not translated for the audience. This opening sequence of three successive shots ends with a close-up of the stylus reading the grooves of the spinning record. Then there is another cut to black and the film's title flashes on-screen in white lettering.

Opening the film with a series of shots of a man, who we later learn is both the director and the narrator, captured listening to the phonograph saliently evokes the visual iconography of protodocumentary filmmaking and its entanglement with early ethnographic imagery. Consider once again Austrian ethnographer Rudolf Pöch's 1908 *Buschmann spricht in den Phonographen* (Bushman speaking into the phonograph). A film of just three minutes and thirty-six seconds stages the scene of a man in present-day Botswana speaking into the phonograph. This was also the first film that was later synchronized with original sound. Consider further one of the first (silent) documentaries, American Robert J. Flaherty's 1922 ethnographic *Nanook of the North* about the life and struggles of an Inuk man living in the Canadian Artic. One of the most notable scenes of the film portrays Nanook's first encounter with a phonograph, the technology of which appears to delight and baffle him to such an extent that he picks up the record with his hands and bites into it in a childishly oral attempt to understand the source of the sound. These depictions of the phonograph and the Indigenous subject display what Michael Taussig calls "white man's magic" and "primitive" wonder.[1] At this mythical site, a constellation of colonial encounter and technological recording and reproduction emerges in full force.[2] *Bontoc Eulogy* evokes this history. Citing Lisa Lowe, Jan Christian Bernabe describes Fuentes's re-enactment in the opening scene of the film as an exacting capture of the trope of "the simultaneous imbrications of civilization and barbarism."[3]

In its explicit re-enactment of a colonial image of the cinematic past, the employment of this historically charged mise-en-scène at the start of *Bontoc Eulogy* catches our attention. By no means a homage to this visual legacy, this opening sequence and its repetition of shots nevertheless set a historical mood. The film to come, *Bontoc Eulogy*, is not an ethnographic film, bound to a rigid sense of objectivity and veracity, not to mention predicated on "the production of Otherness."[4] But it does concern itself with ethnography and appears to recognize its inheritance of the theoretical burden of ethnographic representation.[5] Bill Nichols classifies the film as "reflexive documentary," which he characterizes as a documentary mode concerned with the historical world as well as the challenges of the filmmaker to represent it.[6] The audiovisual ethnographic materials comprising much of this film are both albatross and opportunity from which Fuentes creates an autoethnographic film that listens.

Not dissimilar to listening to noise in the previous chapter, autoethnography serves as another strategy of the decolonizing ear that asserts the Indigenous subject's self-representation through the seizure and reimagination of voices and sounds recorded by colonial ethnographers. Thus, it challenges erstwhile power relations insofar as the one once listened to (and recorded) becomes the listener, not in a passive scene of technological first encounter discussed in earlier chapters but in a commanding act of both rendering sound and taking it in. Autoethnography in this film does not simply reverse power relations; it turns the whole order of colonial listening on its ear.

The first film by Philippine American filmmaker and photographer Marlon Fuentes, *Bontoc Eulogy* was released in 1995. It is a sombre testimonial about the colonial history of the Philippines and the plight of the Bontoc Igorots under colonial rule. It draws out the exploitation of the Philippines and especially its Indigenous groups on the occasion of the 1904 St. Louis World's Fair through a personal narrative about coerced emigration, displacement, and transgenerational memory. Similar to Philip Scheffner's *The Halfmoon Files* discussed in the previous chapter, *Bontoc Eulogy* also presents a scouring of the archives as a means of piecing together a story of a man compelled to leave his home, brought to a foreign land under false pretences, exploited as a spectacle, subjected to numerous ethnographic studies, and finally condemned to an unknown fate. Both films are ghost stories in their own right. The harrowing annals of colonialism present many such narratives, most famous perhaps that of the South African figure Sarah Baartman, the best known of the Khoikoi women forced to travel to Europe and put on display as the "Hottentot Venus" for the voracious appetites of European crowds. Scheffner's and Fuentes's respective films part ways in their respective approaches. For Fuentes the voice of a man recorded on the phonograph becomes the impetus for story-making in the guise of searching. He does not look for ghosts so much as he creates them. Indeed, *Bontoc Eulogy* is not a true documentary. It is rather a docudrama or a mockumentary. That is, it gives pretences of a documentary and bases its content on historical fact, but its tale about a Bontoc warrior by the name of Markod and grandfather to the director and narrator is fictional. We only learn this when the end credits roll with the boilerplate set of statements: "This story is inspired by actual events. Any similarities to persons living or dead are purely accidental." As established in the previous chapter, *The Halfmoon Files* searches for the image and the identity to fill out the voice. In *Bontoc Eulogy* a similar search for the man behind the voice unfolds, but Fuentes allows memory fragments and imagination to bolster archival material, and an oneiric tale comes to form as postcolonial and autoethnographic critique. Although *Bontoc Eulogy* does not directly return to the Lautarchiv at the Humboldt University in Berlin and the collection of the Royal Prussian Phonographic Commission (RPPC), this book's study of the latter provides a significant conceptual context for understanding colonial listening, its development, its preservation, and its persisting authority, which in turn permits new and unexpected pathways into this film.

A more thematically relevant comparison for Fuentes's compilation docudrama might be Kidlat Tahimik's nearly three-hour-long diary film *Why Is Yellow the Middle of the Rainbow?* (Philippines, 1993). Likewise framed within a transgenerational narrative in the form of a fragmentary dialogue between father and eldest son (at the time, an eight-to-ten-year-old child), this family tale of life in the Philippines in the 1980s unfolds against the backdrop of the nation's sustained anticolonial struggle against the enduring presence and influence of the United States. A gamut of visual reminders and objects of the longer colonial history of the Philippines and the plight of the Indigenous communities, especially the Igorots, comes into relief. Unlike Fuentes, Tahimik dispenses with archival ethnographic materials almost altogether. If anything, his own body presents itself as a site of historical indexicality. Like Fuentes, the filmmaker also descends from the Igorots. Occasional scenes show the filmmaker in traditional Igorot dress and re-enacting historical events. In one scene of the film, Tahimik and his family, who reside in Baguio in the northwest region of the country, visit an Igorot community in the interior of the Cordillera mountains. The film demonstrates the community's rich culture and heritage during a day of festivities as well as its sustained resistance to the colonial and neocolonial powers, as a community that has long faced persecution and land dispossession. In a singular talking-head interview with Lopez Na-uyac, an Igorot living in the community, Na-uyac alludes to the history of the St. Louis World's Fair and the various ethnographic exploitation shows, especially in the United States, for which Igorot members were recruited. He explains that the government in Manila treats the Igorots as tourist attractions and not a community of people. Watching the two films chronologically with respect to their release dates, one is struck by the thought that *Bontoc Eulogy* could serve as a historical prequel to *Why Is Yellow the Middle of the Rainbow?*

Yet there are also significant differences between the two films. This slightly earlier film rejects the ethnographic gaze and ear outright.[7] Further, Tahimik's presence in the Philippines means that he does not have to rely on the archive to access the country and its past.[8] *Why Is Yellow the Middle of the Rainbow?* reads the past through the actions of the present. *Bontoc Eulogy*, by contrast, repeatedly employs archival ethnographic materials housed in a foreign land not only to tell the story of colonialism but to do so through the machinery of the colonizer and from the exilic context. Resistance to this machinery is performed from within. Demonstrating what Bernabe conceptualizes as an "archival imperative," the film is a creative, political practice that, in his words, "troubles the certainties of knowledge production of American empire."[9] Similar to the experience of exile itself, as Edward Said has taught us, the film teeters on a condition of absolute loss and a condition of creative freedom.[10]

In the prologue to *Bontoc Eulogy*, the voice that finally emerges from the phonograph on the third try symbolically ushers in the film. An imaginary interview revised for the collective volume *F Is for Phony: Fake Documentary and Truth's Undoing* (2006) articulates Fuentes's own interpretation of the visual imagery of the prologue described at the outset of the chapter. Instead of conjuring a colonial scene of encounter and capture, according to Fuentes, the image of the man (himself) listening to the phonograph recalls the famous logo of "His Master's Voice," an image of the mixed terrier Nipper leaning inquisitively into the funnel of a phonograph. This famous logo demonstrates the phonograph as a preservation device, for Nipper presumably hears his dead master's voice and therefore responds with a confused gesture.[11] However, I am certain it is not lost on Fuentes that this iconography also exploits the pooch's inability to decipher between reality and recording, what Taussig refers to as "the alleged primitivism of the mimetic faculty" in a manner not unlike ethnographic imagery of the Other ostensibly baffled by the technology of the phonograph.[12] Fuentes's prologue is complex. Even if he is not the direct descendant of the fictionalized protagonist of this story, as a diasporic subject of Philippine descent Fuentes is still also the subject of postgenerational memory and the trauma of colonialism. Purposefully seating himself in front of the phonograph and thus visually mimicking a position of subjugation within the ethnographic constellation of colonialism, Fuentes reappropriates the image and thwarts expectations and strategically reverses the hierarchy of listening. For it is the filmmaker who works the machine and who listens, not in marvel or confusion but with perception, understanding, and careful, deliberate actions. As Bernabe writes, "Rather than conveying the native body's ignorance with technology, Fuentes's actions are strikingly fluid, lacking any sort of spontaneity" (figure 4.1).[13]

A film composed of montage and the aesthetics of collage consisting of found footage and images from such locations as the University of Pennsylvania Museum of Archaeology and Anthropology, the National Archives at the Library of Congress, and the Smithsonian Institution Archives, *Bontoc Eulogy* "functions," according to Fuentes, "as an autoethnographic document that reconstructs an internal reality based on the flotsam and jetsam of cultural history."[14] We find immense clarity and insight in just this brief formulation of the autoethnographic as a "reconstruction" of the personal from the refuse of history. Mary Louise Pratt establishes the terms "autoethnography" and "autoethnographic

Figure 4.1. Marlon Fuentes in *Bontoc Eulogy* (Marlon Fuentes, Philippines/ US, 1995). Courtesy of Marlon Fuentes.

texts" as inverse concepts. As she puts it, these "refer to instances in which colonized subjects undertake to represent themselves in ways that engage with the colonizer's terms. If ethnographic texts are a means by which Europeans represent to themselves their (usually subjugated) others, autoethnographic texts are texts the others construct in response to or in dialogue with those metropolitan representations."[15] Following Pratt, Jeannette Hoorn explains the use of the genre of autoethnography specifically in the case of *Bontoc Eulogy* in this way: "[The filmmaker] positions himself as both a colonised subject and a diasporic intellectual. By turning around the premises of ethnography, Fuentes provides himself with an appropriate position from which he is able to take a tool of western imperialism, namely ethnographic film-making, and do what Gayatri Spivak thought impossible, namely represent his own alterity."[16] Seizing the authorial power to forge one's own narrative and to draw the parameters within which one may be represented, autoethnography subverts the designs of traditional ethnography.

Since its inception as a concept, autoethnography has been heavily anchored in the visual. It has worked against the "imperial eyes" of the white Euro-American, dubbed "the seeing-man," the one who "looks out and possesses."[17] This chapter seeks to analyse the autoethnography of *Bontoc Eulogy* through sound and thus bring an old concept into a new context. The tool of Western imperialism explicitly at stake in this film is phonographic recording. Perhaps this calls for playing with the prefix "auto-" by exchanging it for "oto-." The latter relates to the ear as an organ of perception. In a reading of Friedrich Nietzsche's autobiography *Ecce Homo*, Jacques Derrida famously displaces "autobiography" for "otobiography." If autobiography is the narration of self for oneself, then otobiography, according to Derrida, is the narration of self for the Other, or more specifically, for the *ear* of the Other.[18] I will stop short of introducing the term "oto-ethnography," as this, while evocative, is redundant or at least self-fulfilling in this context. Brought into presence via this simple act of visual mimicry, the film sets forth its intention and force from the beginning. The most instructive aspect of Fuentes's own discussion of this prologue concerns not the image but the sound – moreover, the sounds emitting from the phonograph. As Fuentes himself puts it, "This prologue suggests the possibility that the whole film, the whole story about to follow, is really a concoction of the character's imagination – a fleshing out of the sound artifacts he has heard."[19] Here again, we might ask: What sound precedes this image? Or better, what sound precedes this film?

A Film Based on a Sound

Fuentes silently waits for the phonograph to speak. A voice eventually resonates amid the reverberating hiss of static and then rumbling percussion. At first, the audience receives no indication of the owner or the original provenance of this voice. The appearance of the analogue machine and the degraded sound quality of the recording suggest that this sound and this voice are old. This is, we are given to believe with the development of the film, the recorded voice of the narrator's grandfather. But like the authenticity of the story itself, the recording of the narrator's grandfather also gives rise to speculation. As the story goes, this recording and others throughout the film were made of the narrator's grandfather in 1904 during the St. Louis World's Fair at the behest of on-site ethnographers. We learn, however, that the recordings are also re-enactments. Unable to find phonographic recordings of Indigenous Philippine informants from that period, Fuentes instead procured translations of transcriptions of recordings made of a Bontoc Igorot, Chief Fomolaey of Bontoc, who had been part of the original group at the St. Louis World's Fair and subsequently performed on Coney Island, where he apparently told the story of his life and his experiences in the United States and was recorded. According to Peter X. Feng, Fomolaey narrated his story via an interpreter to the magazine

The Independent in 1905, which then published it. Reprinted as part of a collection in 1906, Fomolaey's story can be found today in *Life Stories of Undistinguished Americans As Told by Themselves*, edited by Hamilton Holt and most recently reprinted in 1990.[20] The content of the volume's chapter "The Life Story of an Igorrote Chief" does bear many similarities to Markod's story. Were the recordings made not for anthropological but rather journalistic purposes? Reportedly representative of "the humbler classes of the nation," as the introduction notes, this collection holds to a certain ethnographic ethos.[21] From this transcribed account of "the Igorot experience," Fuentes reconstructs the original recordings through their textual traces.

In interviews, Fuentes explains that he had these stories retranslated into old Bontoc and read by a Bontoc elder in Los Angeles by the name of Fermina Bagwan. Her voice was recorded and then altered to sound more androgynous. Finally, a "synthetic patina" of digital noise was added to replicate the sound of the degraded wax cylinder. This vibratory hiss created the right historical, etic effect of difference and distance.[22] The drumming, however, is authentic and hails from recordings of Bontoc percussion taken from the University of Washington's ethnomusicology collection. To reject these recordings as simply forged representations would not take us very far.[23] There is much more at stake here. What Fuentes provides is a process of close listening, even decolonial listening, that makes the once-recorded speech accessible beyond ethnographic ambitions. Consider again the video project of the Language Keepers and the Maliseet elder, mentor, and song keeper Maggie Paul's rendition of the Wolastoq song extracted from the wax cylinders, described in chapter 2. After listening closely and attentively, Paul describes how she was able to decipher the tune of the song and reperform it for members of her community. I draw important parallels between these examples of listening and re-rendering for new purposes. Overall, the challenge posed by the absence of actual recordings seems to have presented an opportunity, if not a testament to the political context of these early sound recordings, which would have likely been deemed too unimportant to preserve. Indeed, archival film work always involves dealing with levels of absences.

That the narrator does not begin to speak right away and instead presents himself as a mere silent listening figure evokes what Fatimah Tobing Rony describes as "the conflict of sound versus silence" that is "set up at the very beginning of the film."[24] The act of listening appears confined to the experience of the narrator in the film's prologue. But his attentive listening mediates our own as a process of auratic experience in lieu of linguistic or semantic understanding. Curiously, the words of the recorded voice are not translated in this early sequence, although they will be later on. The voice seems to speak to the narrator alone, and in turn the narrator delivers the story that will take shape as this film. Operating within a less semantic deduction, the sounds emitting from the phonograph still reveal much from a media archaeological perspective. Each scratch, hiss, and hum divulges insight from the archive of noise, regardless of whether it was rerecorded or not. This film is not only an archaeology of the colonial history of the Philippines, it is also what Rony formulates as "an archaeology of cinema," one that, I propose, reminds us of cinema's phonographic forebear.[25] The sound that precedes *Bontoc Eulogy* is the sound that precedes cinema, perhaps ethnographic cinema in particular.

Employing a vast range of ethnographic photographs and silent footage recovered from the archives, Fuentes nonetheless opens his film with sound and the reminder that sound recordings and the technology of the phonograph were not only a significant form of colonial capture of Philippine subjects but also the beginnings of what was to become cinema. Indeed, signs of cinema's early days make themselves apparent throughout the film. Replete with found footage frequently shot from a single camera position and focused on a frontal performance spectacle in a wide-angle framing, the film repeatedly reminds us of instances of the early "cinema of attractions."[26] These demonstrated for the first time how movement could be captured. Devoid of narrative, this kinesthetic spectacle was framed and celebrated. *Bontoc Eulogy* also offers a remarkable homage to Georges Méliès, one of the early pioneers of cinema and of cinematic special effects and illusion. Two children (purportedly, those of the narrator) perform a magic act for the camera and through the style of an original jump cut make a rabbit appear out of a black top hat. Likewise, the nod to early documentary and Flaherty's 1922 *Nanook of the North*, as indicated at the start of the chapter, adds to the film's citation of cinema history. But do not be fooled by this pretence of teleology of mechanical recording and cinema history. *Bontoc Eulogy* does not begin with the analogue as a point of departure to be moved beyond. Rather, the advent of sound recording becomes a repeated point of engagement for the film. Fuentes reinforces Friedrich Kittler's theory of the nonlinearity of media history. The phonograph did not evolve into the kinetoscope, even if the two were rendered by Thomas Edison's selfsame hands.[27] A more instructive approach to the entanglement of the phonograph, that rather short-lived invention, and cinema is their discursively aligned origins at the turn of the twentieth century.

Bontoc Eulogy does fan out the full span of Edison's machines and their ethnographic misrepresentations. His Kinetograph, appropriately later referred to as his Wargraph, becomes implicitly inscribed in the film. Fuentes inserts footage from Edison's 1899 short films of several key battle scenes during the Philippine-American War. These include "Filipinos Retreat from Trenches" and "Capture of Trenches at Candaba." Both render re-enactments of the historical events and were filmed not in the Philippines but in the United States. At the time, efforts were not spared to make the re-enactments appear "authentic" to their American audiences. As Joseph Palis indicates, they were staged "in the lushly vegetated region of New Jersey to represent the conquered lands, and 'peopled' by African Americans" playing the Filipino soldiers. The films served propaganda purposes to promote American imperialism and militarism, not to mention inscribe the militarized Western seizure as a means of converting the "alien" space of the "Orient" into "colonial space."[28] But let us return to the phonograph and what I perceive as the colonial instrument on display.

The sounding of the phonographic recording opens the film and carries it forward. It is a noisy reminder of the colonial past that haunts the film. Throughout, speech is interwoven with an almost constant extradiegetic musical track, beginning with mouth harp music performed by the Ramon Obusan Folkloric Group and followed by music composed by Douglas Quin. Both compositions bear influences of Cordilleran folk music.[29] Markod's voice resurfaces in the film after fifteen minutes with the narrator's implicit enunciation of the film's central motive: "I haven't given much thought about Markod since I was a child. But I suspected there was a much larger story behind his disappearance. I wanted to find out what really happened to him." As though a calling into voice, the narrator's solemn words cut to the sibilant sound of static and a voice speaking in another tongue. This time the recording is translated almost simultaneously by the narrator himself. Two voices become layered but remain discrete, enveloped in an intense auditory hum. The voice of the narrator as it translates does not undermine or eclipse the recorded voice but symbolically engages it in a transmedia, transhistorical dialogue. This double voicing, to extrapolate on a Bakhtinian term, reflects what Trinh T. Minh-ha calls "speaking nearby." It is "a speaking that does not objectify, does not point to an object as if it is distant from the speaking subject or absent from the speaking place. A speaking that reflects on itself and can come very close to a subject without, however, seizing or claiming it."[30] In hesitant, somewhat monotone speech, the pre-recorded voice speaks briefly of the distinct cosmology of the Bontoc Igorots, one threatened by the devasting tripartite of Christianity, modernity, and coloniality. The voice then fades to the soundscape of nature and birds chirping. This "recording" both sets the historical tone of the story and offers an auditory experience of authority and authenticity, notwithstanding its material deception. Returning after a brief interval, the degraded voice then narrates the story of the arrival of the Americans and the dawn of a new phase of colonial rule in the Philippines in the early 1900s, after nearly four centuries of Spanish colonial rule. Markod describes the Americans first as inducing fear through the threat of violence and then as ostensibly benevolent, even friendly. "When the Americans first came to our village, we were afraid of them. Their guns made a lot of noise and scared everyone, including the animals in the forest. We did not like them visiting our villages. Later, we realized that they wanted to be our friends. They wanted us to go with them to America, where many were gathered, so we could build a village and show our ways of living." Encapsulated in this narrated description is the constellation of military might and anthropological exploitative curiosity cloaked in benevolence, the twin pillars of colonial violence. Following the defeat of Spain in the Spanish-American War in 1898, the Philippines (a fledgling independent republic since its own recent anticolonial revolution) was surrendered to the United States under the 1898 Treaty of Paris. Despite Philippine resistance, the country fell to the United States in 1902. The concurrently burgeoning field of anthropology and its branch of documenting culture – namely, ethnography – were integral to this new phase of colonialism.[31] Fuentes reveals that at the dawn of American colonial rule the anthropologists Albert Jenks and Daniel Folkmar led the recruitment of over twelve hundred individuals from different Indigenous Philippine communities to travel to the United States and construct and perform in the "Philippine Reservation" for the 1904 St. Louis World's Fair.[32] Bringing Indigenous Filipinos to the United States en masse greatly facilitated the studies of anthropologists and ethnographers. Once there, they were essentially enslaved. For the eight-month-long duration of the World's Fair, the Filipinos were not permitted to leave the fairgrounds, which were heavily guarded. Unable to escape, the study subjects for the anthropologists and ethnographers consistently and conveniently remained at their disposal. As so often was the case, anthropology and ethnography likewise provided "scientific" legitimacy and justification to the fair's exploitative pursuits. The World's Fair was, as Robert Rydell expresses it, "an anthropologically validated racial landscape."[33] As Fuentes adds of the fairgrounds, "They also had laboratories for anthropometric and psychometric assessments of these tribal subjects, primarily for proving what scientists then thought were race-related characteristics of intelligence, physical ability, and personality."[34] In these laboratories no doubt phonographic recording took place. The narrator leads us to believe this is where Markod's voice was also recorded.

Midway through the film, the static returns and with it the same voice. This time it reports from St. Louis. The tone of the voice and the manner of its speech do not appear greatly altered, but its content reveals disenchantment and despair at this new setting, whose modern inventions are a source not of wonder but of distress and even pity. According to the narrator, Markod was promised some money to speak into "the machine that would record his voice." Although the auditory yields of these recording sessions resonate from the start, at a later point in the film there is a visual re-enactment of Markod speaking into the phonograph. In a mise-en-scène unmistakably similar to that which opens the film, we see the actor Enrico Obusan playing Markod squatting in front of the funnel of the phonograph. At first, he appears to listen, and then he speaks. Clothed only in a traditional *wanes* (G-string cloth) and a rattan cap, the nearly nude Indigenous Igorot man at the phonograph set against a white cloth background is a spectacle that directly inscribes the ethnographic imaginary within the film. For this image of Obusan as Markod unequivocally calls to mind a myriad of similar images that offer visual evidence of the irrevocable link between the phonograph and ethnography. Even early marketing for the phonograph capitalized on this colonial fantasy and what Brian Hochman refers to as "the origins of the phonograph's privileged ethnographic status."[35] (See figures 4.2 and 4.3.)

It is worth comparing the image of Markod in figure 4.2 to the 1909 marketing art poster for the National Phonograph Company in figure 4.3.[36] In the latter's painted image we see a group of Indigenous people in ceremonial regalia gathered around a phonograph with a large and ornate funnel positioned on the stump of a tree. This does not appear to be a typical ethnographic phonograph designed for fieldwork but one for well-to-do bourgeois households. The group gathered around the machine appears cheerfully in awe. As Brian Hochman remarks, the advertisement signals two distinct attributes of the discursive culture of the phonograph corresponding to its two discrete mechanical functions: to record and to play sound. First, the image draws the connection with the firmly established practice of ethnographic sound recording among ethnographers in the United States by that time. Second, its slogan "Original and Aboriginal" seems to suggest the promise of authenticity and sound fidelity of the machine

Figure 4.2. Enrico Obusan as "Markod" in *Bontoc Eulogy* (Marlon Fuentes, Philippines/US, 1995). Courtesy of Marlon Fuentes.

and its quality of sound reproduction. In Hochman's words: "The advertisement also posits Native Americans (or at least, a romantic idea about Native American cultural difference) as a necessary ideological middle ground in the construction of phonographic sound fidelity."[37] Interpreted as such, the actual pun of the slogan appears without intention, because while "Aboriginal" might simply be taken as a (somewhat dated) substitute for "Indigenous," next to the word "original" the prefix of the former comes into focus. "Ab-" indicates precisely the negation of the word in its definition of "away." Therefore Ab-original semantically becomes the "absence" of the original. Is not the invention of phonographic sound recording based on the unprecedented reproduction of sound in the absence of its original source? Hochman points to the ambivalence of the advertisement insofar as it is unclear whether the group is speaking into the phonograph or listening to it.[38] I suggest that the ambivalence also lies in the double entendre of the advertisement's messaging, not to mention the incongruence of the image.

Such twofold ambivalence brings us back to the image of Markod, who in the film both listens to and speaks into the phonograph funnel. Further, if absence and presence form the antagonistic plot of the iconographic imagery of the Othered subject at the phonograph, then they also reflect the structure of *Bontoc Eulogy*. This is a film about

Figure 4.3. The Edison Company "Original and Aboriginal" advertisement poster for the National Phonograph Company (featured in *Profitable Advertising*, April 1909, 1128). Rights holder unknown. Courtesy of the University of Wisconsin-Madison Memorial Library.

memory and history full of voids and fissures. In Laura U. Marks's analysis, intercultural artists such as Fuentes "are in a position to interrogate the historical archive, both Western and traditional, in order to read their own histories in its gaps, or to force a gap in the archive so that they have a space in which to speak."[39] Fuentes speaks into the gap, as does Markod. To be sure, there are no archival images of Markod (the imaginary grandfather and Bontoc warrior) speaking into the phonograph. Yet similar images do exist in the archive. Fuentes even inserts one later in the film as part of a montage of random images. Uncertain of the fate of his grandfather, Fuentes concludes his "eulogy" of Markod with speculation that he may have never returned home from the United States. "My investigation opened up

Figure 4.4. Archival photograph of an Indigenous Filipino and an American soldier with phonograph in *Bontoc Eulogy* (Marlon Fuentes, Philippines/US, 1995). Courtesy of Marlon Fuentes.

other leads. It was possible that Markod never returned home, that he joined other Igorots who were placed on display in other fairs and expositions around the country. For many years, all across America, from San Francisco to Coney Island, Indigenous Filipinos brought money and fame to their promoters." As visual documentation to these words, Fuentes presents a roughly two-minute photo montage that continues even after the extradiegetic music has broken off. Frontal ethnographic images of Igorots flash across the screen like a gallery of lost souls who uncannily return the viewer's gaze.[40] Fuentes's spoken statement above suggests that the fate of these captured figures is uncertain. If colonialism is the "blind field" of these photographs, to borrow Roland Barthes's term, as that context often severed by the frame, in these photographs it is repeatedly activated.[41] Violence permeates these images and becomes reprised in this presentation of randomness, anonymity, and lack of context. The soundtrack's mysterious and melancholic music accentuates the effect. The montage disturbs. Among these images is a single one of an Igorot man squatting in front of the funnel of a phonograph and on the other side a white man in military uniform (figure 4.4). This photograph offers indexical proof of the colonial first-encounter phonographic constellation. While the wax cylinders containing phonographic recordings of Indigenous Filipinos may not physically (or at least readily) exist in the US archives, this does not mean that these recordings were not made. Is this image meant to stand in for Markod or vice versa? The contextual anonymity of this later photo montage threatens to pull us out of the narrative of Markod and its promise of specificity. In the film's literal re-enactment of the ethnographic image of the "primitive" and the "white man's machine," we find presence in absence. But this "live" visual representation also threatens to reduce the film to the machinery of colonial fantasy of cultural difference. Though it is less romantic and pastoral in the design of its mise-en-scène than is the Edison advertisement, the parallels of the two images presented above are nonetheless evident. The film ultimately warns us not to succumb to a hierarchy of vision. Tina M. Campt would suggest, instead, that we need to listen to these images.[42]

To begin, the film's images of Markod listening to and later speaking into the phonograph are accompanied by the voice of the narrator as he tells the story of Markod's encounter with the phonograph. Here and elsewhere, the narrator offers apparent intimate knowledge of Markod, his thoughts, and his feelings. Unlike his fellow Igorots, Markod was evidently not afraid of losing his voice to the phonograph and willingly participated in the recordings. The narrator proclaims: "He had heard of this contraption, the one that allowed the man's voice to travel over many miles. Over the course of several months, Markod told the story of his people and his experiences at the fair." Paired with the narrator's voice, we hear Andrew B. Sterling's 1904 song "Meet Me in St. Louis, Louis," as originally sung by William F. Denny and performed on a zonophone. There is cruel irony at play in this layering of the narrator's solemn tone and the peppy ragtime-style song that celebrates the event of the World's Fair, in reality a prohibitive and unapologetic spectacle of imperialism and colonialism. Eventually, the noise of the machine and the grainy recorded voice previously heard extradiegetically return to dovetail with the image. But as in so much of the film, sound and image tracks do not find synchrony. The movement of Markod's lips does not match the speech. Over-performance and artificiality mark the sequence. At once articulated as an instrument of scientific and cultural subjugation, within the context of the film the phonograph as the colonial ear is also turned back on itself. Sound itself becomes a fabrication and symbolic at best. The instrument of the "white man's magic" becomes a casualty to its own mechanical reproduction. One cannot help but consider Walter Benjamin's famous essay "The Work of Art in the Age of Mechanical Reproduction" ([1936] 1968) at this turn. As we are reminded at closer reading, mechanical reproduction did not destroy the aura so much as invented it. In a footnote, Benjamin inserts a definition of the aura that supports the assertion of its retroactive nature:

> Precisely because authenticity is not reproducible, the intensive penetration of certain (mechanical) processes of reproduction was instrumental in differentiating and grading authenticity. To develop such differentiations was an important function of the trade in works of art. The invention of the woodcut may be said to have struck at the root of the quality of authenticity even before its late flowering. To be sure, at the time of its origin a medieval picture of the Madonna could not yet be said to be "authentic." It became "authentic" only during the succeeding centuries and perhaps most strikingly so during the last one.[43]

Put briefly, the idea of an original only arose simultaneously with its wane; the aura is thus contingent upon mechanical reproduction. Allow me to riff on Joni Mitchell with a slight variation: we only recognize something when it's gone. Jonathan Sterne goes so far as to claim that "aura is the object of nostalgia that accompanies reproduction."[44] Sterne's reading of Benjamin's essay is instructive and thematically relevant. In the case of recording machines, such as the phonograph, Sterne writes, "The possibility of sound reproduction reorients the practices of sound production; insofar as it is a possibility at all, reproduction precedes originality."[45] But as much as the phonograph shaped sound, not to mention listening practices, it also opened itself up to endless processes of reproduction, what Benjamin might call the allegory of historical representation. *Bontoc Eulogy*'s profilmic process of procuring transcriptions of historical recordings (not to mention translations) in the archive and then retranslating and rerecording them as historical representation for film could not exemplify this better.

By reperforming the act of colonial phonographic capture in which the ethnographer is now absent from the scene, *Bontoc Eulogy* blurs the line between roles, and the distinction between the recording ethnographer and the recorded Other becomes indecipherable. In the film's repurposing of archival ethnographic materials, who exactly is recording whom? These moments represent the broader project of the film and its authoethnographic mode as it stages new encounters with history and memory in an assertion of self-determination, what Catherine Russell has also classified as a kind of "antidocumentary."[46] Thus, the sound that precedes this film is, to paraphrase Campt again, the hum that is both presence and absence.[47]

Autoethnography: Countering the Salvage Paradigm

Fuentes calls his film autoethnography. He inserts himself into the archival historiography of US colonialism and thereby asserts his own subjective narration of the ethnographic materials that form the film. His accented voice-over resonates with a certain vulnerability but is also exhilaratingly interventional in its performance of identity as it destabilizes the omniscient narrator and the hegemonic narrative system of film, to borrow from Hamid Naficy's concept of accented cinema.[48] According to José Esteban Muñoz, autoethnography entails "inserting a subjective, performative, often combative, 'native I' into ethnographic film's detached discourse."[49] But if, on the one hand, autoethnography appears to personalize the characteristically "detached," objective, and realist mode of ethnography, on the other hand it seeks to bring these personal histories into the public sphere.[50] Critical to autoethnography is the blending of the personal and the political, a point Fuentes himself raises in his previously noted definition of the practice: "Reconstruct[ing] an internal reality based on the flotsam and jetsam of cultural history."[51] While Mary Louise Pratt is often cited as the first scholar to employ and define the term "autoethnography," in truth this credit more accurately belongs to Françoise Lionnet, who introduced the term in her writing on the anthropologist and novelist Zora Neale Hurston. Lionnet rather discreetly sneaks the term into her analysis as a more nuanced alternative to "autobiography." Autoethnography, in her words, is "the defining of one's subjective ethnicity as mediated through language, history, and ethnographical analysis ...[,] a kind of 'figural anthropology' of the self."[52] This figural anthropology of the self is a reflection of the scepticism both about the ethnographic project and about autobiography, one that returns us to the circular movement of autoethnography from the historical to the personal and then back again. Lionnet writes of Hurston, "Her skepticism about the writing of culture would permeate the writing of the self, the autobiography, turning it into the allegory of an ethnographic project that self-consciously moves from the general ... to the particular ... and back to the general."[53] Such a description of autoethnography as allegory of an ethnographic project befits *Bontoc Eulogy*. This film reflexively performs a fictionalized account of personal memory as a means of accessing and addressing what Doris Sommer refers to in another context as the equally "foundational fictions" of colonial rule and historiography at the turn of the twentieth century.[54]

Lionnet's important distinction between autobiography and autoethnography was extended just a few years later with Pratt's distinction between ethnography and autoethnography, as we saw above. She writes, "If ethnographic texts are a means by which Europeans represent to themselves their (usually subjugated) others, autoethnographic texts are texts the others construct in response to or in dialogue with those metropolitan representations."[55] Pratt's formulation presents another illustration of the significant work of autoethnography as not just an alternative but now also a riposte to ethnography, insofar as it takes an oppositional course. Autoethnography confronts and disrupts the inviolable, unmarked, scientific perspective from outside that had long conditioned ethnographic representations. Influenced by disciplinary turns in the late 1980s and early 1990s, autoethnography emerged through a series of developments. Across the humanities and social sciences, interdisciplinary, self-critical, collaborative approaches and methods emerged, fueled by postmodern thinking and the breakdown of the regime of "grand theory." As a result, the discipline of anthropology experienced a "crisis of representation."[56] One central issue of dispute was the ethnographic authority long underpinning the discipline. From within documentary film studies, Pooja Rangan reflects back on this moment and cites the crisis of ethnographic representation as the important shift towards autoethnography, which provided an alternative and "privileged site for such methodological reflection," insofar as it "precipitated the imperative toward self-examination, reflexivity, and experimentation."[57]

Likewise a corollary of postcolonial studies and its early engagement with the foundational work of Edward Said, Homi K. Bhabha, and Gayatri Chakravorty Spivak, autoethnography furthermore responds to the totalizing perception that the colonial matrix of power is an unshakeable force. Muñoz likens autoethnography to Bhabha's notable concept of mimicry as that which at once a presents a mode of appropriation of colonial discourse and a strategic disavowal. Contra Said and his wholesale thesis of the irreversible imbalance of power between Orient and Occident, Bhabha famously alerted us to the ambivalence of power in colonial discourse that opened up space for the possibility of resistance.[58] Following Hoorn's evaluation cited earlier in this chapter, autoethnography also similarly defies Spivak's argument that the colonized subject can never represent its own alterity with the weighted conclusion to her critical essay: "The subaltern cannot speak."[59] This impossibility is underpinned by "an injunction to silence" and an "affirmation of non-existence" under the double subjugation of patriarchy and imperialism, which, as she maintains, "consequently states that of all this there is nothing to say, to see, to know."[60] Autoethnography asserts authorship of one's own history as a colonized subject not as a means of resubjugation but as a historiographical mode of self-expression that is both reflexive and unsettling.

Muñoz's autoethnographic discussion of Richard Fung's video work provides a helpful bridge from Lionnet and Pratt, who concentrate on autoethnography in writing rather than filmmaking. Muñoz's definition of autoethnography in the context of the audiovisual instructively reads as follows: "Autoethnography is a strategy that seeks to disrupt the hierarchical economy of colonial images and representations by making visible the presence of subaltern energies and urgencies *in* metropolitan culture. Autoethnography worries easy binarisms like colonized and the colonizer of subaltern and metropolitan by presenting subaltern speech through the channels and pathways of metropolitan representational systems."[61] Muñoz emphasizes autoethnography's resistance from within what he calls, following Pratt, "metropolitan culture" by shuffling visual hierarchies and foregrounding the voice of the colonized subject. Muñoz further identifies the specific audiovisual strategies employed by Fung that establish his autoethnographic style. These include voice-over monologues, found familial objects such as home movie footage, and the special effect of video keying.[62] Catherine Russell also indicates that first-person voice-over is critical to autoethnographic film- and video-making, but for her this voice-over "is intently and unambiguously subjective."[63] Overall, Russell expands on the repertoire of autoethnographic film techniques put forward by Muñoz in her own broader study of experimental video. Also mentioning Fung's work, Russell identifies the origins of much autoethnographic filmmaking as both queer culture and the experiences of "displacement, immigration, exile, and transnationality." Such themes are common in autoethnographic filmmaking, what Russell dubs "journeys of self."[64] Along such lines, Peter X. Feng describes *Bontoc Eulogy* as "one man's personal journey from primary archival and presumably authentic documents to increasingly fanciful stories inspired by them."[65]

Bontoc Eulogy is curiously not mentioned among Russell's numerous examples of autoethnography, but it fits in to what, for instance, Russell characterizes as the subgenre of "contemporary personal cinema." Including works such as Richard Fung's *The Way to My Father's Village* (Canada, 1988) and *My Mother's Place* (Canada, 1990), Mona Hatoum's *Measures of Distance* (Lebanon, 1988), Rea Tajiri's *History and Memory* (US, 1991), and Ngozi Onwurah's *The Body Beautiful* (UK, 1991), this is what Russell describes as "the staging of an encounter with the filmmaker's parent(s) or grandparent(s) who embody a particular cultural history of displacement or tradition."[66] According to Russell, transgenerational divides bear out over media difference. She elucidates further that "the difference between generations is written across the filmmaker's own inscription in technology, and thus it is precisely an ethnographic distance between the modern and the premodern that is dramatized in the encounter – through interview or archival memory or both."[67] In accordance with what we know about *Bontoc Eulogy* and its fictionalized account, Russell acknowledges the unreliability of the autoethnographic form and its dependence on memory and testimony, which always opens up onto a plane of imagination where truth is supplemented with impressions and echoes formed through trauma and longing.

In sum, Fuentes's autoethnography, an imaginary encounter with his grandfather framing the archival piecing together of a narrative about a country and culture subjugated and exploited through colonial rule, is both personal and public. It relies, furthermore, on an interweaving of fact and fiction. Most importantly for the present study, as autoethnography *Bontoc Eulogy* explores and troubles the technological divide between generations. As a film that consists in large part of found footage and archival images as well as footage that is made to appear found, *Bontoc Eulogy* dims the distinctions between past and present and bestrides the analogue and digital. Its extensive use of ethnographic material, frequently without direct engagement or contextualization, casts it precisely in the grey zone of ambivalence between resistance and enthusiasm, thus supporting Russell's proclamation that autoethnography is inherently oxymoronic.[68] Fuentes seems to be aware of this; he wilfully plays with the politics of the reappropriation of colonial documents and the tensions of ethnographic representation as well as its reversal. Although its visual track might appear to provide a broader horizon for exploring the autoethnographic impulse in *Bontoc Eulogy*, I return to sound and especially the encounter of the voice-over narrator and the inserted audio file allegedly of the narrator's grandfather in the balance of this chapter. Significantly, the remediation of the sound recordings works against the mythologizing salvage paradigm of ethnography, the directive to record and save "primitive" cultures before they vanish, and instead allows them to serve as a part of a personal narrative that begins to decolonize listening.

As James Clifford critiques it, the salvage paradigm is the pervasive assumption by anthropologists that primitive (read: precolonial) cultures are diminishing and must be preserved by ethnography in a kind of "last-chance rescue operation."[69] While this logic no longer directly informs ethnographic work the way it did in the pioneering age of Franz Boas, it permanently shaped the conception and practice of ethnography and continues to reverberate through ethnographic materials from the past.[70] Clifford remarks that the most problematic principle of the salvage paradigm was its inscription of a culture as disappearing, or even of another era. "This 'pastoral' encodation [of the salvage paradigm] is its relentless placement of others in a present-becoming-past."[71] Such an inscription negates subjectivities, knowledges, and cosmologies outside of the narrow parameters of logocentric knowledge regimes. "The salvage paradigm placed 'primitive' peoples back along a linear timescale predicated on post-Enlightenment notions of the progress of social evolution, with modern 'western' culture as its apotheosis. It has been argued that the salvage paradigm robs these Other peoples of their own complex and ever-changing histories."[72] Condemned to a vanishing existence by anthropologists, cultures were denied their coexistence and became fodder for the self-serving practice of ethnography to develop and expand the knowledge archive of the West.[73] Phonographic recordings of Indigenous languages and music were also motivated by this specious ethnographic paradigm of salvage and accordingly came to fill the shelves of the Western archive. Disappearing cultures not only meant disappearing languages but also oral cultures. If the diminishment of a culture might hold some truth, ethnography and its entanglement with colonial structures are constitutive of this problem and not simply a derivative. Colonialism destroys cultures and records their last echoes as well.

As a film that relies heavily on archival ethnographic materials, *Bontoc Eulogy*'s autoethnographic method might also be described as media archaeological. Notwithstanding the overall more apolitical approach of media archaeology, it does hold relevance in its effort to reveal the historical conditions of existence for media practices. Their motivations might be distinct, but both autoethnographer and media archaeologist return to the archive in search of multimedia memories. In the European context, these are the audiovisual recording projects that developed into, for instance, the Lautarchiv or Albert Kahn's infamous Archives de la Planète. One of the largest-scale salvage projects of photography and film in history, the latter was a multimedia archival project initiated by the wealthy French investment banker Albert Kahn and intended as a private collection. Between 1908 and 1931, cinematographers and photographers were sent out under the direction of Sorbonne geographer Jean Brunhes to capture and store the scenes of everyday life across the globe before they became irrevocably altered by modernity.[74] Consistent with his "cold gaze," Wolfgang Ernst rather callously (perhaps naively) refers to the yields of this project and others as "global memories."[75] To be fair, his interest lies beyond semantic content and original objectives of the archives of salvage ethnography to save the last traces of doomed cultures. For Ernst, these new multimedia archives, distinct from their print predecessors, no longer presented a collection of dead materials but constituted a source of reproductive creation of the new. "Frozen voices, banished to the analog and long-forgotten storage media, wait for their (digital) defreezing."[76] The media archaeologist always dreams in digital. The metaphor of frozen voices of the sound archive calls to mind a satirical and fantastical quote by Renaissance author François Rabelais:

> Here, here, said Pantagruel, here are some that are not yet thawed. He then threw us on the deck whole handfuls of frozen words, which seemed to us like your rough sugar-plums, of many colours, like those used in heraldry; some words gules (this means also jests and merry sayings), some vert, some azure, some black, some or (this means also fair words); and when we had somewhat warmed them between our hands, they melted like snow, and we really heard them, but could not understand them, for it was a barbarous gibberish.[77]

Instead of warming the words between one's hands, the media archaeologist and the autoethnographer alike employ technology to thaw the voices of the past and their mysterious languages. This thawing is the act of digitalization, what Anette Hoffmann calls a "refiguring." In her account, "This refiguring has several aspects, one of which is the atomisation or disaggregation of the sound recording: the digitalisation of, say, the recording on an Edison wax cylinder, entails a fragmentation of the sounding object into an acoustic (digital) file and – in the ideal case – several digital images that show the cylinder, and the cardboard box with its captions and labels (or lack thereof)."[78] The thawing of voices not only implies their sounding but also their disaggregation, their splitting into various parts.

In his own autoethnographic practice, Fuentes thaws the voices of the past. How he uses these thawed voices is another story. In *Bontoc Eulogy* he takes recourse to the archival multimedia materials not just to wangle the material details for his story but to pursue the very basic germinal glimmers of memory. When Fuentes explains in voice-over at the start of the film that he only has "flickering afterimages" of home, black-and-white footage from the colonial Philippines appears. Evidently, Fuentes himself possesses no or scant personal memories of the country where he was born and lived until young adulthood. Through this audiovisual pairing (though not synchronicity), Fuentes tacitly positions memory and its reproduction at the site of the archive and its reproduction, rather than himself as remembering subject. However, this long opening monologue is also riddled with apparent contradictions. A final reflexive return to his own image among the seamlessly sutured collage of archival ones brings the phrase: "One day I'll be gone. And these memories will be lost." The irony of these words may be read in a twofold manner. Despite its serious tone, on the one hand this line invokes the fabrication of the film's overarching narrative; on the other hand it flippantly evokes the salvage paradigm as a grounding for the film's creation. The narrative of Fuentes as the so-called native informant must be recorded and saved before the knowledge and memory he possesses disappear forever. Yet the memories in question do not directly belong to Fuentes. These are scenes from an earlier era before he was alive; they are derived from the ethnographic archive and its hegemonic historiography. They serve as the fabricated memories of fabricated memories – memories accorded by the salvage paradigm. Is Fuentes suggesting we salvage ethnography itself? Is *Bontoc Eulogy* structured like an elaborate joke? Jaimie Baron argues for such a reading.[79] Certainly, the autoethnographer reperforms the salvage project with no less than a dash of mockery. In *The Archive Effect*, her study of a vast array of found-footage films, Baron proposes that films such as *Bontoc Eulogy* question the assumed reality of the filmic document itself. By drawing a line of difference between archival artifacts and the archive-based film – that is, between document and documentary – through aesthetic strategies of misuse and misappropriation, in the form of jokes and irony, *Bontoc Eulogy* reveals the utter illusion underpinning our desire for a coherent and linear history.[80]

Most striking and elaborate among Fuentes's fabricated or reproductive memory creations are the phonographic sound recordings that usher the film into presence and repeatedly accent its soundtrack. By recreating and digitally altering the written transcriptions of ethnographic sound recordings, Fuentes demonstrates both media archaeology's imagination and its ear. Authentic or not, his sound recordings bear the indexicality of early mechanical reproduction via the noise that signals to the listener the preservation of the past. This provides at the very least a simulated version of what Baron labels "the archive effect," insofar as even a fictionalized account can engender an *"experience of reception"* regardless of its lack of indexicality to an officially sanctioned and stored "archival document."[81] Along these lines, a fairer description of *Bontoc Eulogy* and its creation of "found" sound recordings might be "meta-archival." The film reflexively represents how the archive came into existence. That the archive itself as a source of history must be troubled comes perhaps most forcefully in a later scene of the film, in which Fuentes takes us to the space of the archive for the first time. Strolling through the University of Pennsylvania Museum of Archaeology and Anthropology, Fuentes directly confronts the physical

archive containing the skeletons and body parts of deceased Philippine Igorots preserved in glass jars and plasticized three-dimensional
images. Uncanny point-of-view shots reveal the empty stares of count-
less skulls on display in vitrine cabinets, partial facial objects, profiles,
and crania, all in disturbingly proximate close-ups. Bodies are quite literally reduced to parts and consequently to anthropological taxidermy.
Unmasked as an unapologetically and thoroughly pathological enterprise of extreme violence, archival logic surpasses itself in this scene.

Fuentes's autoethnographic film invokes ethnographic memory as
a totalizing ersatz for personal memory. Intensely inundated with the
images and sounds of centuries of colonial rule, cultural memory itself
ebbs and becomes substituted by the materials of empire. From within
the treachery of archives of the West and their knowledge regimes, of
colonialism and salvage ethnography, Fuentes tells a story. Yet despite
their accreted plentitude, these archives cannot always provide the
material evidence upon which they mount their history and authority, and Fuentes's own story must be supplemented. In its re-sounding
of the phonographic recordings made by ethnographers, *Bontoc Eulogy*
acoustically reminds us of the machinery of colonial listening without
reinscribing the process. Fuentes tells his own version of history. Classify *Bontoc Eulogy* as you like, but its documentary promise does not
fail. For as Nichols defines it, "In documentary, an event recounted
is history reclaimed."[82] In this chapter, I have sought to demonstrate
how the film brings forth another mode of decolonial listening in its
autoethnographic intervention of reflexivity as well as self-expression
and assertion that works against the colonial rules of engagement of
destruction and salvage.

Further throwing the colonial ear into relief, the following and final
chapter turns to Adele Horne's documentary *The Tailenders* (US, 2005).
Distinct from *The Halfmoon Files* and *Bontoc Eulogy*, this last film takes
a turn to a more recent phenomenon of colonial listening and to different recording and playback devices. *The Tailenders* tracks the work
of the Global Recordings Network, an evangelical Christian missionary organization devoted to translating and disseminating Bible stories
to remote areas of the world through the instrumentalization of rudi-
mentary sonic machines that are at once weird and utterly resourceful.
The film demonstrates how sound recording has evolved to continue
to play a central role in the colonial and neocolonial project of the West.
Ultimately, I return to the topic of the voice and its unfading echo in
documentary film. Horne's film examines the affective ramifications
of prescriptive orality and aurality. The mechanized and instrumentalized voice of catechizing not only becomes systematically severed from

an identity and a story but also loses its humanity. It becomes its sole message. This final chapter offers yet another dimension to the arsenal of the decolonizing ear that builds from noise to autoethnography in chapters 3 and 4. In a twofold material approach, first, the machine itself becomes the subject of direct scrutiny. To scrutinize the machine detracts from its message, and in the context of audio evangelism, this detraction is highly subversive. Second, the nature of the emitted voice of the machine comes under fire.

Chapter Five

Weird Machines and Disembodied Voices: Audio Evangelism in *The Tailenders*

Adele Horne's 2005 documentary film *The Tailenders* begins much the same way Marlon Fuentes's *Bontoc Eulogy* does, enigmatically with a sound machine and its emission of a disembodied voice. In this later film, the fade-in and -out of the film's title on a black screen accompanied by mysterious instrumental sound is followed by a cut to a close-up of a square piece of cardboard labelled "CardTalk" resting on a white surface. Two hands reach into the frame and unfold the cardboard, propping up one side. They then place a small phonographic record onto the horizontal piece of cardboard, which is equipped with a short spindle. A hardly visible stylus protrudes from the bottom edge of the propped-up side of the cardboard. The hands place the stylus on the record's grooved edge. One hand then inserts a pen into a small hole in the record and begins to rotate it clockwise. A canned male voice emerges and in English states: "I would like to ask you a question: what is a Christian?" The same voice, or perhaps another male voice, in a slightly higher-pitched tone, launches into a concise but lengthy definition to this catechism: "A Christian is ..." All the while, the hand continues to rotate the record with the pen. Once the voiced definition winds down, a sharp cut in image and sound follows. This opening scene introduces us to a machine, a captivating, improvised record player (figure 5.1).

The Tailenders is a documentary film about Gospel Recordings, now called Global Recordings Network (GRN), a Christian missionary group founded in Los Angeles in 1939 that uses low-tech audio devices to spread the evangelical message to Indigenous communities across the globe. The communities the GRN targets encounter extreme precarity with the impending loss of land, language, and culture as a result of global capitalism. It calls these target audiences "the tailenders" because they represent groups not yet reached by missionaries. *The Tailenders* is also a film invested in weird machines. As the first scene

Figure 5.1. The CardTalk opens *The Tailenders* (Adele Horne, US, 2005).
Courtesy of Adele Horne.

demonstrates, these objects play a central role. What is brought forth
through the inaugural demonstration of the CardTalk is not merely the
evangelical message emitting from the machine but rather the machine
itself, its properties, and its simple functionality. According to Horne, it
was the machine and not the message that incited the project of making
this film. She reveals in an interview that the CardTalk was an object she
recalled from her own childhood, given to her parents from missionary
friends. This weird machine, if we can even call it that, stuck with her.
Eventually she was compelled to investigate its origins.[1]

In this final chapter, I seek to examine the history and role of language and the voice in missionary work, which have resulted in the
weird sonic objects that make regular appearances in *The Tailenders*.
The film's focus on these machines, now mostly in disuse, presents an
unorthodox approach to listening to the messages of audio evangelism.
Such an approach ultimately challenges the original intentions of these
machines, insofar as it draws the listener's attention away from the content of their messages. Decolonial listening in this film takes another
media archaeological turn through the unsettling exploration of the

machine. Prioritizing the machines with abundant focus on the practicality, ideology, and hiccups of using them, this film refuses to take their proselytizing messages at face value. As GRN members themselves have charged, the film does not take their work seriously. For the film's insistence that the medium is the message foregrounds aspects of this missionary work meant to remain invisible and especially inaudible. A return to the multimedia archive of the GRN thus becomes a subversion of its objects. Beginning with these weird sonic machines, the chapter finally makes it way to the phenomenon of the disembodied voice. Not a mere complement to the sonic machine, the disembodied voice is a powerful phenomenon that draws a through line from evangelism to machines and finally to documentary's classic voice-of-God narration. Horne employs the latter in her film but not without irony and reflexivity. Although the disembodied voice is a device present in all of the films explored in this book, *The Tailenders'* direct thematization of it opens up a fecund space for auditory and ideational exploration.

In this rather conventionally structured documentary with its talking-head interviews, expository voice-over narration provided by the filmmaker herself, location and identificatory captions, and the low-tech reality aesthetics of the DVCam footage, Horne traces the history of the GRN and accompanies three different groups on missionary trips to the Solomon Islands, Mexico, and India, respectively. Like Philip Scheffner's *The Halfmoon Files* and Marlon Fuentes's *Bontoc Eulogy*, *The Tailenders* is also Horne's first feature-length film, for which she provides the narration as well. Horne's film also returns to a sound archive, but this one diverges in different ways from the Lautarchiv at the Humboldt University in Berlin or the public US-American archives such as the Smithsonian Institution Archives or the American Library of Congress. To begin, *The Tailenders* presents an archive of recorded voices still very much in use. Further, this ever-accreting archive of sound recordings compiled by the GRN does not consist of turn-of-the-twentieth-century phonograph wax cylinders or shellac records but of reel-to-reel audio tape recordings. Finally, the archive of the GRN is private and explicitly oriented towards a theological universalism. Despite these obvious distinctions, however, the sound archive in *The Tailenders* shares many of the features of the Ur-European colonial archive. Therefore, thinking about this film within a longer history of colonial listening and in the shadow of the Lautarchiv deepens and expands our understanding of the project of the GRN and the politics of *The Tailenders*.

In this film the colonial ethnographic logic of recording for preservation and collection becomes partly supplanted – or supplemented – by the operative logic of missionary evangelizing. Voices from around the world are recorded and collected in order to disseminate the word of God to others. Colonial listening thus assumes a circular directive. Missionaries enlist first-language speakers to translate and speak the Gospels into recording devices, which are later played back to Indigenous speakers with proselytizing objectives. Ana María Ochoa Gautier puts forward a lucid description of the transition of roles from convert to informant constituted through listening: "The indigenous person is no longer one to be converted but an informant, an aide to the constitution of a literary and scientific paradigm instantiated by listening to the aesthetic and scientific elements of language and to the data the informant provides."[2] While the historical context for this described shift emerges from the development of comparative grammar to linguistics underpinned by the pull of secularization in the late nineteenth century, this did not nullify the missionary project. The latter merely altered its strategies.[3] Thus, I offer a slight variation to Ochoa Gautier's account: the Indigenous person is now *both* one to be converted *and* an informant. Early in the film, Horne narrates the scene of recording in a contemplative, almost essayistic, tone against a collage of all-too-familiar archival photographs of Indigenous individuals and groups flanked by audio-recording equipment and often overly eager, smiling white faces: "The missionaries come with machines from the wealthy first world. The Indigenous people whom they target are losing their land and their languages to the onslaught of global capitalism. The product of this encounter is an audio recording." Between image and verbal message, we easily recognize the unequal positions of those who produce the sounds and those who record them. An enduring scene of what Marie Louise Pratt has notably referred to as "zones of colonial contact," those spaces of colonial encounter are where, as she indicates, "peoples geographically and historically separated come into contact with each other and establish ongoing relations, usually involving conditions of coercion, radical inequality, and intractable conflict."[4] The material product of this encounter of unequal power relations, the audio recording, is then checked, edited, and sometimes manipulated by the missionaries. Finally, it is copied and disseminated to speakers of the same language group, who are then encouraged to listen to its messages over and over again. If the content of the speech acts performed for the phonograph had been of scant interest to the ethnographers of the past as explored in previous chapters, then here the content of the message is what matters most. For the scripted evangelical message always remains the same.

Yet there is still room for error, even when the act of recording, its process and message, appears infallibly categorical and buttressed by new technologies. Noise and the (mostly) unbidden errata of recording sound and speech thematized in chapter 3 through an analysis of *From Here to Here* and *The Halfmoon Files* likewise come into the play in *The Tailenders*. Ingeniously pragmatic as ultra-low-tech recording and sound equipment employed by the GRN may be, it not surprisingly opens the floodgates to inevitable slips and glitches. As Friedrich Kittler has taught us, with sound recording came the recording of noise. That first recording and playback machine, the phonograph, did not, in Kittler's account, "filter voices, words, and sounds out of noise," and for the first time, "register[ed] acoustic events as such."[5] This was of course a bane of the work of ethnographers and missionaries alike and guaranteed that any sound archive would also be what Mary Ann Doane in her reading of Kittler refers to as an "archive of noise."[6] While the machines and their products may have become quieter with the invention of new audio devices and the possibility of postrecording editing, missionaries still cannot entirely winnow or suppress the undesired soundscape of a recording setting in the field, often without access to quiet spaces. The background noise of nature, children playing, and domestic animals often seeps through in the recordings. Ambient sound disturbs the intended message. Horne offers acoustic and visual evidence of this: she plays some recordings of speaking voices simply blending into broader soundscapes. Zooming into the labels accompanying these recordings, we can also read the penned indications of the background noise.

Challenges of recording in other languages and the difficulty of translating the Gospels into Indigenous tongues also arise when speakers insert their own interpretations of the evangelical stories. In one extended scene, GRN missionary Philip Young, whose group Horne accompanies to Baja California, Mexico, works with Mario Gracido, a native Oaxacan and a first-language speaker of the Mixtec language. The task is to translate and record "The Good News Picture Booklet," a script reportedly about punishment, pain, and suffering. But a direct translation proves impossible, for, as Mario explains to an incredulous Philip, these concepts do not even exist in Mixtec. In prolongation of the semantic trouble that frequently arises in the work of biblical translation, another scene shows Philip in conversation with a volunteer solicited to check a recording. Here he discovers that instead of conveying the message that God can wash away our sins, the narrative has been comically reversed. The listeners instead are told that *they* must wash away *God's* sins. Humour heightens when Philip shares yet another anecdote of mistaken translation from the story of "The Prodigal Son" that unbeknownst to the missionaries becomes rendered as the comically profane, not to mention blasphemous, story of

"The Prodigal *Pig*," about a wayward swine who leaves home in search of adventure.

Calling attention to the archive of noise in *The Tailenders*, Jaimie Baron describes both the ambient sounds and the (in)voluntary translations of the biblical stories that filter through the recordings, as part of the function of archival irony in the film.[7] Baron understands this as contributing to the structure of the joke of the film, not unlike the joke of *Bontoc Eulogy*, a point I also consider in the previous chapter. According to Baron, the joke of *The Tailenders* lies in the fugitive nature of the archives it presents and the indexical traces these archives seek to preserve. She indicates that "[these] often escape the control of the archons." While noise poses a threat to the missionary work and the archives it seeks to create, maintain, and instrumentalize to disseminate knowledge, the film instead appears to "celebrate its liberatory effect in the breakdown of the missionaries' control."[8] Foregrounding the noise of the archive, literal or metaphorical, as *The Tailenders* does, becomes for Baron a "productive 'misuse' of its materials."[9] Such a productive misuse of the archive is an approach that permeates all of the films in the present study and merits scrutiny in its provision of critique of the sound archive and its processes of archivization. Yet as this chapter seeks to show, Horne's film and its relationship to the archive congeal most forcefully at other sites of heterodox listening. An unearthing of these sites demands an investigation of the longer history of missionary work, language, and evangelical dissemination through the voice, which gradually (over history) becomes disembodied through technology's machines.

A Brief History of Language, Translation, and Missions

At the time of this film's making, the GRN boasted an archive of recordings containing 5,485 different languages and dialects from around the world.[10] Many of these languages are no longer spoken or are at risk of extinction. One of the initial scenes in *The Tailenders* presents Horne's visit to the GRN's original archive in Los Angeles, where the organization was founded by Joy Ridderhof, herself a Quaker missionary, in 1939. There we are greeted by Sandy Milligan, the de facto archon, who presides over what she calls "the vault." By way of introduction, she vaunts: "I believe in this vault you are in the presence of more languages in audio form than anywhere else on earth." The camera zooms in to examine some of the audio cassette tape labels. Milligan's explanations follow in voice-over. What strikes the viewer upon seeing these audio cassettes and reels are the almost infantile scribbles that accompany them, with scratched-out letters and words. The labels appear unofficial, inconsequential, even a bit silly. In casual dress and with modest manners, Milligan herself does not immediately fit the picture one might have of the archon of the world's largest collection of audio language recordings. From the beginning, it is difficult to take this archive and its objects seriously. If in Baron's account the film produces an ambivalence about the missionaries' archive, then this is made vivid in this scene.[11] Horne unsettles the authority of the archive by revealing its amateurishness. But Horne does this without downplaying the severity of its entanglements. Baron is correct to conclude that "Horne is able to use Gospel Recordings' archival mission to trace the legacy of colonialism and the flow of evangelism, in concert with the spread of global capitalism and consumerism."[12] However, Horne consistently draws our attention to the cracks in the foundation of the archive and its authoritative power.

Joseph Errington traces the history of missionary language work and its inextricable link to colonial rule from the Catholic missionaries in the sixteenth and seventeenth centuries to the Protestants in the nineteenth, and finally to their post- and neocolonial counterparts. In the unapologetic words of the German Roman Catholic missiologist and founder of the Internationales Institut für missionswissenschaftliche Forschungen (International Institute for Research in Missiology) Joseph Schmidlin: "To missionize is to colonize and to colonize is to missionize."[13] The missionary project not only proved to be a consequence of colonialism but worked with it hand in glove. As early as 1513, the Spanish monarchy drew up the Requerimiento (Spanish Requirement) declaring divine legitimation for the conquest of the so-called New World, one that sought to convert its inhabitants to Christianity. An appallingly blatant perversion of Catholic theology, the Requerimiento solidified religion's place in the devasting project of colonialism. Language too must be inserted into this equation of catastrophe of enslavement, displacement, and genocide. Errington writes, "In Spain the question of language was central for resolving the status of *los indios* so as to legitimize the conquest."[14] This did not always result in the direct enforcement of language acquisition, although that certainly evolved as a corollary. Instead, Catholic friars took it upon themselves to learn some of the more widely spread Indigenous languages in order to pen God's word in their own versions of Indigenous literary languages. Establishing a grammar and writing system of Indigenous tongues based on the Latin vernacular, missionaries returned these written languages to the colonized with new messages of Christianity.[15] But their efforts were not only self-serving; they also exercised another unique kind of violence, the violence of the displacement of spoken language in favour of orthography. For Walter Mignolo, this illustrated the darker side of literacy, one that promoted "the letter," in his words, "to an ontological dimension with clear priority over the voice, as well as other writing systems."[16] Indeed, Franciscans systematically ignored the pre-existing script of classic civilizations. The letter refers not to all writing systems but to Greco-Roman alphabetic forms of writing, which displaced earlier and other forms. The specification of the letter as opposed to writing tout court resonates with Jacques Derrida's famous declaration of the "violence of the letter," which, inter alia, bore witness to the systematic rejection by European anthropologists and philosophers (he famously names Claude Lévi-Strauss and Jean-Jacques Rousseau in particular) of non-alphabetic forms of writing.[17] To be clear, Indigenous languages did have collective forms of writing, they were just different from European letters.

With the Protestant missionaries in later centuries the interdependence of evangelizing and colonialism did not loosen, but approaches altered. Distinct from the Catholic universal strategy, Protestants sought to engage with communities more directly. The message of God needed to speak to converts' experiences and interests in a way that was personal and "unmediated." Missionaries pursued this strategy through translation. Errington underscores this in his study: "Protestants understood that biblical truth could only come directly to individuals through personal knowledge of that text, and so that they were called to provide translations which could produce internal conversions of mind, imagination, and soul."[18] Unlike their Catholic counterparts, Protestant missionaries saw the value in learning individual Indigenous languages with a certain fluency as a means to bridge communities with the Christian faith. They were thus much more committed to learning the languages of their target communities, spending time with them, and developing an understanding for their culture. This did not come without its challenges. The effort and time required for such an endeavour were profound. Further, as Errington explains, Protestant missionaries were faced with "a double paradox of translation and conversion," which presented the difficult task of deciding what elements of the Indigenous culture could be preserved and what had to be dismissed in the translation and re-presentation of biblical texts.[19] *The Tailenders* offers explicit examples of this double paradox. The question of flexibility versus fidelity (and the obligation to literally understand the divine inspiration of God's word) arises for instance in contemplation of the translation of the first miracle story, the Marriage of Cana, in which Jesus turns water into wine. What if, for instance, beer is the preferred celebratory beverage? But is it wise to share such a story with a community that suffers from alcoholism? Several similar discussions arise throughout the film. These reflect the enduring challenges of translating biblical texts for the purposes of evangelism.

In the aftermath of New Imperialism in the late nineteenth century and the early twentieth century, the vast majority of missionary enterprises hailed from the United States and English was their lingua franca. As Errington indicates, many missionary groups continued where their Protestant colonial forbears left off, maintaining an emphasis on the importance of spreading the Gospel and engaging people through their own native tongues. One such organization is SIL International (formerly, Summer Institute of Linguistics), founded in 1934 and based in Dallas, Texas. The founder, Cameron Townsend, recognized that one could reach more people and foster greater literacy by providing written material in the Indigenous languages of the communities one sought to target.[20] Founded just five years later, GRN follows a similar logic but advanced its strategies through the employment of multimedia technology. By dint of technology and audio recording, missionaries could reach their audiences much more efficiently. Further, they could even appeal to children and illiterate adults. Beginning with Spanish and then expanding to multilanguage phonographic records in the late 1930s, GRN founder Joy Ridderhof quickly gained success and by the mid-1940s had employed engineers to design machines explicitly for her organization's missionary endeavours.[21] Now instead of investing time and energy in learning and understanding the language groups they addressed, missionaries could delegate this work to first-language speakers, whose recorded and mechanized voices could disseminate God's word in the target language for them. This model directly instantiates Horne's reflection in voice-over, citing David Himrod, that "American Protestantism is a syncretism between Christianity and technology."[22] In his article bearing the same title, Himrod elaborates that "technology has encompassed Protestantism; and the symbols of technological activity and Protestantism have coalesced into one religious system, which has promoted republican technology."[23] Horne distills this further, narrating, "[Protestantism] is a fusion in the belief in the power of God and the power of machines." As Himrod indicates, a turn to technology does not intimate a secular turn, as one may be wont to believe, but simply a transformation of Christian symbols.[24] The machines that facilitate this transformation warrant further examination.

An Archive of Weird Objects and Sonic Machines

The Tailenders spends significant time in the archive. Indeed, the GRN boasts two archives, or at least two distinct parts of a larger one. The first contains the audio recordings of the canon of biblical stories in nearly six thousand different languages and assumes the appearance of a small library of tightly ordered audio cassette tapes. The other is a repository, or even private museum space, of technology of prototypes and discontinued machines once used to disseminate the missionaries' message. Here one can tinker with the strange devices. Although they have fallen into disuse, in many cases these machines are still in working order. These sonic machines of the GRN are simple, motorless, and hand-cranked. They also do not rely on electricity or batteries to operate. According to Jacob Smith, "the engineers at Gospel Recordings, like those at RCA and the U.S. military, were called on to develop playback devices that had 'the utmost ruggedness, stability with temperature, and ability to keep working under adverse climatic conditions.'"[25] The curious machine that opens *The Tailenders* and returns later for further demonstration, the CardTalk, was developed in 1964 with precisely this ambition of "ruggedness" and "stability" in mind (see figure 5.1). It was furthermore cheap and easy to produce and transport. Thus, it provided the perfect tool for missionary fieldwork to reproduce the word of God from a single speaker to many pairs of ears.

Jury-rigged gramophones, cassette players, and the like comprise the GRN archive of weird objects (figure 5.2). In the film, George Bowers, a GRN missionary and engineer, demonstrates these strange and fascinating machines for the camera. They include among others the "Phonette," a small hand-crank gramophone; "Cassette Talk," a strip of cardboard equipped with supply and take-up reels for an audio cassette; "Tape Talk," a hand-wind cassette player; and the wooden-armed gramophone. In his spirited manner, Bowers explains the GRN strategy: "We take what the man makes and we revamp it to do what we want it to do." These devices look like toys, and Bowers like an adult child at play as he winds, cranks, and listens with pricked ears. The film contains several scenes of machine demonstration. Later on David McNaughton, a similarly long-time missionary and engineer for GRN, displays and demonstrates a bright-red gramophone. The colour, he elucidates, is intentional; it attracts attention. First, the people see the machines; then they listen; finally, they recognize the voice as one of their own. McNaughton describes it like a marketing strategy: "The novelty factor is the point of the hook." Indeed, the eccentricity of these machines is part of their appeal. These audiovisual tours to the archive evoke the experience of taking a stroll through the Media-Archaeological "Fundus" at the Berlin Humboldt University Institute for Media Studies, which is full of machines from previous eras. Both earn the description of "an archive of media-epistemological toys" and "a repository and a tinkering space for old media technology."[26] But Bowers's playful attitude towards the archive does not obviate its nexus

Figure 5.2. GRN missionary and engineer George Bowers tinkering in the archive, from *The Tailenders* (Adele Horne, US, 2005). Courtesy of Adele Horne.

with the context of colonial history. Instead, the gravitas of the archive continues to waver. Over decades, these machines facilitated the neo-colonial encounter between missionaries and Indigenous communities throughout the world. The GRN archive is, to put it in Siegfried Zielinski's words, just as much "the externalization of historical consciousness, thereby documenting a consciousness fundamentally tied to power."[27]

Horne displays an acute awareness of the imbrications of machine and mastery. Beyond the effective real-time talking-head interviews with missionaries and members of communities targeted by the missionaries, she provides a potent example of the callousness of missionary mechanisms. In one instance, with more than a hint of irony, Horne displays a series of three photographic images: the first two feature a woman with a child in Guatemala, and the third features of a group of four children from Nicaragua. In all three images, the subjects clutch small machines. In voice-over, Horne comments that they had all been given solar-powered, fix-tuned radios by an evangelical organization called Galcom International, based in Canada, which, according to their website, produces "durable, technical equipment for communicating the Gospel worldwide."[28] Horne explains that these radios cannot be tuned and they receive only one evangelical radio station that broadcasts throughout the region. Instead of showing the caption attached to the third image of four children posing for the camera, Horne reads it aloud: "Children from Nicaragua lost their parents in a flood but were given solar, fix-tuned radios for some hope." That this is the last thing these children need is an axiomatic addendum that goes unspoken. Many analogous instances come to surface throughout the film and via the missionary work. Injustice, privation, and dispossession worldwide are met with prayer and the pedagogy of acceptance, reconciliation, and hope, rather than subsistence, resistance, and collective political action.

The GRN archive is nevertheless worthy of exploration. Horne seems compelled by its weird media objects and invites us to look and listen more closely. These are not simply familiar relics or artifacts of audio technology come to repose; rather, they are uniquely engineered devices that often appear to defy technological capability. How could a record or a tape emit recorded sound without a loudspeaker, electricity, or batteries, for that matter? These machines are utterly analogue but simultaneously outlandishly inventive, wireless, and portable. Further, what do we make of the fact of their inextricable ideology? We cannot forget that these machines, frivolous as they may seem, were designed with the sole intention of evangelizing. This motive is built into their structure and functionality. They neither play standard records or audio cassettes nor have a record button that would allow their recipients to override the messages on the cassettes or create their own messages. They are strictly one-way media with a one-way message.

In sum, the GRN has generated an archive of weird machines whose operation appears technically impossible and whose usage is restrictive and ideological. Notwithstanding their improvised nature, these odd archival objects came into being as part of a body of knowledge, complex relations, positive conditions, and a set of practices; in other words, discourse. As we have learned from Michel Foucault, objects do not precede or exist outside of discourse. Is it the evangelical or the technological discourse that gave these objects the very status of objects, or in Foucault's words, made them "manifest, nameable, and describable"?[29] As Horne indicates, it appears to be both, imbricated in the congruity of American Protestantism. This is more than just coincidence or serendipity, even. According to Horne in a post-film interview, the missionaries of the GRN believe that the machines and the inventive craft of their retooling have been provided by God: "GRN sees their work as enacting a mechanical Pentecost. They feel that God has provided recording technology to make it possible to spread the gospel message more efficiently, with record players acting as sort of robot missionaries. GRN is incredibly interested in gadgetry. They devote a lot of energy to inventing and producing machines, and to retooling existing machines for their own purposes. The spirit of invention and ingenuity is nearly as strong a current within their organization as the evangelical impulse."[30] The approach of the missionaries might appear antidiscursive, insofar as they understand the weird media objects of the GRN to be divine gifts from God rather than products of an unfolding complex system of knowledge. However, such a challenge does not take into consideration the broader discourse of the syncretism of Protestant popular religion and technology. Himrod calls this syncretism the coalescence of Christian and technological symbols.[31] The techniques of the GRN typify this coalescence.

More curious in its approach than critical, the film's mere attention to the sonic machines of the GRN apparently struck the most subversive chord. The organization's own distancing from the film upon its public release attests to this. Even beyond concerns about the film's implicit critique of evangelical missionary work tout court as exploitative and rooted in a colonial tradition and history, the disapproval voiced by the GRN surprisingly centred on the film's apparently misleading portrayal of the network's employment and dependency on low-tech media objects.[32] What Horne portrays as innovative and pragmatic for the purpose of missionary work, the GRN views as a discrediting focus on the primitive and the analogue nature of their devices. Perhaps more than in any other film examined in this study, in *The Tailenders* the machine really is the message.

One is left to wonder what the GRN expected from Horne's documentary. Certainly, there exists a plethora of missionary documentary films. Beginning as early as the 1920s, it was not uncommon for missionaries to film their expeditions. Rev. John G. Magee's documentary films in China are perhaps among the most famous early examples. His 16 mm documentation of the Nanjing Massacre between 1937 and 1938 is without doubt historically groundbreaking.[33] It is unclear if the GRN anticipated a more promotional film through the lens of a missionary-minded filmmaker. Horne notes in interviews that her parents are evangelical Christians and even worked as missionaries.[34] This would have fostered initial knowledge and interest and perhaps provided the necessary connection to the GRN. It goes without saying that the organization may have been less inclined to cooperate with someone inexperienced with or openly critical of its faith and practices. Horne has also noted that during the trips she took with the various groups to the Solomon Islands, Mexico, and India, she was perceived as part of the respective missionary groups by the locals. However, *The Tailenders* is not an observational, fly-on-the-wall documentary. Despite Horne's own claim that this film is a kind of ethnography of the missionaries, thought to provide (at least, aesthetically) unmediated representation of the activities of the subject group, her own hand as a filmmaker in the form of sound, cinematography, and editing belies or at least troubles this.[35] Horne may be for the most part physically invisible in the film, but she does participate in the production of images and speech. Her take and voice on the events are carefully formulated and presented.

By focusing on the ingenuity, peculiarity, and playfulness of the machines rather than the biblical messages they were constructed to emit, Horne does not so much downplay the severity of the evangelical missionary practices of the GRN as she refuses to afford them the seriousness and truthfulness they seek. The Gospel stories and fragments played at various points throughout the film do not find intended addressees and thus their semantic meanings fail to arrive. The opening scene with the CardTalk is a case in point. In thrall to the medium itself, the audience ceases to listen to the verbal message. In this way, the strange machine hinders its own transmission. To riff on Mladen Dolar, the film and its audience do not recognize themselves as addressees of the Gospel messages but as receivers of another message about the existence and functionality of this strange machine.[36] One begins to contemplate an equivalent situation of missed meaning or interpellation among the communities targeted by the missionaries too. Were communities likewise too consumed with marvel at the machines to care about the message? The film tacitly presents this possibility as conceivable. Unlike in the other films, the audio recordings Horne remediates are not translated, save for through discussion with translators or language checkers. The opening message played on the CardTalk, "What is a Christian?," is in English but the voices are canned and sound almost cartoonish. In one scene, we witness the editing of native speaker Mario's audio file in Mixtec, a process involving the deletion of the Spanish-language prompting of the missionary and of any undesirable pauses, sighs, breath, and so forth. *The Tailenders* appears less interested in reading and deciphering these involuntary utterances and disturbances, which with the phonograph would have been left unedited and simply tolerated because early technology did not allow otherwise. The machines serve greater appeal. Above and beyond the inveterate colonial history of the phonograph, the performative pitch of the invention of the GRN's weird objects as missionary machines, created solely to convey the message of Christianity to isolated Indigenous communities, takes the mechanics of colonial listening to another level. The film brings this forth with equal doses of curiosity and irreverence.

Disembodied Voices of the Machines

Returning once again to the opening scene of the film and its inaugural object, the CardTalk, one cannot help but be seized by an appreciation of what it might have been like in centuries past to have heard a phonograph for the first time, or perhaps Wolfgang von Kempelen's even earlier invention, the Sprechmaschine. A certain rush of disbelief, shock, and marvel sets in, if just negligibly, at the beginning of *The Tailenders*. By now, we are more than accustomed to the disembodied voice of audio technology, but its emission from this weird object made of cardboard and cranked with a pen still puzzles. While the film's focus on the materiality of the GRN's sonic machines might intentionally distract from their evangelical messages, the phenomenon of the disembodied voice is not as easily hushed.

The disembodied voice could be taken up as part of any one of this book's chapters. All the films in focus here present worthy objects of study with regard to this topic. And it stands to reason that the matter of the voice has long been a central element of documentary studies.[37] But until now I have skirted the voice and orality to concentrate on the ear and audition. With *The Tailenders*, the irrevocable entanglement of the ear and the voice, not to mention documentary's foregrounding of the spoken word, powerfully comes to form. If the disembodied voice found symbolic visual representation via the black screen or through the close-up of the equally black shellac record spinning on the turntable in *The Halfmoon Files* and *Bontoc Eulogy*, respectively, here its mechanical representation achieves creative new heights. Numerous close-ups of audio machines permeate the image track. But the visualizing of sound goes beyond showing the machines. In one curious scene, Horne allows the film frame to fill with the digital signal produced by a recording in an unidentified language. There are no subtitles; the audience listens only to the prosodic qualities of the disembodied voice and its production of stereo imaging, what Bill Nichols might describe as moiré-like patterns in the form of rising and falling white waves against a black background.[38] Not simply a visual metaphor for the voice, this image presents its legible audio signal. A similar scene of visually documenting the disembodied, recorded voice emerges later in the film. In this case, Horne provides previously missing details. Before launching into the recording, the film shows the text in English translation, labelled "Script #112: 'The Good Spirit,'" and reveals the language and provenance of the recording: "Yei language, Botswana." Once the recording begins, the visual track horizontally layers what appear to be black-and-white negative voice-prints in a montage of auditory sliding textures that appears eerily spectral. Once the recording has ended, Horne's own voice follows in a reflection on the GRN's archive of language recordings, which in some cases present remaining traces of languages already vanished, now reduced to a single coerced recording of a Bible story, in her words, "fed line by line into the mouth of a speaker." Horne's attentiveness to the reverberations and textures of the voice – both physically and ideologically – shapes the film in significant ways.

With well-nigh fervour, Horne pursues the disembodied voice and recognizes the importance of its uncanny presence of authority. She directly speaks to it, as she reflexively throws doubt on her own voice-over narration and its ontological and epistemic purview. The emergence of voice-over narration in documentary film, commonly equated with the voice-of-God technique promoted by documentary pioneer John Grierson, historically aligns with the founding of the GRN in the 1930s and 1940s. In its early conceptualization, voice-of-God narration sought to achieve a position of objectivity and detachment from above, with which the audience could align and approach the subject matter of the film with critical detachment.[39] The historical connection between the documentary medium and the subject of her film is not lost on Horne. Not dissimilar to the mechanical and mechanized voices of the GRN, the disembodied voice in documentary has represented a powerful mode of authority, communication, and exposition. A turn here to Charles Wolfe's account of voice-over narration in documentary proves insightful: "Disembodied, this voice is construed as fundamentally unrepresentable in human form, connoting a position of absolute mastery and knowledge outside the spatial and temporal boundaries of the social world the film depicts."[40] Importantly, the disembodied voice could speak truth to the filmic text. One should note, of course, that voice-of-God narration has also long been a source of scepticism and an impetus for scholarship eager to challenge it. Paul Bonitzer and Mary Ann Doane have pointed to the troubling non-referential charge of the voice-over, which disengaged itself from the body and thereby assumed transcendental dimensions attesting to an unquestionable authority. Doane's commentary on the disembodied voice-over is unsurpassed:

It is its radical otherness with respect to the diegesis which endows this voice with a certain authority. As a form of direct address, it speaks without mediation to the audience, by-passing the "characters" and establishing a complicity between itself and the spectator – together they understand

and thus *place* the image. It is precisely because the voice is not localizable, because it cannot be yoked to a body, that it is capable of interpreting the image, producing its truth. Disembodied, lacking any specification in space or time, the voice-over is, as Bonitzer points out, beyond criticism – it censors the questions "Who is speaking?," "Where?," "In what time?," and "For whom?"[41]

The unmoored voice, unattached to the film's diegesis, its image, or even to a body, becomes omnipresent and therefore also omniscient on account of its invisible source. It can speak the truth without question, because it "sees" all, "hears" all, and "knows" all. Therefore, it also cannot be questioned or doubted. It is incontestable. This very inviolability is, according to Bonitzer, the essence of the disembodied voice's power.[42]

With zeal, evangelists took up the all-powerful disembodied voice described by Doane. They found great appeal in the possibilities of this voice for the project of spreading the word of God. Horne dramatically brings this connection into focus in her film. An extreme close-up shot of a rotating cassette tape accompanies the sound of proselytizing speech of what we may have come to recognize as televangelist drones. This voice cuts off and Horne's contrasting, almost demurely quizzical voice takes over. Punctuated with thought-provoking pauses, Horne contemplates the appeal of disembodied voices:

> Why are disembodied voices so captivating? [*pause*] In the dark of our mother's womb, sounds seem to come from nowhere. [*pause*] The first voices we hear have no bodies. And then there's God's voice emanating from a burning bush, Bin Laden's voice circulating and spreading via audio- and videocassette, as the Ayatollah Khomeini's did in the years prior to the revolution in Iran. Hitler claimed that without the loudspeaker, he would never have conquered Germany. [*pause*] Separated from its body, a voice becomes superhuman. [*pause*] It can speak to more people than any single person could. [*pause*] Evangelists began using the disembodied voice in the twenties and thirties.

Perhaps the most sentient commentary in the entire film, Horne's interrogation of the disembodied voice is made possible (and performative) through its very mobilization. The reflexivity of this speech act registers more on the level of the essay film than documentary. But to what degree irony plays a role here remains ambiguous. Baron proposes that Horne implicitly mimics the CardTalk with its opening question and didactic technique. She classifies Horne's narration in this scene as part of the joke structure of the film.[43] Horne's reflexive question arrives via her own disembodied voice. An occasional disembodied hand notwithstanding, we never see her in the film nor hear her voice as a diegetic voice-off (out of the film frame but not extradiegetic), even when she pursues talking-head interviews and her subjects are presumably responding to her questions or verbal prompting.[44] Within the frame of this rhetorical ruse, Horne presents the complex nexus of the disembodied voice, to which we are, according to her, even biologically predisposed. From the maternal voice to God's voice to those political leaders who sought apotheosis, and finally to the machine, the scope and influence of the disembodied voice are inescapable and all powerful. What is fascinating about the machines of the GRN is, according to Baron, their capacity to *"literalize* the notion of the 'voice of God.'"[45] Objects such as the CardTalk were designed to speak the word of God, not simply as placeholders, but as the real deal. How can the voice-over narration of documentary compete with such conviction?

The truth be told, Horne's own voice-of-God narration ultimately falls short of its promise and purview, and she is undoubtedly well aware of this. In her interview with Elizabeth Castelli, to which I often return, Horne reveals that she originally had no intention of including voice-over narration. Later she decided that narration was necessary to draw out some relevant themes. She furthermore did not at first seek to narrate the film herself but apparently reached this decision on account of her audible "curiosity and passion for the subject," which in her words, "comes through in my voice."[46] Certainly, these qualities of "curiosity and passion" resonate beyond the patronizing authority so frequently linked to voice-of-God narration, or at least perceived as its default. Notably, Horne's voice is also distinct from the unaccented, detached, authoritarian, anonymous, male voice so inextricably linked to this phenomenon and invested with dubious power.[47] Hers is the female voice, which in Kaja Silverman's view is "associated with unreliable, thwarted, or acquiescent speech."[48] While it might seem old hat to bring this up, the credibility bias of non-male, accented voices doggedly holds and it persists as a topic in scholarly discussions of the narrative voice in cinema.[49] By employing her own voice, Horne consciously destabilizes the perceived authority of the (male) voice-over. Her voice further contrasts with the other disembodied voices presented in the film. While one cannot say for certain that the majority of the voices recorded for the purposes of dissemination by GRN were male, all of the examples Horne remediates in *The Tailenders* are. Is this just coincidence? All of the recordings made by the Royal Prussian Phonographic Commission (RPPC) during the First World War (see chapter 1) were similarly exclusively male voices. Ethnographic phonography and its sound archives have relied predominantly on male voices. The reasons for this seem obvious enough but are no less worth contemplating. Why is the disembodied male voice more powerful, more authoritative, more compelling? By extension, why might it be perceived as the more authentic example of linguistic expression? Ironically, Silverman suggests that the linguistic status of a woman is "analogous to that of a recorded tape, which endlessly plays back what was spoken in some anterior moment, and from a radically external vantage."[50] That is to say, a woman's speech is always already deemed a copy and lacking in significance and novelty. This is not to suggest that recorded voices, perforce, become feminized. But it does attest to the unequal power relations of the missionary (or the ethnographer, for that matter) who records the voice and the subject who feels compelled to speak into the recording equipment.

But I wish to return to Horne's protracted reflection on the disembodied voice cited earlier and how quickly biology (an infant's gestational relationship to the maternal voice) and theology (the voice of God arising from the burning bush for the sake of Moses's ears) transforms into, or is actually always underpinned by, technology. Here soundtrack and visual track appear to part ways but also ally. From the extreme close-up shot of the cassette tape spinning in the tape deck, there is a cut to a sketch of the famous logo "His Master's Voice" featuring Nipper the terrier listening to the phonograph funnel, confused by the acoustic yet invisible presence of his deceased master. This was an early and renowned advertising logo for the Gramophone and Typewriter Company. Still iconographic for the representation of the power of the machinic voice, the logo evokes the erstwhile draw of the phonograph as a machine capable of raising the dead. At first glance, the pairing of this image with the audio commentary about the biblical story of the voice of God emanating from the burning bush seems merely erratic, but Horne draws an important parallel and reinforces the link between religion and machine. Edison not only made it possible for the dead to speak, but for God himself to speak – and be heard too (figure 5.3).

The disembodied voice of God and machines unite through the concept of the acousmatic voice, the voice whose source is invisible and often unknown. Popularized and expanded by Michel Chion through his work with the voice and cinema and conceptually borrowed from the composer and sound theorist Pierre Schaeffer, the acousmatic voice has been taken up by a number of thinkers in recent decades.[51] Many of these thinkers hark back to the much older history of this phenomenon. The acousmatic voice derives from the philosophical legend of

Figure 5.3. "His Master's Voice" logo; still from *The Tailenders* (Adele Horne, US, 2005). Courtesy of Adele Horne.

Pythagoras, who believed that his disciples (the *akousmatikoi*, Greek for "auditors" or "listeners") could learn free from distraction by listening to his lectures without seeing him in the flesh.[52] Predating any kind of audio playback machine, Pythagoras achieved this pedagogical practice by lecturing from behind a curtain, hanging, veil, or the like. His disembodied voice assumed an aura and authority that dramatically approached the theological. As the story goes, this marked the founding of the first philosophical school, and Pythagoras's approach brought him cultlike status; he was "revered as a dignity."[53] With the invention of audio playback machines, however, the acousmatic voice proliferated and lost its sui generis. With the departure of its novelty followed part of its magic. According to Dolar, the "His Master's Voice" logo is the lasting visual reminder of the auditory enchantment evoked by the disembodied voice.[54] That Horne would insert this reminder in her film at the mention of God's burning bush is revealing. She tacitly conjures this historical imbrication of religion, philosophy, and technology: Moses listening to God's voice, Pythagoras's disciples listening to their teacher, Nipper listening to his dead owner. The history of listening to the disembodied voice manifests itself as a history of obedience – of listening to the master. Dolar traces the etymological links of listening and obeying. For instance, in German the linguistic connection between *hören* (both to listen and to hear) and *gehorchen* (to obey) appears self-evident.[55] Horne traces this connection between audition and obedience through further examples of authoritarian leaders of the twentieth and twenty-first centuries (Osama Bin Laden, Ayatollah Khomeini, Adolf Hitler). Their instrumentalization of audio machines to summon the auditory attention of their followers and to disseminate their ideologies unites them through strategy as well as politics. As Rey Chow indicates, in the contemporary period the Pythagorean curtain is the site where technology and ideology are located.[56]

But to suggest that to listen is to obey contradicts much of what this book argues throughout its pages. Impassioned or indoctrinated listening is certainly not the same as the colonial listening of ethnographers, whose Boasian sound-blindness resulted in scientific indifference or simply utter disdain.[57] Need we be reminded of the earlier example of Alexander von Humboldt's protracted griping about the allegedly angry chants of the *bogas* on the Magdalena River or even R. Murray Schafer's notorious comments about Inuit throat singing as a sound akin to clearing one's throat?[58] Representing a long historical arc, Humboldt's and Schafer's pernicious observations demonstrate the tenacity of racialized thinking that has long extended to linguistic heritage, from German comparative philology and the interpretation of "language as evidence of ethnic descent" to Darwinian-influenced eugenics of language.[59]

The instrumentalization of listening to disembodied voices put into operation by the GRN and the process by which the organization "listens" with an audio recorder to first-language speakers as a means to control and then disseminate this voice for the purpose of preaching to diverse linguistic and cultural communities offers yet another example of the tangled and sinister process of colonial listening. In the context of colonial encounter, white colonialists have long listened with a wilfully indifferent tin ear, as Dylan Robinson reminds us, and colonial subjects have conversely been conditioned to a mode of listening that disciplines, because as Jennifer Lynn Stoever similarly contends, listening is racialized and the sonic colour line, as she calls it, is real.[60] Stoever compellingly argues that sound and listening, as much as sight and vision, have enabled racism's evolving persistence. "Far from being vision's opposite," she writes, "sound frequently appears to be visuality's doppelgänger in U.S. racial history, unacknowledged but ever present in the construction of race and the performance of racial oppression."[61] Not dissimilar to my own exploration of a history of colonial listening, Stoever examines how US white supremacy "has attempted to suppress, tune out, and willfully misunderstand" certain sounds and their makers.[62] Beyond merely laying out the injurious history of the sonic colour line, she also brings forth many important examples of resistance to this long line of silencing and disciplining as demonstrated through literature, music, and film.

The Tailenders similarly informs us of how colonial listening continues to function in more recent decades through the project of evangelism hailing from countries such as the United States and Australia. The film enlightens its audience about this subject matter while also signalling a cautionary critique. Unspoken as the film's critique may be, it serves to unsettle a straightforward portrayal of the GRN and similar organizations, their motives, and their practices. The film concludes not with Horne's voice but with a series of talking-head interviews. Advertently or not, she abandons the disembodied voice and voice-of-God narration at the end and embraces the style of direct cinema and cinema verité. Historically, documentary filmmakers adopted more observational styles in the 1950s and 1960s as a conscious rejection of the dogmatically ideational techniques of traditional documentary and voice-of-God narration as its linchpin.[63] Following Bill Nichols's more metaphorical approach to voice, these new kinds of documentaries did not relinquish their "voice" as such, for the voice-of-documentary is precisely that which "conveys to us a sense of a text's social point of view, of how it is speaking to us and how it is organizing the materials it is presenting to us."[64] Therefore, these films continued to express ideas and points of view but without a narrative voice-over. Their approach was more indirect and variegated; furthermore, they found expression in a multitude of voices. In the interviews pursued by Horne, individuals in Baja California discuss the mounting burden of evangelical Christianity on their community. At this location, in particular, Horne was able to return to speak to community members without the presence of the missionaries. Her interviews extend to a range of people with different views on the issue. Some of the members express themselves as staunch Protestant believers and others are sceptical, even critical, of the changes brought by way of the teachings of the missionaries. The latter group underscores how with Protestantism came individualism, materialism, and the lack of community spirit. Divisiveness and the weakening of collective social and political sovereignty have transpired as a result. Despite the precarious circumstances under which many of these community members live and survive, converts to Protestantism seek guidance and deliverance from God and not politics or collective action. In a sense, Christianity's pedagogy of forbearance has silenced them.

The film's closing sequence tracks Mario Gracido again. Earlier in *The Tailenders*, scenes of Mario cross-cut between a talking-head interview in which he reflects on his family's hardships and footage of him labouring in a field, picking strawberries. As mere children, he and his sister had to stop attending school in order to work in the fields to help pay the debts incurred by his mother's hospital bills. What appears to be the same talking-head interview returns and continues in this later sequence, but this time it cross-cuts with footage of Mario attending church. He emerges from a one-story house in Santa Maria, California, wearing a black suit, quite literally his "Sunday best," and clutching what appears to be a Bible. He climbs into his 1980s Lincoln Continental luxury car parked in the driveway. As he drives, his voice continues to narrate in voice-over. Mario now relates his own story of upward social mobility and economic prosperity through conversion to evangelical Protestantism. "Puedo ir a qualquier restaurante … Si yo trabajo aquí, puedo pagar mi renta o puedo comprar un carro" ("I can go to any restaurant … If I have a job, I can pay my rent, or I can buy a car").[65] Arriving at his destination, the Santa Maria Community Church, Mario cheerfully greets another parishioner at the door and then enters. Inside the atmosphere is animated. There is live music, clapping, and movement. A group of children bounces around in the back of the church. Then there is prayer. The minister preaches loudly and with heavy emotion to his congregants, who respond in piece. Some even dramatically weep. Mario emotionally calls out in response, praying to God, his hands raised and his eyes closed: "En tí encuentro soluciónes a mis problemas" ("In you I find solutions to my problems"), he utters with powerful conviction. But his voice-over narration re-sounds and competes with his diegetic prayer. In his final words, he attests not without a tinge of regret, possibly even disappointment, that people who convert to Protestantism are often no longer welcome in their communities. This is because they reject the teachings of their ancestors, he explains. Then a final pan to the front of the church and the minister cuts to black and the end credits begin to roll. The film's closing turn to more observational-style documentary allows Horne space for critique without being didactic; that is, without imposing her own discursive power through the employment of her disembodied voice. At the same time, the ending should not be reduced to the paternalistic principle of documentary, famously polemicized by Trinh T. Minh-ha, of "letting others speak for themselves."[66] Horne does not "let her subjects speak"; she simply does not speak directly in voice-over in this later sequence and thereby offers no verbal commentary. Instead, Mario speaks. The event speaks as well, to evoke Bonitzer. That is to say, the events of the film unfold for the audience to piece together in the absence of direct commentary.[67] Mario, a convert, translator for the GRN, and someone who at the missionaries' behest also contributed his voice to the archive of multilanguage Bible recordings, appears for better or for worse to have fully embraced the organization's evangelical pedagogy.

As a film, *The Tailenders* begins with a weird object, a sonic machine that delivers a singular Gospel message, and concludes with the complex reverberations of that message. In Horne's poetic account: "Every word spoken reverberates through time. The pulsation of air set in motion by a spoken word has ever-expanding ripples in all directions." This film traces the ripples of spoken words from production and recording to dissemination and coerced listening. It also returns to the machines that continue to ease the passageway of these spoken words. It urges us to listen to the mechanical and mechanized disembodied voices produced throughout time and to stay attuned to their theological and ideological effects in sustained critique. Despite this final chapter's more explicit turn to the voice, it does not relinquish the book's broader focus on what it means to listen. Put another way, it does not replace the auditory with the oral. If anything, an examination of Horne's film demands that we not separate the two. *The Tailenders* speaks and listens. Ultimately, the film's audibility refuses to let us lose earshot of the discursive histories of the sonic machines and their voices.

Sinister Listening and Its Afterlives

I began this book with an image, a still from Rudolf Pöch's short ethnographic film *Buschmann spricht in den Phonographen* (Buschmann speaking into the phonograph, Austria, 1908). With this opening, I sought to invoke many of the issues this film raises, not least its colonial entanglements. The film stages a scene of an Indigenous man in what is present-day Botswana speaking into a phonograph. It performs the European myth of the first encounter and the perceived ignorance of the Indigenous subject vis-à-vis technology. Beyond that, the film reminds us of the early employment of recording technology and its collusion with colonial ethnography, a historical collusion from which neither phonograph nor cinematograph emerged above suspicion. Finally, this image alerts us to the long and charged cinematic fascination with the phonograph. *Buschmann spricht in den Phonographen* provides evidence that film is not always counterarchival or emancipatory. For a book about the decolonizing possibilities of filming the sound archive, this final point is critical.

The idea for this book began with Philip Scheffner's film *The Halfmoon Files* (2007), which I investigated in chapter 3. It opened out as a historical curiosity about the Lautarchiv of the Humboldt University in Berlin and its infamous collection of speech recordings of colonial prisoners of war produced by the Royal Prussian Phonographic Commission (RPPC) during the First World War as explored in Scheffner's film. Thereafter, the book project unfolded into a search for corresponding films that also tackle colonial sound recordings through techniques of remediation and recodification. I found just a few other examples. My corpus proved narrow in content but nonetheless rich in scope, yielding such divergent films as Madhusree Dutta and Philip Scheffner's *From Here to Here* (2005), Marlon Fuentes's *Bontoc Eulogy* (1995), and Adele Horne's *The Tailenders* (2006). All linked through their prodding of a colonial sound archive and their variations on the documentary mode, these films do exhilaratingly different things with audio recordings. With the exception of *The Halfmoon Files* and *From Here to Here*, I treat the films within discrete rubrics and highlight their individual themes, treatment of documentary, cultural context, period, and to a minor extent their distinct concrete archival sources (as they do not all return to the Lautarchiv). They all proffer a different approach to the decolonizing ear. The disrupting phenomenon of noise becomes central in my examination of *From Here to Here* and *The Halfmoon Files*. Auto-ethnography as a creative and subjectivizing strategy to sound comes into play in *Bontoc Eulogy*. Finally, the materiality of off-the-beaten-path audio machines and their imbrication with the disembodied voice take over in an analysis of *The Tailenders*. From chapters 3 to 5, I approach the sui generis nature of the films to first discern what each one does on its own, and in due course I ask how they contribute to the book's broader arc and offer examples of the decolonizing ear. By the same token, the films converge through topics both major and minor, and among the chapters the reader can detect critical overlap. Indeed, a comparative study of these films within the context of colonial listening permits new and exciting entryways into each, which in turn reveal hitherto unexplored dimensions. Through this study, the films at once offer compelling examples of audiovisual modes of decolonial listening and reveal themselves as unique objects of analysis.

To gain an understanding of the discursive context to which these films respond, I trace the history of colonial listening in Germany with a focus on the RPPC and its preserving and legitimating domicile, the Lautarchiv. Paradigmatic in its formation and creation of knowledge, this archive provides a fitting example of the operative measures involved in ethnographic listening. These are measures informed by colonial and imperial politics. Broadly speaking, the archive is both product and principle of these politics. While not all the films return directly to the Lautarchiv, its substantive material history and irrefutable ties to the hallmarks of the Western colonial enterprise more broadly establish it as an instructive entity and point of departure for thinking beyond its own national context and generalizing its representational potential. Significant studies of the Lautarchiv are altogether recent and exist almost exclusively in the German language, authored especially by Britta Lange, whose toil in this archive has been illuminating. Bringing our attention to the Lautarchiv, and especially the specificities of the RPPC collection, through her method and strategy of close listening, Lange has laid the groundwork for further study.[1] But I did not want to simply reproduce the critical archival undertakings of

Lange and her colleagues; tracing this history as an example and frame suffices. Instead, I was drawn to what artists, and filmmakers in particular, have made of both this sound archive and others. I have sought to ask, riffing on Jennifer Culbert, what the terms of "counter-archival sensibility" sound like in the context of the colonial sound archive.[2] I have landed somewhere between new information and further reflection. For artistic work tout court tends towards this threshold. But so much of what has been written on archival or counterarchival work responds to specifically creative *visual* work. Drawing on these insights, I have sought to subsequently address the creative work of film with sound and the sound archives through a means more specific to the auditory experience.

The concept of decolonial listening and what that entails unfolds along a rather jagged line. While more recent studies on sound and listening have critically uncovered the deep and gnarled roots of colonialism and white supremacy, sustaining what Jonathan Sterne calls "regimes of listening practices," from Jennifer Lynn Stoever's sonic colour line to Dylan Robinson's hungry listening, the notion that listening could be as ideologically influenced as, for instance, looking remains an unwonted truth.[3] For does not listening prompt an unintrusive attunement to someone or something outside oneself and therefore a gesture of openness, plentitude, sincerity, even non-sovereignty? Though the answer is no, not always, such a conjecture tarries. Thus, working out a methodology of the decolonizing ear became a challenge and, perforce, a sleight-of-hand endeavour. Chapter 1 interrogates the history of colonial listening and its legitimation through the sound archive. In riposte, all efforts are brought to bear on its possible decolonization in chapter 2. Weaving together insights from sound studies, decolonial and Indigenous studies, and archival studies and taking a final, unorthodox turn to media archaeology, this chapter lays out a method and practice for tackling the vast epistemological reaches of colonial listening. The answer is not to seal one's ears to sound – indeed, that would be almost impossible – but to listen in a manner that delinks (to borrow Walter Mignolo's term) the ear from its colonial trappings. Here audiovisual media facilitate the process. But before delving further into film this book takes a moment to consider how other art forms, such as Indigenous music, already have an established tradition of reappropriating and reperforming sound formerly seized by settler-colonial listeners-cum-ethnographers. Jeremy Dutcher's musical reworking and digitalization of wax cylinder recordings from the turn of the twentieth century as a means of recovering the voices and songs of his forebears offers a significant case in point.

I am well aware that decolonizing the sound archive is not an endeavour unique to film. Yet the added dimension of the visual and the challenge of representation makes film an exciting place to unwrap and set apart this study. Much scholarship exists on the voice and film. Consider most prominently Michel Chion's and Mary Ann Doane's respective work. Bill Nichols and Trinh T. Minh-ha have also written extensively on the voice within documentary studies. To my surprise, however, far fewer studies exist on the phenomenon of audition and film. Pooja Rangan's important intervention on listening and documentary presents one of the few exceptions.[4] Taking this one step further to colonial listening and film hurls the present study into far-flung solitude. Even writings on the individual films I examine, which are diverse, do not occasion more comprehensive thinking on the topics of colonial and decolonial listening. Thus, the treatment of decolonial listening in film, not least documentary film, is altogether new.

The audiovisual repurposing of materials from the archive upholds a lengthy tradition, and certainly with the arrival of digital filmmaking this undertaking became much less demanding and far more accessible. Scholars have conceptualized different methods for this process. Earlier on, Jay David Bolter and Richard Grusin introduced the concept of remediation, which has since become shorthand for all appropriation of analogue media in the digital realm.[5] Catherine Russell's more nuanced archiveology designates the practice of borrowing images and audiovisual material from the archive and brings them into new filmic creations.[6] She develops this technique from media archaeology alongside Walter Benjamin's vast theoretical oeuvre on history, media, the archive, and beyond. The present project ultimately turns to the insights of media archaeology. Despite its pronounced eschewal of culture and politics in favour of the cold gaze (or better, dispassionate ear) of media, it accounts for the materiality as well as the instability of media throughout history and especially the vicissitudes of sound technology. In particular, Wolfgang Ernst's interest in what he refers to as "sonicity" and the possibilities of processuality of sonic media offers a significant means of approaching archival sound recordings and their machines as unique objects in the first place.[7] The media insights of these thinkers and many others guide my analyses of the individual films through the themes and practices previously summarized of noise, autoethnography, weird sonic objects, and the disembodied voice. Essentially, I examine how these filmmakers challenge the colonial archive and its epistemic traditions. This subterfuge can take the shape of reviving already-present emancipatory moments of the past when subjects themselves dared to subvert colonial listening regimes, and it can also take the shape of new ruptures through differently appropriating materials in ways that alter erstwhile intended meaning. In sum, these films perform counterarchival work, but I stop short of calling them counterarchives. If anything, they invite us to think beyond the form of the archive and its positivist impulses.

Coda

Returning to the catalyst of the broad theme of sinister listening, which also briefly served as a working title for this book, I will close on this line of thought.[8] The larger project on sight and audition I had originally conceptualized included multimedia examples of the sinister ear from film to installation and even literature. This quickly became unfeasible and inconsistent. Therefore, I settled with film, and this has allowed me to think more profoundly about the medium and the mode of documentary. However, I append this brief coda in order to conclude with the work of Dubai-based contemporary audio artist Lawrence Abu Hamdan, who has much to say about sinister listening and the detriment of its afterlife. On his website, Abu Hamdan describes himself as a "private ear," as a variation of a "private *eye*" detective, investigating, inter alia, unjust cases of forensic listening. His work focuses on sound, politics, and listening. As he importantly reminds us, "Listening is never simply a passive, objective, and receptive process, but rather an act that plays a fundamental role in the construction and facilitation of the speech of the interlocutor (whether subject or object)."[9]

One topic he explores in several of his projects is the highly controversial practice of what is called "Language Analysis for the Determination of Origin" (LADO), instrumentalized in asylum application cases by many European governments as well as in Australia and New Zealand since 1993.[10] The apparent motivation behind this instrument is to establish national origin in cases of asylum applicants who cannot provide documentation.[11] However, as critics have pointed out, this is far from an exact science. Asserting the nation of origin of a person based on how they pronounce certain sounds, or even their word choice, is highly speculative if not impossible. As Emily Apter concludes, this operation reflects the myopia of nations in which "monolingualism is the standard and [which] bring with them a reflexive tendency to regard hybrid speech as aberrant, outside the norms of language."[12] In two of his more renowned projects from 2012, *Conflicted Phonemes* and *The Freedom of Speech Itself*, Abu Hamdan explores the procedure and ramifications of LADO as eugenics of the voice and a violent attempt to reduce spoken language to a set of arbitrary rules. As a result of this procedure of listening, asylum seekers could face acceptance or rejection for asylum status. Such a modus operandi comes across as controversial if not archaic. Indeed, it evokes nineteenth-century German comparative philology and the idea that language is not only an indication of ethnicity but also the sole, true marker of national identity.[13]

LADO presents a mode of listening whose strategies resemble those of the colonial ear. Asylum applicants are commanded to speak at the edict of the government officials; their voice is recorded and is subsequently analysed for authenticity. Is the language they claim to be their mother tongue really their mother tongue? Listening becomes an act of profiling and policing the voice of another person. LADO applies a kind of shibboleth test to catch speakers who might use or "mispronounce" words perceived as integral to that language and dialect. Not unlike the linguists in the RPPC, the "language experts" in the case of LADO ascertain the quality and legitimacy of the language spoken. The difference lies merely in the consequences of such an assessment.

Abu Hamdan's *The Freedom of Speech Itself* consists in part of a thirty-minute audio essay in which language specialists, lawyers, asylum seekers, and immigration officials offer testimonies of their experiences with the practice of LADO and the devastating repercussions of wrongful deportation. The other component of the project consists of an undulating physical model containing sculptural forms of voiceprints made with sound-absorbent foam. Cartographically rendering speech, the model gives physical presence to the frequency and range of voices uttering the word "you."[14] According to Abu Hamdan, the model serves as a reminder of the act of forensic listening, which "fundamentally stretched the role of the juridical ear from simply hearing words spoken aloud to actively listening to the process of speaking, as a new form of forensic evidence."[15] It represents both the speech of the subject and the ear of residual power. In cases of LADO procedures, in which the outcome of the asylum process can be decided based on speech analysis, there is no habeas corpus, no day in court, no physical evidence for examination whatsoever. This model stands in for the denied material rights of the asylum seeker.[16]

Through a slightly disparate, certainly more tactile, audiovisual mode, Abu Hamdan interrogates and criticizes sinister listening; that is, listening with harmful intentions. His understanding that "we are not free to choose the ways we are being heard," as uttered by the narrator at the close of the audio essay of *The Freedom of Speech Itself*, offers a declaration of the social and political injustice and deprivation of freedom of speech for certain individuals and groups in our present world. Comparable to so many injustices of the present, the inequalities of freedom of speech trace their roots back to a long genealogy of colonial listening and its abuses. Throughout his artistic and scholarly work, Abu Hamdan has maintained that the universal human right of freedom of speech can only truly exist when accompanied by the right to silence.[17] Neither the utterance nor the silence of a person may be at the decree of another. But while speech may be a universal human right, silence is not. Abu Hamdan's private ear is not unlike the decolonizing ear. Both are attuned to auditory injustice as a result of centuries of unequal power relations and strive to address this injustice through creative means of listening differently.

Concluding with the example of Abu Hamdan's work does not serve as a means to move away from film. This book learns from film, and if it contains a single truth it is that films can teach us how to listen reflexively and critically. Rather, this coda serves as concomitant reflection. It demonstrates that colonial listening is more than just a historical phenomenon. Colonial listening endures in our contemporary world in only slightly different forms. This final excursus into Abu Hamdan's work furthermore extends the opportunity to generally assess the ways in which multimedia art can also evoke the possibilities to decolonize listening in a manner both unbounded by the limitations of a single-screen format and even rendered physically tangible for the auditor. *A Decolonizing Ear* thus unfolds as an ongoing project and not simply a completed work. At this provisional end point, to turn and survey the chapters of this book is to observe how we may (and indeed need to) learn from the insights of film and its audiovisual offshoots. For the imperative of decolonizing listening continues to hold relevance both in our treatment of the past and our tackling of the present. This book began with an image yet concludes with much more. Closing thus, it is my hope that at the very least the contents of this work stimulate further inquiry and have offered some tools with which to get started or, as the case may be, to continue in this direction.

Notes

Introduction: The Phonograph on Film

1 Fuhrmann, "Ethnographic Films," 338.
2 As Anette Hoffmann indicates, "Kubi" is the name Rudolf Pöch uses, but there is no other evidence to confirm the veracity of this name. See Hoffmann, *Kolonialgeschichte Hören*, 38, 105–6.
3 Henley, *Beyond Observation*, 38–9.
4 Taussig, *Mimesis and Alterity*, 207.
5 Rony, *Third Eye*, 112.
6 Okslioff, *Picturing the Primitive*, 32.
7 Hoffmann, *Kolonialgeschichte Hören*, 14.
8 Henley, *Beyond Observation*, 36–7. Wolfgang Fuhrmann also implicitly draws this connection. See Fuhrmann, "First Contact," 3–8.
9 This film was also titled *Die Fortschritte der Zivilisation in Deutsch-Ostafrika* (The progress of civilization in German-East Africa) and was produced by Pathé Frères and Germania Film in 1912. It was principally intended as a propaganda film to showcase the success of the "civilizing" mission of German colonialism. The director is unknown. See Fuhrmann, "Propaganda und Unterhaltung," 362. (All translations from German to English are my own unless otherwise indicated.)
10 I am grateful to Wolfgang Fuhrmann for a discussion of the intertitle and its translation in English, which I also cite from his study. Fuhrmann, *Imperial Projections*, 210. See also Fuhrmann, "Filmaufnahmen in Afrika," 156. The connection between phonograph and film extends to production. Now principally a film production company, at the turn of the twentieth century Pathé was a major distributor of both film production equipment and phonograph records.
11 Rony, *Third Eye*, 69; Okslioff, *Picturing the Primitve*, 4; see also Fuhrmann, *Imperial Projections*. Rony dedicates an entire chapter to

Félix-Louis Regnault and Charles Comte's early ethnographic films. These chronometric tableaux focused on the movement and gestures of photographed ethnographic subjects, particularly in West Africa. See Rony, *Third Eye*, 45–73.

12 Tobias Nagl offers a sharp analysis of these two films and their representations of the "first encounter." Nagl, *Die unheimliche Maschine*, 328–41.

13 Taussig, *Mimesis and Alterity*, 203.

14 Koepnick, *Fitzcarraldo*, 54.

15 John Grierson coined the term "documentary" in 1926 in a review about Flaherty's later film *Moana*. In this review Grierson writes of *Moana*'s "documentary value." See Nichols, *Introduction to Documentary*, 10, 165.

16 The potential staging of this scene is reinforced by a possible (German) visual precursor. A 1907 advertisement for the German company Beka Records titled *"Ein Koloniales Ereignis!"* (A colonial event!) features a German salesman with a Prussian-style moustache peddling phonographs and records apparently to local buyers in Africa (the exact location is unclear). Just beyond the main group, a man can been seen biting into a record. See *Phonographische Zeitschrift* 9, no. 26 (1907): 635. See also Fuhrmann, *Imperial Projections*, 222n61.

17 Rony, *Third Eye*, 112.

18 Gunning, "Doing for the Eye," 16.

19 Feaster and Smith, "Reconfiguring," 311–25, 311.

20 Wurtzler, *Electric Sounds*, 46.

21 Mèhèza Kalibani introduces the term *"das koloniale Ohr"* in his master's thesis "Das koloniale Ohr: Phonographische Aufnahmen aus deutschen Kolonien und ihre Bedeutung im (post)kolonialen Kontext am Beispiel der Smend-Sammlung im Berliner Phonogramm-Archiv" (2019) (The colonial ear: Phonographic recordings from German colonies and their significance in the [post]colonial context through the example of the Smend Collection at the Berlin Phonogram Archive) completed at the University of Siegen. He employs the term to describe the phonographic recordings made by colonial ethnographers in the German colonies between 1900 and 1914. He summarizes his study in a recent article, cited here: "The Less Considered Part," 43–53, 51.

22 I must add a caveat to this statement. In 2020, Ernst Karel and Veronika Kusumaryati's US documentary *Expedition Content* premiered at the Berlinale (Berlin International Film Festival). The film explores the photographic, film, and audio collections of the archive of the 1961 Harvard Peabody Expedition headed by Robert Gardener to Netherlands New Guinea. During this expedition Michael Rockefeller

made ethnographic audio recordings of the Hubula people. This film also repurposes these recordings in a critical new way. Unfortunately, due to its very recent release I only had the opportunity to watch and listen to it well after the manuscript for this book was written; therefore I will not discuss it at length in this study. However, it could serve as a further example to my modest corpus of films and certainly merits mention here. I am grateful to Philip Widmann for drawing my attention to the film.

23 Rony, *Third Eye*, 17.
24 A term used in more recent studies in psychoanalysis, "the third ear" connotes careful listening for deeper meaning. See Reik, *Listening with the Third Ear*, 144–7. Reik's usage, although distinct in meaning, is derived from that of Friedrich Nietzsche. In his criticism of German as a scholarly language, Nietzsche writes in *Beyond Good and Evil* that anyone with a third ear will be tortured by reading books in German. For him, the third ear (*"das dritte Ohr"*) is a metaphor for refined perception. Nietzsche, *Beyond Good and Evil*, 182.
25 Nagl, *Unheimliche Maschine*, 9–10.
26 Nancy, *Listening*, 7, 10.
27 Doane, "Ideology," 61. This is an argument that Doane also addresses in her work on the voice in cinema ("The Voice in Cinema," 1980) discussed later in this book and later in the production of space in cinema. In the case of the latter, I refer to a lecture given at the Institute for Cultural Inquiry in Berlin in 2016, entitled "The Trope of the Turn and the Production of Sound Space," in which she argues, inter alia, that sound provides depth to the cinematic space and its two-dimensional screen. The lecture can be listened to online in video format courtesy of the Institute for Cultural Inquiry, https://www.ici-berlin.org/events/mary-ann-doane/.
28 Sterne, *The Audible Past*, 15, 16.
29 Stadler, "On Whiteness," n.p.
30 See Stadler, "On Whiteness"; Stoever, *The Sonic Color Line*; Radano and Olaniyan, *Audible Empire*; Robinson, *Hungry Listening*; Schmidt, "Rassismus in der Klassik." In Schmidt's article, she references meLê yamomo's work on colonial listening in her article about the history of classical music. According to yamomo, colonialism determines who will be heard and who will be silenced, who defines what music is and what sound is. I have been unable to find the direct quote in yamomo's own work – namely, what he calls *"die Kolonialisierung unserer Ohren"* (the colonialization of our ears), and presume it is derived directly from an interview or conversation with the scholar and artist. However, his monograph *Theatre and Music in Manila and the Asia Pacific, 1869–1946: Sound Modernities* is an excellent resource in this regard. See also Kalibani,

"Less Considered Part," 51. Finally, Kira Thurman's very recent study *Singing Like Germans: Black Musicians in the Land of Bach, Beethoven, and Brahms* explores the sonic colour line that shaped the history of classical music and especially opera in Germany.

31 Sterne, *Audible Past*, 91.
32 Robinson, *Hungry Listening*, 53.
33 Robinson, *Hungry Listening*, 47.
34 Stadler, "Never Heard Such a Thing," 87–105, 89, 92.
35 Most issues of the magazine have been digitally archivized and are available to view online through the Münchener DigitalisierungsZentrum /Digitale Bibliothek, https://www.digitale-sammlungen.de/index.html?c =sammlung&projekt=1386147579&l=en.
36 Ames, "The Sound of Evolution."
37 Since I will be discussing two Berlin sound archives, I will refer to this sound archive hereafter as the "Phonogramm-Archiv."
38 Ziegler, "Historical Sound Recordings," 145–6.
39 Lange, "Archiv," 239.
40 Kalibani, "Less Considered Part," 48.
41 To avoid confusion with the previously mentioned Berlin Phonogramm-Archiv, I will refer to this archive hereafter as the "Lautarchiv."
42 The website of the Lautarchiv is very informational and provides some digitalized examples of archived recordings: https://www.lautarchiv .hu-berlin.de.
43 Indeed, recent monographs in German Studies speak to a new "auditory turn" in recent German Studies modernist discourses, to which *A Decolonizing Ear* loosely contributes. These include Tyler Whitney's *Eardrums: Literary Modernism as Sonic Warfare*; Kata Gellen's *Kafka and Noise: The Discovery of Cinematic Sound in Literary Modernism*; and Thurman's *Singing Like Germans*. These follow and expand on earlier studies on sound in the German context that appeared with the emergence of the field of sound studies. See Alter and Koepnick's groundbreaking edited volume *Sound Matters: Essays on Acoustics of Modern German Culture* and David Schwarz's *Listening Awry: Music and Alterity in German Culture*.
44 Elsaesser, *Film History as Media Archaeology*, 17.
45 In the closing line of his short but illuminating article on the archive, Mike Featherstone reminds us via Michel Foucault and Jacques Derrida that the archive must be treated as "paradigmatic entity as well as a concrete institution." Featherstone, "Archive," 591–6, 596.
46 Derrida, *Archive Fever*, 12.
47 Stoler, *Along the Archival Grain*, 1.
48 Freshwater, "Allure of the Archive," 740.

49 Freshwater, "Allure of the Archive," 740.

50 Stoler, *Archival Grain*, 1.

51 Stoler, *Archival Grain*, 53.

52 Lange, *Gefangene Stimmen*, 25–6; Hoffmann, "Introduction," 75.

53 Hoffmann, "Introduction," 75 (emphasis in original).

54 Lange, *Gefangene Stimmen*, 25.

55 Since the announcement of the construction plans nearly a decade ago, many groups have protested against the building of the Humboldt Forum. The collective "No Humboldt 21!" has been central among the detractors. The collective's website clearly delineates the motivations and aims of the project: https://www.no-humboldt21.de/resolution /english/. It might be added that Felwine Sarr and Bénédicte Savoy's clarifying response to the restitution of cultural artifacts from countries formerly under colonial rule in the French context has been equally influential in the German context, especially in light of the recent opening of the Humboldt Forum. See Sarr and Savoy, "Restitution of African Cultural Heritage." For a follow-up discussion more specific to Germany, see Kuster, Lange, and Löffler, "Archive der Zukunft?"

56 Foucault, *Archaeology of Knowledge*, 138–40.

57 Foucault, *Archaeology of Knowledge*, 6–7.

58 Foucault, *Archaeology of Knowledge*, 13.

59 Parikka, *What Is Media Archaeology?*, 6; Kittler, *Discourse Networks 1800/1900*, 264.

60 Parikka, *Media Archaeology*, 7.

61 Ernst, *Digital Memory*, 25.

62 Ernst, *Digital Memory*, 127.

63 Ernst, *Digital Memory*, 128.

64 Bolter and Grusin, *Remediation*.

65 Hoffmann, *Kolonialgeschichte Hören*, 45.

66 Russell, *Archiveology*, 1, 95.

67 Baron, *The Archive Effect*, 13.

68 Derrida, *Archive Fever*, 9.

69 Azoulay, *Potential History*, 2.

70 Azoulay, *Potential History*, 2.

71 Chion, *Audio-Vision*, 68.

72 Tuck and Yang, "Decolonization Is Not a Metaphor."

73 John Grierson famously called the documentary a "clumsy" description. Grierson, "From 'First Principles of Documentary,'" 453. See also Kahana, *Documentary Film Reader*, 1.

74 Attali, *Noise*, 7.

75 Mignolo, "Delinking."

76 Parikka, *Media Archaeology*, 33.
77 Attali, *Noise*, 33–4.
78 Lionnet, *Autobiographical Voices*, 99–100.
79 This draws both on the voice-over commentary of Horne in the film and the article whose title and main argument she cites. See Himrod, "The Syncretism of Technology."
80 Featherstone, "Archive," 596.

1. Colonial Listening and the Making of a Sound Archive

1 Nancy, *Listening*, 9, 12, 22.
2 Nichols, *Representing Reality*, 31; Gaines, "Introduction, 17.
3 This should not be confused with the colloquial term "acoustocophilia," which is defined as sexual arousal through sound.
4 Robinson, *Hungry Listening*, 2.
5 Boas, "On Alternating Sounds," 47.
6 Hochman, *Savage Preservation*, 96.
7 It is critical to note that Édouard-Léon Scott de Martinville actually invented the first sound recording device called the Phonautographe in 1857; however, with his phonograph, sound was phonetically recorded but could not be played back.
8 Hochman, *Savage Preservation*, ix.
9 Fewkes, "On the Use of the Phonograph," 267.
10 Gitelman, *Scripts, Grooves, and Writing Machines*, 1.
11 Kaplan, "Voices of the People," 288.
12 Brady, *A Spiral Way*, 62.
13 Brady, *A Spiral Way*, 62, 130n3.
14 In his film, Fuentes draws on the University of Pennsylvania Museum of Archaeology and Anthropology, the National Archives at the Library of Congress, and the Smithsonian Institution Archives.
15 The most well-known historical sound archives in the world are as follows: in Vienna (since 1899), Berlin (since 1900), St. Petersburg (since 1903), and Paris (since 1911). Lange, "Archiv," 236–40.
16 Some sources indicate that Carl Stumpf founded the archive and others that it was co-founded with Erich Moritz von Hornbostel, who also became director in 1905 and maintained that position until 1933. In any case, the establishment of the archive was largely funded by Hornbostel's estate. Ames, "Sound of Evolution," 299.
17 According to Walter Graf, in 1900 the Musée Phonographique of the Société d'Anthropologie de Paris also established a phonogram archive. See Graf, "Phonogrammarchiv der österreicherischen Akademie der Wissenschaften." However, other sources indicate that the Paris archive

was initiated only in 1911 as part of the Albert Kahn archive project; see Lange, "Archiv," 239.

18 Ames, "Sound of Evolution," 299–300. In a footnote, Ames notes (319n16) that between 1901 and 1914, many other sound archives were established in cities across Europe and the United States.

19 In 1999, this archive was included in the UNESCO's "Memory of the World" register. For a comprehensive catalog of Phonogramm-Archiv, its history and its holdings, see Ziegler, *Wachszylinder*.

20 Ames, "Sound of Evolution," 300–1. Carl Stumpf would go on to become of one of the founding figures of ethnomusicology, whose discussions about the pitch distinctions between speech and song (by example of yodeling) proved instrumental to the field. Rehding, "Quest for the Origins of Music," 351–2; Ochoa Gautier, *Aurality*, 45.

21 Ziegler, "Historical Sound Recordings," 146; Kalibani, "Less Considered Part," 48–9; Ziegler, *Wachszylinder*, 21.

22 Stumpf, quoted in Radano and Olaniyan, *Audible Empire*, 10.

23 Ames, "Sound of Evolution," 309.

24 Mahrenholz, "Recordings of South Asian Languages," 187.

25 Doegen, *Kriegsgefangene Völker*, III, 3; Kaplan, "Voices of the People," 281. One source suggests that the RPPC selected thirty-one camps for the collection of their samples; see Mahrenholz, "Recordings," 190.

26 Doegen, "Denkschrift," 20.

27 Kaplan, "Voices of the People," 291.

28 Some sources suggest that there were many more recordings made during this period, even up to 4,500. Susanne Ziegler writes that there were total of 1,651 sound plates and 1,020 wax cylinders made. See Ziegler, "Historical Sound Recordings," 143. See also Kaplan, "Voices of the People," 292.

29 Doegen, *Unter fremden Völkern*, 12–13.

30 The entire archive was to be moved to the Humboldt Forum, housed within the newly constructed City Palace. This is something I will discuss further in a later section. However, due to the COVID-19 pandemic, plans to move the archive were temporarily postponed.

31 Both the Phonogramm-Archiv and the Lautarchiv have been scheduled to move to the Humboldt Forum.

32 Germany enlisted soldiers from its African colonies as well, but they were deployed to fight solely on the African continent. Lange, *Gefangene Stimmen*, 15. As Heather Jones explains, there was a specific German discourse of fear with regard to colonial soldiers of colour, which stigmatized them as brutally violent and inhumane. See Jones, "Imperial Captivities," 181.

33 See Doegen, "Vorwort," in *Kriegsgefangene Völker*; Jones, "Imperial Captivities," 179; Evans, *Anthropology at War*, 182.

34 Doegen, *Unter fremden Völkern*, 6.

35 Mbembe, "The Power of the Archive," 21.

36 Ochoa Gautier, *Aurality*, 31–2.

37 Humboldt, *Reise auf dem Río Magdalena*, 69–70.

38 In her study, Ochoa Gautier offers an excellent translation originally rendered from the Spanish. I cite this translation in slightly abbreviated form with minor adjustment. See Ochoa Gautier, *Aurality*, 32.

39 Kittler, *Gramophone, Film, Typewriter*, 21.

40 Ochoa Gautier, *Aurality*, 32.

41 One could pursue a longer discussion about Humboldt's approach to Enlightenment thinking and his troubling of the mechanism of the Cartesian mind-body division through what has been referred to as his "enlightened vitalism." There was a broader perception of and appreciation for the reciprocity of nature and humanity. Reill, *Vitalizing Nature*, 148, 238.

42 Zantop, *Colonial Fantasies*, 170.

43 Friedrichsmeyer, Lennox, and Zantop, "Introduction," 22.

44 Ochoa Gautier, *Aurality*, 33.

45 Radano and Olaniyan, *Audible Empire*, 8.

46 Hanslick, *Vom Musikalisch-Schönen*, 183–4.

47 Stumpf, "Tonsystem und Musik der Siamesen," 129. See also Ames, "Sound of Evolution," 306.

48 Stumpf and Hornbostel, "On the Significance of Ethnological Studies," 3.

49 Otto Wiener cited in Kittler, *Gramophone, Film, Typewriter*, 77.

50 Kittler, *Gramophone, Film, Typewriter*, 22–3.

51 Kaplan, "Voices of the People," 288.

52 Adorno, "The Form of the Phonograph Record," 56.

53 Evans, *Anthropology at War*, 3.

54 Zimmerman, *Anthropology and Antihumanism*, 7.

55 Evans, *Anthropology at War*, 50. Felix von Luschan also headed the anthropological studies conducted at the prisoner-of-war camps in Germany.

56 Said, *Orientalism*, 19.

57 Zantop, *Colonial Fantasies*, 4; Evans, *Anthropology at War*, 51. It bears mentioning that Germany's late turn to colonial politics precipitated the nation's eventual aggressive, even genocidal, colonial tactics.

58 Errington, *Linguistics in the Colonial World*, 15.

59 Evans, *Anthropology at War*, 51.

60 Zimmerman, *Anthropology*, 15.

61 Rony, *Third Eye*, 10. The topic of these imperial exhibitions is something I return to in my analysis of Marlon Fuentes's film *Bontoc Eulogy* and the St. Louis World's Fair in 1904.

62 Zimmerman, *Anthropology*, 18. Eric Ames's study on Carl Hagenbeck, *Carl Hagenbeck's Empire of Entertainments*, is also a tremendous resource.

63 Kim, "Task of the Loving Translator," n.p.

64 Zimmerman, *Anthropology*, 18–19.

65 Doegen, *Unter fremden Völkern*, 5.

66 Dettelbach, "The Face of Nature," 474.

67 Kittler, *Gramophone, Film, Typewriter*, 23.

68 Hornbostel, "Formanalysen an siamesischen Orchesterstücken," 314–15.

69 Scheer, "Captive Voices," 305.

70 Doegen, *Bericht über mein Wirken*, n.p.

71 Lange, "South Asian Soldiers and German Academics," 166; Evans, *Anthropology at War*, 138.

72 Doegen, *Bericht*, n.p.

73 Scheer, "Captive Voices," 306. Scheer notes that prisoners were instructed to practise the texts before recording in order to parry deviation, pauses, or silence.

74 Evans, *Anthropology at War*, 141.

75 Jones, *Violence against Prisoners of War*, 93.

76 Roy, "South Asian Prisoners of War," 55, 58–9.

77 Serge, *Men in Prison*, 31.

78 Gordon, *The Hawthorn Archive*, 303.

79 Lange, "South Asian Soldiers and German Academics," 155.

80 Novak and Sakakeeny, *Keywords in Sound*, 1.

81 Kaplan, "Voices of the People," 281.

82 Doegen, "Denkschrift," 11.

83 Doegen, *Jahrbuch*, 33. It may be noted that the project of RPPC was not made public during the war. Ziegler, "Historical Sound Recordings," 143.

84 Schaeffer, *In Search of a Concrete Music*, 132.

85 Lange, *Gefangene Stimmen*, 16.

86 Lange, "Südasiatische Positionen und europäische Forschungen,'" 11.

87 Hoffmann, *Kolonialgeschichte Hören*, 16.

88 Chion, *Audio-Vision*, 28–9.

89 "On records is thus the living language, in which the soul of a people shows itself in the most meaningful way, and as commentary to it in the present work the description of these cultural identity traits in customs and in practice, in history and origin, according to type and ancestry!" Doegen, *Unter fremden Völkern*, 5.

90 Doegen, *Unter fremden Völkern*, 13–15.

91 Errington, *Linguistics*, 83.

92 Jones, "Imperial Captivities," 179.

93 Lange, *Gefangene Stimmen*, 93.

94 Kaplan, "Voices of the People," 287; Scheer, "Captive Voices," 291. Note that Scheer suggests expeditions started with phonographs but eventually most switched to using the "gramophone." Allow me to draw a critical distinction here: in much of the literature regarding the RPPC, the term "gramophone" is used when I believe "graphophone" is intended. It is important to note that gramophones were not able to record sound.

95 Lange, *Gefangene Stimmen*, 10; Ziegler, "Historical Sound Recordings," 143.

96 Graf, "Phonogrammarchiv," n.p.

97 Freshwater, "Allure of the Archive," 730.

98 Featherstone, "Archive," 592. In a slightly earlier study, Richard Harvey-Brown and Beth Davis-Brown also alert us to the role of the archive in formation of national identity. See Harvey-Brown and Davis-Brown, "The Making of Memory," 17.

99 Freshwater, "Allure of the Archive," 730.

100 Steedman, *Dust*, 2.

101 Derrida, *Archive Fever*, 1.

102 Derrida, *Archive Fever*, 12.

103 Derrida, *Archive Fever*, 81; Foucault, *Archaeology of Knowledge*, 7.

104 Sterne, *Audible Past*, 327.

105 Sterne, *Audible Past*, 325–32.

106 Stoler, *Archival Grain*, 44.

107 Foucault, *Archaeology of Knowledge*, 129.

108 Stoler, "Colonial Archives," 92.

109 Lange, "Archiv," 239.

110 Scheer, "Captive Voices," 281, 292.

111 Taylor, *Archive and the Repertoire*, 19.

112 Taylor, *Archive and the Repertoire*, 19.

113 Lange, *Gefangene Stimmen*, 17.

114 Monique Scheer calls this preservation of the documents "salvage mentality." This is a curious re-employment of the term, given its loaded application as a driving force of ethnography. The salvage mentality or "preservationist ethos" buttressed the project of ethnographic recording of Indigenous languages and ways of life under the assumption that they were endangered and needed to be preserved, what James Clifford has referred to as the "relentless placement of others in a present-becoming-past." This is a topic I explore further in chapter 2. See Scheer, "Captive Voices," 282; James Clifford, "On Ethnographic Allegory," 115.

115 Here I paraphrase Azoulay, *Potential History*, 178–9.

116 Azoulay, *Potential History*, 182.

117 Thomas, *Imperial Archive*, 7.

118 Thomas, *Imperial Archive*, 1.
119 See Zantop, *Colonial Fantasies*.
120 Steedman, *Dust*, 8–9.
121 See Derrida, *Mal d'archive*; Steedman, *Dust*, 8.
122 Azoulay, *Potential History*, 366.
123 El-Tayeb, "Universal Museum," 79.
124 El-Tayeb, "Universal Museum," 74.
125 This surpasses the unspoken European, certainly German, gesture to account for some past oppressions in the historical canon and thereby absolve its longer history of colonial guilt. A number of scholars have addressed this issue. For the German context, see Friedrichsmeyer, Lennox, and Zantop, "Introduction," 4. For the European context, see Kirn, *Partisan Counter-Archive*, 65. It bears noting that at the ceremony for the opening of the Ethnological Museum and Museum for Asian Art in its new location within the Humboldt Forum in 2021, German president Frank-Walter Steinmeier did indicate the reality of the violent colonial history of the collections enclosed within these museums. Further, he noted the blind spot of the German colonial past in national and collective memory and the imperative to address it. The speech is available online: https://www.youtube.com/watch?v=toL5gbOK__4. Echoing Jürgen Habermas, Steinmeier states that remembering the Holocaust does not prevent us from remembering other histories of injustice.
126 Kalibani refers to these recordings as "immaterial heritage." See Kalibani, "Less Considered Part," 42–53.
127 Mahrenholz, "Recordings," 195.
128 Lange, *Gefangene Stimmen*, 10–11, 12.
129 Lange, *Gefangene Stimmen*, 25.

2. Decolonizing Listening: A Methodology in Three Parts

1 A few prominent studies that position vision as central to Western paradigms of knowledge and power are Crary, *Techniques of the Observer*; Levin, *Modernity and the Hegemony of Vision*; and Rony, *Third Eye*. Bringing attention to the often-dismissed connection between the history of the African diaspora and sound technology, Alexander G. Weheliye similarly addresses the hegemony of the visual in discourses of Western modernity. He pursues the invention and development of sound recording as both central to the imagination and circumscription of racial formation in Western modernity and to self-defined Black identity and culture. Weheliye, *Phonographies*, 2, 5.
2 Attali, *Noise*, 3

3 Sterne, *Audible Past*, 15.
4 Erlmann, "Ethnographic Ear?," 3–4. For the reference, see Clifford and Marcus, *Writing Culture*, 12. In *Aurality: Listening and Knowledge in Nineteenth-Century Colombia*, Ana María Ochoa Gautier also indirectly provides a response to Erlmann's question about the ethnographic ear. In chapter 3 of her book, titled "On the Ethnographic Ear," Ochoa Gautier proposes that the ethnographic ear is inextricably linked to language and the efforts made by missionaries and German comparative philology of the nineteenth century to rethink the orthography of Indigenous word sounds. This is something I also explore in chapter 5. See Ochoa Gautier, *Aurality*, 126.
5 Adorno and Horkheimer, *Dialektik der Aufklärung*, 62–99. Michael Bull (*Sound Moves*, 19) characterizes this scene as the Ur-example of "the privatization of the experience of sound." See also Hagood, *Hush*, 12–13.
6 Wolfgang Ernst (*Sonic Time Machines*, 49) poses a similar question with regard to proof. In other words, how can we really know what Odysseus heard if we have no phonographic recording?
7 Basu, "Archives of German Anthropology," 731.
8 Campt, *Listening to Images*, 9.
9 Gitelman, *Scripts*, 2.
10 Taussig, *Mimesis and Alterity*, 199–200.
11 Feaster and Smith, "Reconfiguring."
12 A thinking process, which Kittler derives from Michel Foucault, the notion of the non-linear or non-evolutionary history of media is present throughout his work, but perhaps most clearly articulated in *Discourse Networks 1800/1900*. See p. 264.
13 My own first and only encounter with a historical (albeit no longer functional) phonograph was at the Grand Hotel Londres in Istanbul (also Büyük Londra Oteli). Originating in the late 1800s, this hotel opened shortly after the launch of the Orient Express in 1893 and, like a mausoleum, it has maintained its colonial atmosphere, loaded with colonial-era bric-a-brac for time-travelling tourists. In their novel *Außer sich*, 303, Sasha Marianna Salzmann aptly refers to the hotel as a "Kolonialzeit-Sarg" (colonial-period coffin).
14 Seider, "Postcolonial Historiography," 45–6.
15 Lange, *Gefangene Stimmen*, 11.
16 See Lange, *Gefangene Stimmen*, 25–6; Hoffmann, "Introduction," 75; Hoffmann, *Kolonialgeschichte Hören*, 28–39.
17 Hoffmann, *Kolonialgeschichte Hören*, 16.
18 Stumpf and Hornbostel, "Ethnological Studies," 2.
19 Hornbostel, "Formanalysen an siamesischen Orchesterstücken," 320.
20 Kittler, *Gramophone, Film, Typewriter*, 3–4.

21 Steintrager and Chow, *Sound Objects*.
22 Schaeffer, *Treatise*, 67.
23 Schaeffer, *Treatise*, 213 (emphasis in original).
24 Steintrager and Chow, *Sound Objects*, 8.
25 Schaeffer, *Treatise*, 212.
26 Steintrager and Chow, *Sound Objects*, 8.
27 Steintrager and Chow, *Sound Objects*, 8.
28 Benjamin, "Work of Art"; Auslander, *Liveness*, xii. See also Sterne, *Audible Past*, 220.
29 Schaeffer, *Treatise*, 211.
30 Lange, *Gefangene Stimmen*, 30 (emphasis in the original).
31 Serge, *Men in Prison*, 30.
32 Chion, *Sound*, 15.
33 Novak, "Noise," 125.
34 Parikka, *Media Archaeology*, 90–112.
35 Britta Lange's study is significant to the present book for myriad reasons. Her book is the culmination of over a decade of work as an archivist in the Berlin sound archive. With my own plans to visit the archive hindered by the migration of the Lautarchiv from the Humboldt University to the Humboldt Forum, as well as the global pandemic, I am immensely grateful for and reliant on Lange's original work.
36 Lange cites the total 482 as the combined number of recordings made in the Wünsdorf camps: the Halfmoon camp and neighbouring Weinberg camp. See Lange, *Gefangene Stimmen*, 16.
37 Lange, *Gefangene Stimmen*, 50.
38 Barthes, "Grain of the Voice," 505.
39 Lange and Scheffner, "The Halfmoon Files," https://transversal.at/transversal/0708/lange-scheffner/en.
40 Leimbacher, "Hearing Voice(s)," 293.
41 Parikka, *Media Archaeology*, 93.
42 Stoler, *Archival Grain*, 50.
43 Lange, *Gefangene Stimmen*, 18.
44 Stoler, *Archival Grain*, 53.
45 Fanon, *Wretched of the Earth*, 2.
46 Quijano, "Coloniality and Modernity/Rationality," 176.
47 Quijano, "Coloniality," 177.
48 Ngũgĩ wa Thiong'o's slightly earlier work on colonial language bears mentioning here as well, in particular his *Decolonising the Mind: The Politics of Language in African Literature* (1986).
49 The concept of "border thinking" was first introduced by Gloria Anzaldúa in her path-breaking *Borderlands/La Frontera: The New Mestiza* (1987).
50 Mignolo, "Delinking," 455.

51 Mignolo and Walsh, *On Decoloniality*, 146–7.
52 Mignolo and Walsh, *On Decoloniality*, 148.
53 Consider for instance the network LANDBACK, https://landback.org/.
54 Fanon, *Wretched*, 9.
55 Tuck and Yang, "Decolonization," 21.
56 Tuck and Yang, "Decolonization," 31.
57 Hoffmann, *Kolonialgeschichte Hören*, 42.
58 Robinson, *Hungry Listening*, 11.
59 Oliveros, *Deep Listening*, xxiii.
60 In his reading of Franz Kafka's short story "Der Bau" ("The Burrow," published posthumously in 1931), Mladen Dolar describes the feelings of absolute anguish experienced in the face of acousmatic sound. See Dolar, "Burrow of Sound," 115. Many other authors have since discussed Kafka's story as a significant modern literary illustration of acousmatic sound. See Kane, *Sound Unseen*; Whitney, *Eardrums*; Gellen, *Kafka and Noise*.
61 Singh, *Unthinking Mastery*, 30.
62 Schaeffer, *Treatise*, 65. See also Kane, *Sound Unseen*, 180.
63 Sterne, *Audible Past*, 15.
64 One cannot help but consider Kafka's broader oeuvre and the recurring theme of colonialism. See for instance Zilcosky, *Kafka's Travels*.
65 Woloshyn, "Reclaiming the 'Contemporary' in Indigeneity," 216.
66 Clifford, "On Ethnographic Allegory," 115.
67 Between 2008 and 2015, the Truth and Reconciliation Commission of Canada (TRC) investigated the Indian residential school system. This investigation determined that this system perpetuated nothing less than "cultural genocide." See TRC's report *Honouring the Truth, Reconciling for the Future*, http://www.trc.ca/assets/pdf/Honouring_the_Truth _Reconciling_for_the_Future_July_23_2015.pdf.
68 For further details about the Indian residential school system see the TRC report, 85n248.
69 Dutcher in interview with Greene, "Jeremy Dutcher's Innovative 'Wolastoqiyik Lintuwakonawa,'" https://exclaim.ca/music/article /jeremy_dutchers_innovative_wolastoqiyik_lintuwakonawa_is_really _about_the_future. This raises a fascinating issue about early ethnographic recording and the apparent predominance of male voices. This is also the case of the RPPC collection, whose subjects were all prisoners of war and therefore also all male.
70 Woloshyn, "Reclaiming the 'Contemporary' in Indigeneity," 15.
71 Bolter and Grusin, *Remediation*, 5.
72 This refers to *Campbell v. Acuff-Rose Music* (92–1292), 510 US 596 (1994). See Baron, *Reuse, Misuse, Abuse*, 10.
73 Russell, *Archiveology*, 5.

74 Diamond, "Tradition and Modernity," 256.

75 Bhabha, "Of Mimicry and Man," 126.

76 Hochman, *Savage Preservation*, 178–9. This video features Deanna Francis, Alice Tomah, Maggie Paul, Donald Francis, Mary Larkin and her sister, and Joyce Tomah. It is available through the Language Keepers website in the Passamaquoddy-Maliseet portal, https://pmportal.org/videos/lets-all-sing.

77 Following Hochman, 179–83, though, I looked for the song in the digitalized archive in the American Folklore Centre at the Library of Congress, where he claims to have listened to it. I do find "Esunomawotultine" ("The Trading Song"; https://www.loc.gov /item/2015655578/) as part of the Jesse Walter Fewkes Collection, labelled as SR29. But like Hochman, I am unable to detect the melody present in Maggie Paul's song. Perhaps there is another "Trading Song" captured by William H. Mechling to which Paul refers.

78 Hochman, *Savage Preservation*, 178.

79 Hochman, *Savage Preservation*, 178.

80 Parikka, *Media Archaeology*, 33.

81 Spivak, "Can the Subaltern Speak?"

82 Parikka, *Media Archaeology*, 10.

83 Ernst, *Digital Memory*, 36.

84 Parikka, *Media Archaeology*, 8.

85 Sengupta, "Towards a Decolonial Media Archaeology," 4.

86 Zielinski, *Variations on Media Thinking*, 37.

87 Elsaesser, *Film History*, 59.

88 Elsaesser, *Film History*, 58.

89 Culbert, "Counter-Archival Sensibility," 16; Foucault, *Archaeology of Knowledge*, 128–9.

90 Elsaesser's contribution to media archaeology has focused on cinema. For him, the crisis in question is the death of cinema. However, his approach invites us to consider crisis more broadly – the crisis of history, of memory, of media, et cetera. See Elsaesser, "Media Archaeology as Symptom."

91 Parikka, "Archival Media Theory," 25.

92 Indeed, Ernst coins the neologism "sonicity" in lieu of "acoustics" in his discussion of sound as a rhetorical means around anthropocentric approaches to sound. Ernst, *Sonic Time Machines*, 31, 102. Consider Gilles Deleuze and Félix Guattari's famous notion of "body without organs," in *Anti-Oedipus: Capitalism and Schizophrenia*, 9–15.

93 Ernst *Digital Memory*, 181.

94 Ernst, *Sonic Time Machines*, 139.

95 Adorno, *Current of Music*, 114.

96 Kittler, *Discourse Networks*, 206; Ernst, *Digital Memory*, 182 (emphasis in the original).

97   Denning, *Noise Uprising*.

98   Stoever, *Sonic Color Line*, 13.

99   Parikka, *Media Archaeology*, 33.

100   Ernst, *Digital Memory*, 60.

101   Robinson, *Hungry Listening*, 258.

102   Feld, "Acoustemology," 12.

103   Feld, "Acoustemology," 15.

104   Feld, "Acoustemology," 14.

105   Although Walter Benjamin was not referring directly to the "barbarism" of modernity and coloniality but rather to the history of production relations in his critique of the collector Eduard Fuchs, the pronouncement may be applied here. Benjamin, "Eduard Fuchs," 35.

106   Rony, *Third Eye*.

107   Amad, *The Counter-Archive*, 5.

108   Sobchack, "Media Archaeology and Re-Presencing."

**3.   The Noise of Decolonial Listening: *From Here to Here* and
*The Halfmoon Files***

1   See "who is pong?," *pong*, https://pong-berlin.de/en/1/who-pong.

2   Nichols, *Introduction*, xiii.

3   Of the thirty-one camps visited, 482 discs with 765 recordings were made at the Halfmoon camp. The RPPC made a total of eleven trips to the camp. Mahrenholz, "Recordings," 197–8.

4   Roy, Liebau, and Ahuja, "*When the War Began*," 2.

5   As Jürgen K. Mahrenholz indicates, in 1981 Wilhelm Doegen's collection, of which the recordings of the RPPC were central, faced possible disposal. Mahrenholz, "Recordings," 195.

6   Late in the editing stages, Nicole Wolf's collected volume *Grenzfälle: Dokumentarische Praxis zwischen Film und Literatur bei Merle Kröger und Philip Scheffner* (December 2021) appeared. Unfortunately, I am unable to incorporate it into the present study, but I am certain that it would be a rich resource.

7   For more information about the exhibition, see https://halfmoonfiles.de /en/4/making-of/home. See also Gordon, "I'm Already in Sort of a Tomb"; and Gordon, *Hawthorn Archive*, 293–320.

8   Chion, *Sound*, 15; Novak, "Noise," 125; Balázs, *Early Film Theory*, 185.

9   Schafer, *The Soundscape*, 182.

10   Serres, *Genesis*, 22. See also Serres, *The Parasite*, 13. As he writes in *The Parasite*, "In the beginning was the noise."

11   Attali, *Noise*, 3.

12   Attali, *Noise*, 33–4.

13 Muñoz, "Ephemera as Evidence," 10.

14 In 1916, the first mosque was erected on German soil. Religion was used as part of a larger military experiment to indoctrinate prisoners into turning their backs on their colonial powers at home and embracing jihad against their colonizers. In other words, prisoners were trained as jihadists for Germany's allied power, the Ottoman Empire, and survivors were sent to Istanbul to serve in the Ottoman army. Already in 1914 Max von Oppenheim declared this strategic objective in a "memorandum on revolutionizing the Islamic territories of our enemies," prepared by the German Foreign Office, in which he pens the following argument: "In dem uns aufgedrängten Kampfe gegen England, den dieses bis aufs Messer führen will, wird der Islam eine unserer wichtigsten Waffen werden" (In the war forced on us against England, which it intends to fight to the finish, Islam will be one of our most important weapons). Quoted in Tieke, "Das deutsche Kaiserreich und der Dschihad," https://www .deutschlandfunkkultur.de/geschichte-das-deutsche-kaiserreich-und -der-dschihad.976.de.html?dram%3Aarticle_id=303174.

15 Parikka, "Mapping Noise," 256.

16 Bolter and Grusin, *Remediation*, 31.

17 I am grateful to Ihsan Topaloglu and Christopher Lambie-Hanson for their insight and assistance in acoustically interpreting this perplexing scene.

18 Balázs, *Early Film Theory*, 194.

19 "Acoustic fingerprint" is a term I coined in an earlier article about the *Halfmoon Files*. It offers a variation on the more common term "vocal fingerprint," frequently used in music. Landry, "Searching for a Storyteller," 104.

20 Das, *India*, 4. Santanu Das provides both the Punjabi transcription and the English translation. This translation differs slightly from the subtitled version.

21 Hainge, *Noise Matters*, 13.

22 Muñoz, "Feeling Brown," 79; Robinson, *Hungry Listening*, 258. It might be noted that there is also a documentary film *White Noise* (Daniel Lombroso, US, 2020) about the white nationalist movement in America.

23 The crimes of the Holocaust and the Second World War have long overshadowed all other events of the twentieth century in European and especially German historical discourse. In particular, this has resulted in the public neglect of Germany's brief but devastating stint of colonial rule and its consequences. Friedrichsmeyer, Lennox, and Zantop, "Introduction," 4.

24 Amad, *Counter-Archive*, 4.

25 Baron, *Archive Effect*, 7.

26 Russell, *Archiveology*, 5.

27 Basu, "Archives," 731.

28 Basu, "Archives," 740.

29 This is an issue Tanja Seider raises directly in the context of *The Halfmoon Files*. Seider, "Postcolonial Historiography," 131–2.

30 Gordon, *Ghostly Matters*, 22.

31 Sedgwick, *Touching Feeling*, 139.

32 Hainge, *Noise Matters*, 15

33 Nancy, *Listening*, 5–6, 12, 21.

34 Hainge, *Noise Matters*, 16, 17.

35 Robinson, *Hungry Listening*.

36 Lange, *Gefangene Stimmen*, 16.

37 Foucault, *Archaeology of Knowledge*, 130 (emphasis in original).

38 Derrida, *Archive Fever*, 17.

39 Russell, *Archiveology*, 13; Foucault, *Archaeology of Knowledge*, 129; Derrida, *Archive Fever*, 12.

40 Nichols, "Voice of Documentary," 17–18. See also Nichols, *Introduction*.

41 This is a topic I examine at length in chapter 5. See Rangan, *Immediations*, 139.

42 Derrida, *Archive Fever*, 79.

43 Hutchens, "Techniques of Forgetting?," 37; Zielinski, "AnArcheology for AnArchives," 121–2; Massumi, "Working Principles," 6–7, 6 (emphasis in original).

44 Hutchens, "Techniques of Forgetting?," 45.

45 Roy, Liebau, and Ahuja, "*When the War Began*," 12–13.

46 Doane, *Emergence of Cinematic Time*, 64–5.

47 Doane, *Emergence*, 64–5.

48 Ernst, *Digital Memory*, 174.

49 It bears noting that there are two versions of the film. Both are narrated in voice-over by Scheffner, but one is in German and one is in English. I will cite the English-language voice-over here.

50 Clifford, "On Ethnographic Allegory," 115.

51 Bazin, *What Is Cinema?*, 14.

52 Barthes, *Camera Obscura*, 9.

53 Wolf, "*The Halfmoon Files*: To Be Haunted," *The Halfmoon Files*, accessed 6 February 2021, https://halfmoonfiles.de/en/4/film/be-haunted.

54 Sobchack, *Carnal Thoughts*, 256.

55 Shilina-Conte, "Black Screen, White Page," 501.

56 Wolf, "To Be Haunted."

57 Mahrenholz, "Recordings," 196.

58 Nichols, *Ideology and Image*, 238.

59 Moten, *In the Break*, 203.

60 Agamben, *Remnants of Auschwitz*, 145.

61 Moten, *In the Break*, 235.
62 Moten, *In the Break*, 68.
63 Chion, *Audio-Vision*, 68.
64 Moten, *In the Break*, 200; Campt, *Listening to Images*, 7.
65 Lange and Scheffner, "The Halfmoon Files."
66 Barthes, "Grain of the Voice," 505.
67 Das, *India*, 4.
68 Russell, *Experimental Ethnography*, 65.
69 Das, *India*, 5–6.
70 Daughtry, "Acoustic Palimpsests," 9.
71 Gordon, *Hawthorn Archive*, 296.
72 Schneider, *Performing Remains*, 168 (emphasis in original).
73 Mbembe, *Critique of Black Reason*, 139.
74 Russell, *Experimental Ethnography*, 19.
75 Russell, *Experimental Ethnography*, 18.

4. (Re-)Sounding Autoethnography in Marlon Fuentes's *Bontoc Eulogy*

1 Taussig, *Mimesis and Alterity*, 207.
2 Russell, *Experimental Ethnography*, 86.
3 Bernabe, "Queer Reconfigurations," 736.
4 Russell, *Experimental Ethnography*, 10.
5 Moore, "Marketing Alterity," 127.
6 Nichols, *Introduction*, 125.
7 In a theatrical re-enactment of the story of Enrique of Malacca (the "Magellan slave"), a history to which Kidlat Tahimik's obsessively returns, *Why Is Yellow the Middle of the Rainbow?* places a single archival image of an Indigenous man positioned at the funnel of a phonograph.
8 Catherine Russell offers a comprehensive investigation of *Why Is Yellow the Middle of the Rainbow?* in the context of Kidlat Tahimik's broader oeuvre. See Russell, *Experimental Ethnography*, 295–301.
9 Bernabe, "Queer Reconfigurations," 728.
10 Said, *Reflections on Exile*, 173.
11 See figure 5.3 in chapter 5 for an example of this logo.
12 Taussig, *Mimesis and Alterity*, 213.
13 Bernabe, "Queer Reconfigurations," 738.
14 M. Blumentritt, "*Bontoc Eulogy*, History," 84. It might be noted that this was an imaginary interview conducted by a fictional figure created by Marlon Fuentes himself. The name "Blumentritt" is nevertheless very telling. The Austrian Ferdinand Blumentritt was a wave-migration theorist whose work was foundational for the ethnographic categorization

of Philippine Indigenous groups. See F. Blumentritt, *Versuch einer Ethnographie der Philippinen* (1882). See also Almoroso, "Inheriting the 'Moro Problem,'" 126; Bernabe, "Queer Reconfigurations," 757n56. Here Bernabe also indicates that Blumentritt was actually a supporter of the Philippine Revolution, despite his anthropological ideologies, and that a district in Manila is named after him, one where Fuentes actually lived before leaving the Philippines.

15 Pratt, *Imperial Eyes*, 9.

16 Hoorn, "Captivity, Melancholia," 195.

17 Pratt, *Imperial Eyes*, 9.

18 See Derrida, *The Ear of the Other*.

19 Fuentes, "Extracts from an Imaginary Interview," 124.

20 Feng, *Identities in Motion*, 29.

21 Holt, *Life Stories*, vii.

22 Fuentes, "Extracts," 127; Feng, *Identities in Motion*, 29.

23 Feng, *Identities in Motion*, 30.

24 Rony, "Quick and the Dead," 137.

25 Rony, "Quick and the Dead," 139.

26 Gunning, "Cinema of Attractions," 63–70.

27 Kittler, *Discourse Networks*, 264. See also Kittler, *Gramophone, Film, Typewriter*, 3–4. This is something I discuss at greater length in chapter 2.

28 Here I cite Joseph Palis's interpretation of these same videos and his reading with Edward Said. See Palis, "Ethnographic Spectacle," 229.

29 Feng, *Identities in Motion*, 30–1. I am grateful to Marlon Fuentes for also sharing direct insights about the complex sonic composition of the film via e-mail. Marlon Fuentes, e-mail to author, 6 December 2021.

30 Chen, "Conversation with Trinh T. Minh-ha," 82–91. Regarding "double voicing," see Bakhtin, "Discourse in the Novel," 677.

31 Much has been written on US imperialism in the Philippines and this period of colonialism more globally that could be cited here. David P.S. Goh provides an instructive and illuminating summary of the situation in the Philippines with a specific emphasis on the role of ethnography; see his "States of Ethnography: Colonialism, Resistance, and Cultural Transcription in Malaya and the Philippines, 1890s–1930s," 109–42.

32 M. Blumentritt, *"Bontoc Eulogy,"* 78; Vergara, Jr., *Displaying Filipinos*, 136.

33 Rydell, *All the World's a Fair*, 157. Angela Zimmerman has made a similar observation in the German context. The so-called *Völkerschauen* (human zoos) organized by Carl Hagenbeck and Louis and Gustav Castan worked closely with anthropologists and depended on their partnership and support for approval in order to "attest to the authenticity of their performers and to legitimate them to the police." Zimmerman, *Anthropology*, 18.

34 M. Blumentritt, *"Bontoc Eulogy,"* 77.

35 Hochman, *Savage Preservation*, 110.

36 I am grateful to Brian Hochman for his advice on tracking down this this image.

37 Hochman, *Savage Preservation*, 112.

38 Hochman, *Savage Preservation*, 112.

39 Marks, *Skin of the Film*, 5.

40 Victor Serge uses this expression to describe the imprisoned men who were forced to participate in the anthropometric procedures popular in turn-of-the-twentieth-century France. Serge, *Men in Prison*, 30. I discuss this further in chapters 1 and 2.

41 Barthes, *Camera Obscura*, 57.

42 Campt, *Listening to Images*.

43 Benjamin, "Work of Art," 243n2.

44 Sterne, *Audible Past*, 220.

45 Sterne, *Audible Past*, 221.

46 Russell, *Experimental Ethnography*, 277.

47 Campt, *Listening to Images*, 4.

48 Naficy, *An Accented Cinema*, 6.

49 Muñoz, "Autoethnographic Performance," 87.

50 Muñoz, "Autoethnographic Performance," 87.

51 M. Blumentritt, *"Bontoc Eulogy,"* 84.

52 Muñoz, "Autoethnographic Performance," 99. The notion of a figural anthropology is adopted from Michael Serres's discussion of literature: "Literature made clear, even for the blind, a kind of figural, instructive anthropology that was both accessible and profound, but without theory, without awkward weight, not boring but intelligent." Serres, *Parasite*, 6.

53 Lionnet, *Autobiographical Voices*, 99–100.

54 Sommer, *Foundational Fictions*.

55 Pratt, *Imperial Eyes*, 9.

56 Marcus and Fischer, *Anthropology as Cultural Critique*, 7–16, especially 8–9.

57 Rangan, "Immaterial Child Labor," 148–9. Rangan engages with the earlier scholarship of Faye Ginsburg in the development of her argument. See, for instance, Ginsburg, "Shooting Back."

58 Said, *Orientalism*, 2–3; Bhabha, "Of Mimicry and Man," 126; Muñoz, "Autoethnographic Performance," 96.

59 Spivak, "Can the Subaltern Speak?," 104.

60 Spivak, "Can the Subaltern Speak?," 102.

61 Muñoz, "Autoethnographic Performance," 88 (emphasis in original).

62 Muñoz, "Autoethnographic Performance," 86.

63 Russell, *Experimental Ethnography*, 277.

64 Russell, *Experimental Ethnography*, 278.

65 Feng, *Identities in Motion*, 29.
66 Russell, *Experimental Ethnography*, 278.
67 Russell, *Experimental Ethnography*, 278.
68 Russell, *Experimental Ethnography*, 277.
69 Clifford, "On Ethnographic Allegory," 113.
70 Clifford, "On Ethnographic Allegory," 113.
71 Clifford, "On Ethnographic Allegory," 115.
72 Whitehead, "The Agency of Yearning," 216.
73 Rony, *Third Eye*, 91.
74 For an informative and extensive study on the Archives de la Planète, see Amad, *Counter-Archive*. See also Groo, *Bad Film Histories*, 43–104, and Henley, *Beyond Observation*, 40–2.
75 Ernst, *Digital Memory*, 125.
76 Ernst, *Digital Memory*, 128.
77 Rabelais, *Five Books*, https://www.gutenberg.org/files/1200/1200-h/1200-h.htm#link42HCH0056. Anette Hoffmann begins her article on sound archives with this same quote. I am grateful to her for bringing it to my attention in this context. See Hoffmann, "Introduction," 73.
78 Hoffmann, "Introduction," 74.
79 Baron, *Archive Effect*, 118.
80 Baron, *Archive Effect*, 118–23. See also Löffler, "Medienarchäologie und Film," 9.
81 Baron, *Archive Effect*, 7, 10 (emphasis in the original).
82 Nichols, *Representing Reality*, 21.

5. Weird Machines and Disembodied Voices: Audio Evangelism in *The Tailenders*

1 Castelli, "Interview with Adele Horne," 318.
2 Ochoa Gautier, *Aurality*. 154.
3 Ochoa Gautier, *Aurality*, 146. Tuska Benes, *In Babel's Shadow*, provides a comprehensive study on the historical shift from comparative philology to linguistics in the nineteenth century.
4 Pratt, *Imperial Eyes*, 8.
5 Kittler, *Gramophone, Film, Typewriter*, 22–3.
6 I discuss Doane's concept of an "archive of noise" and its reading with Friedrich Kittler at great length in chapter 3. See Doane, *Emergence*, 64–5.
7 Baron, *Archive Effect*, 114.
8 Baron, *Archive Effect*, 14. Baron draws on Carolyn Steedman's reading of Derrida's *Archive Fever* to conceptualize her own approach to the joke of the archive. In *Dust*, Steedman urges the reader to look beyond the metaphor of "fever" and draws our attention to, for instance, the fact that

nineteenth-century archives frequently contained books within whose leather bindings unbeknownst to the reader lurked the anthrax bacterium. See Steedman, *Dust*, 28.

9 Baron, "Contemporary Documentary Film," 16.

10 According to the GRN website, this has more recently increased to around 6,500 different speech varieties. See https://globalrecordings.net/en /about (accessed 11 May 2021).

11 Baron, *Archive Effect*, 14.

12 Baron, "Contemporary Documentary Film,"17.

13 Issued in 1913, this declaration complemented the statement of the German colonial secretary Wilhelm Solf (1911–18) with the statement "to missionize is to colonize." See Bosch, *Transforming Mission*, 306. See also Rieger, "Theology and Mission," 201.

14 Errington, *Linguistics*, 28.

15 Errington, *Linguistics*, 29.

16 Mignolo, *Darker Side*, 46.

17 Derrida, *Of Grammatology*, 109–10. Errington also makes mention of this. See Errington, *Linguistics*, 32.

18 Errington, *Linguistics*, 96.

19 Errington, *Linguistics*, 96.

20 Errington, *Linguistics*, 153–4.

21 Smith, *Eco-Sonic Media*, 149.

22 In an interview with Elizabeth A. Castelli, Adele Horne notes that this is borrowed from David Himrod. See Castelli, "Interview," 321. See also Himrod, "Syncretism," 49–60.

23 Himrod, "Syncretism," 49.

24 Himrod, "Syncretism," 58.

25 Cited from "Record Players for Gospel Recordings," memo, 4 June 1965, folder 46, box 34, "Records of Gospel Recordings, Inc. – Collection 36," BGC. See Smith, *Eco-Sonic Media*, 149.

26 Parikka, *Media Archaeology*, 131.

27 Zielinski, "AnArcheology," 116.

28 See https://galcom.org (accessed 12 May 2021).

29 Foucault, *Archaeology of Knowledge*, 41.

30 Castelli, "Interview," 321.

31 Himrod, "Syncretism," 58.

32 Scott, "Response to *The Tailenders*," http://archive.pov.org/tailenders /film-update/2/. (Date of publication of response unknown.) See also Castelli, "Interview," 325–6.

33 There is still scant research on these materials, but Joseph W. Ho has more recently drawn our attention to the photographic and filmic work of missionaries in China during the interwar period. See for instance his

essay "Imaging Missions, Visualizing Experience" and his forthcoming monograph *Developing Mission*.

34 See interview with POV accompanying the PBS premiere of *The Tailenders*, 26 June 2006, http://archive.pov.org/tailenders/film-update/. See also Castelli, "Interview," 318.

35 Castelli, "Interview," 320.

36 In the opening of his important study on the voice, *A Voice and Nothing More*, Mladen Dolar discusses the problem of the voice and interpellation via a joke about unresponsive soldiers on the battlefield, too preoccupied with the beauty of the voice of the commander to follow his directions (3–4).

37 Pooja Rangan opens the introduction to her co-edited special issue of *Discourse*, entitled "Documentary Audibilities," with this statement. Indeed, she seeks to turn our attention away from the voice in favour of audibility. Rendering the voice an audibility transforms it into, among other things, "a mode of relation" and "a shared world," not concerned merely with a referent but also with a product (282). See Rangan, "Audibilities," 280. See also Nichols, "Voice of Documentary," 19.

38 Nichols, "Voice of Documentary," 18.

39 Rangan, "Audibilities," 283.

40 Wolfe, "Historicising the 'Voice of God,'" 149.

41 Doane, "The Voice in Cinema," 41.

42 Bonitzer, "Silences of the Voice," 324.

43 Baron, "Contemporary Documentary Film," 17; Baron, *Archive Effect*, 113.

44 I should note that similar to Mary Ann Doane, I distinguish between the "voice-over" and "voice-off." I understand the voice-over as completely extradiegetic and not emanating from the diegetic world of the film, whereas the voice-off indicates a voice that emanates from the off; that is, from out of the frame but not extradiegetic. In the case of the latter, the source of the voice might not be visible but is known. The voice-off frequently occurs in documentary during talking-head interviews when the filmmaker might not be visible in the frame but is audible and poses questions to the subject of the interview.

45 Baron, *Archive Effect*, 113 (emphasis in original).

46 Castelli, "Interview," 323.

47 See Bruzzi, *New Documentary*, 51; Youdelman, "Narration, Invention, and History," 9; Rangan, "Skin of the Voice," 139. It is important to add here that Horne uses voice-of-God narration but never ventriloquizes the recorded voices she presents. In her repeated display of the sound machines, the audience is always reminded of the provenance of the voices. Jaimie Baron's recent study on reusing and misusing archival audiovisual material discusses the topic of "archival ventriloquism" in its second chapter. See Baron, *Reuse, Misuse, Abuse*.

48 Silverman, "Dis-Embodying the Female Voice," 131.
49 At the 2021 Society for Cinema and Media Studies conference, there were several panels and roundtables devoted to the voice and voice-over in documentary film and video essay production.
50 Silverman, "Dis-Embodying the Female Voice," 131–2.
51 Kane's *Sound Unseen* is probably the most comprehensive investigation of acousmatic sound to date.
52 Kane, *Sound Unseen*, 4.
53 Dolar, *Voice*, 61–2.
54 Dolar, *Voice*, 63.
55 Dolar, *Voice*, 75.
56 Chow, "Listening after 'Acousmaticity,'" 117.
57 As mentioned in previous chapters, Franz Boas coined the term "sound-blindness" to indicate the difficulties ethnographers faced to register certain sounds. This often resulted in the subjective judgment of noise. See Boas, "On Alternating Sounds," 47.
58 In chapter 1, I discuss Alexander von Humboldt's extended diary log about the *bogas* music during his trip to what is now Colombia. The intense grumbling of his description of the *bogas* is surprising when contrasted with Humboldt's otherwise open fascination with his experiences during his travels. See Humboldt, *Reise*, 69–70. In a similar derogatory tone, R. Murray Schafer much later compared Inuit throat singing to Winston Churchill clearing his throat. See Schafer, "Limits of Nationalism in Canadian Music," 72.
59 Benes, *In Babel's Shadow*, 10; Ochoa Gautier, *Aurality*, 157.
60 Robinson, *Hungry Listening*, 38–47; Stoever, *Sonic Color Line*, 4.
61 Stoever, *Sonic Color Line*, 5.
62 Stoever, *Sonic Color Line*, 6.
63 Rangan, "Skin of the Voice," 139.
64 Nichols, "Voice of Documentary," 18.
65 Mario speaks in Spanish. Here and elsewhere, I cite him directly and the English-language subtitles that accompany the film.
66 Trinh T. Minh-ha, *When the Moon Waxes Red: Representation, Gender, and Cultural Politics* (London: Routledge, 1991), 60.
67 Bonitzer, "Silences of the Voice," 320–1.

Conclusion: Sinister Listening and Its Afterlives

1 Lange, *Gefangene Stimmen*, 25–6. As I note throughout the book, this method of close listening was developed in collaboration with Anette Hoffmann.
2 Culbert, "Counter-Archival Sensibility," 17.

 3 Sterne, *Audible Past*, 91; Stoever, *Sonic Color Line*; Robinson, *Hungry Listening*.
 4 See, for instance, her co-edited special issue with Genevieve Yue of *Discourse*, entitled "Documentary Audibilities" (2017). See also her introduction to this special issue: Rangan, "Audibilities." She is also currently working on a project entitled "Audibilities: Documentary and Sonic Governance."
 5 Bolter and Grusin, *Remediation*.
 6 Russell, *Archiveology*.
 7 See Ernst, *Digital Memory*; Ernst, *Sonic Time Machines*.
 8 I draw thematic influence from David Toop's literary exploration of listening as a haunting experience in *Sinister Resonance*.
 9 Abu Hamdan, "Aural Contact," 73.
10 Hui, "Cosmopolitan Hospitality and Accented Crossing, 330.
11 Patrick, "Language Analysis," 2.
12 Apter, "Shibboleth, 106.
13 Benes, *In Babel's Shadow*, 10, 211.
14 Apter, "Shibboleth," 105.
15 Abu Hamdan, "Aural Contact," 66.
16 Apter, "Shibboleth," 105. See also Lawrence Abu Hamdan's website for a description of the work: http://lawrenceabuhamdan.com/#/the-freedom-of-speech-itself/ (accessed 13 May 2021).
17 Abu Hamdan, "Aural Contact," 74–5.

Filmography

Am Rande der Sahara. Black-and-white film, 90 min. Rudolf Bierbach and Martin Rikli, Cyrenaica, Germany, South Tunisia, and Tripolitania, 1930. Universum Film AG.*

Bontoc Eulogy. Black-and-white film, 56 min. Marlon Fuentes, Philippines and United States, 1995. Corporation for Public Broadcasting.

Bushmann spricht in den Phonographen. Black-and-white, silent film, 3:36 min. Rudolf Pöch, German South-West Africa, 1908. Österreichische Mediathek.*

Deutsch-Ostafrika: Eine große öffentliche Schule in der Provinz Usambara. Black-and-white, silent film, 4 min. German East Africa. (Filmmaker unknown), 1912. Germania Film/Pathé Frères.*

Fitzcarraldo. Colour film, 158 min. Werner Herzog, Peru and West Germany, 1982. Zweites Deutsches Fernsehen.

From Here to Here. Colour video, 60 min. Madhusree Dutta and Philip Scheffner, India and Germany, 2005. Majilis.

The Halfmoon Files. Colour film, 87 min. Philip Scheffner, Germany, 2007. Pong.

Mit Büchse und Lasso durch Afrika. Black-and-white film, 84 min. Gernot Bock-Stieber and Lutz Heck, Congo, East Africa, and Germany, 1930. Kulturfilm-Produktion Ada van Roon (Kultura).*

Moeder Dao, de schildpadgelijkende. Black-and-white film, 88 min. Vincent Monnikendam, The Netherlands, 1995. Eye International.

Nanook of the North. Black-and-white, silent film, 78 min. Robert J. Flaherty, Canada and United States, 1922. Pathé Exchange.

The Tailenders. Colour film, 72 min. Adele Horne, India, Mexico, Solomon Islands, and United States, 2006. Public Broadcasting Service.

Welt Spiegel Kino. Black-and-white, silent film, 93 min. Gustav Deutsch, Austria and The Netherlands, 2005. Sixpack Film.

White Noise. Colour film, 101 min. Geoffrey Sax, United States, 2005. Universal Pictures.

Why Is Yellow the Middle of the Rainbow? Colour film, 175 min. Kidlat Tahimik, Philippines, 1981–93. Yamagata.

---

* Please note that I indicate the (colonial) location names at the time of filming not to repeat injury but for historical accuracy.

Bibliography

Abu Hamdan, Lawrence. "Aural Contact: Forensic Listening and the Reorganization of the Speaking Subject." In *Forensis: The Architecture of Public Truth*, edited by Forensic Architecture, 65–82. Berlin: Sternberg Press, 2014.

Adorno, Theodor W. *Current of Music: Elements of a Radio Theory.* Edited by Robert Hullot-Kentor. Cambridge: Polity, 2009.

– "The Form of the Phonograph Record." Translated by Thomas Y. Levin. *October* 55 (1990): 56–61.

Adorno, Theodor W., and Max Horkheimer. *Dialektik der Aufklärung: Philosophische Fragmente.* Berlin: Fischer, 1971.

Agamben, Giorgio. *Remnants of Auschwitz: The Witness and the Archive.* Translated by Daniel Heller-Roazen. New York: Zone Books, [1999] 2002.

Almoroso, Donna J. "Inheriting the 'Moro Problem': Muslim Authority and Colonial Rule in British Malaya and the Philippines." In *The American Colonial State in the Philippines: Global Perspectives*, edited by Julian Go and Anne L. Foster, 118–47. Durham, NC: Duke University Press, 2003.

Alter, Nora M., and Lutz Koepnick, eds. *Sound Matters: Essays on Acoustics of Modern German Culture.* New York: Berghahn Books, 2004.

Amad, Paula. *The Counter-Archive: Film, the Everyday, and Albert Kahn's Archives de la Planète.* New York: Columbia University Press, 2010.

Ames, Eric. *Carl Hagenbeck's Empire of Entertainments.* Seattle: University of Washington Press, 2009.

– "The Sound of Evolution." *Modernism/Modernity* 10, no. 2 (2003): 297–325.

Anzaldúa, Gloria. *Borderlands/La Frontera: The New Mestiza.* San Francisco: Spinsters/Aunt Lute, 1987.

Apter, Emily "Shibboleth: Policing by Ear and Forensic Listening in Projects by Lawrence Abu Hamdan." *October* 156 (2016): 100–15.

Attali, Jacques. *Noise: The Political Economy of Music.* Translated by Brian Massumi. Manchester, UK: Manchester University Press, [1977] 1985.

Auslander, Philip. *Liveness: Performance in a Mediatized Culture*. London: Routledge, 2008.

Azoulay, Ariella Aïsha. *Potential History: Unlearning Imperialism*. London: Verso, 2019.

Bakhtin, Mikhail. "Discourse in the Novel." In *Literary Theory: An Anthology*, edited by Julie Rivkin and Michael Ryan, 674–85. Malden, MA: Blackwell, 2004.

Balázs, Béla. *Early Film Theory: Visible Man and the Spirit of Film*. Edited by Erica Carter. Translated by Rodney Livingstone. New York: Berghahn Books, [1924] 2010.

Baron, Jaimie. *The Archive Effect: Found Footage and the Audiovisual Experience of History*. London: Routledge, 2014.

– "Contemporary Documentary Film and 'Archive Fever': History, the Fragment, the Joke." *Velvet Light Trap* 60 (2007): 13–24.

– *Reuse, Misuse, Abuse: The Ethics of Audiovisual Appropriation in the Digital Era*. New Brunswick, NJ: Rutgers University Press, 2020.

Barthes, Roland. *Camera Obscura: Reflections on Photography*. Translated by Richard Howard. London: Vintage Classics, [1980] 2000.

– "The Grain of the Voice." In *The Sound Studies Reader*, edited by Jonathan Sterne, translated by Stephen Heath, 504–10. London: Routledge, [1977] 2012.

Basu, Priyanka. "Archives of German Anthropology and Colonialism in Philip Scheffner's *The Halfmoon Files*." *Third Text* 33, no. 6 (2019): 727–43.

Bazin, André. *What Is Cinema?* Vol 1. Translated and edited by Hugh Gray. Berkeley: University of California Press, [1967] 2005.

Benes, Tuska. *In Babel's Shadow: Language, Philosophy, and the Nation in Nineteenth-Century Germany*. Detroit, MI: Wayne State University Press, 2008.

Benjamin, Walter. "Eduard Fuchs: Collector and Historian." Translated by Knut Tarnowski. *New German Critique* no. 5 (1975): 27–58.

– "The Work of Art in the Age of Mechanical Reproduction." In *Illuminations: Essays and Reflections*, edited by Hannah Arendt, translated by Harry Zohn, 217–52. New York: Schocken Books, [1936] 1968.

Bernabe, Jan Christian. "Queer Reconfigurations: *Bontoc Eulogy* and Marlon Fuentes's Archive Imperative." *positions* 24, no. 4 (2016): 727–59.

Bhabha, Homi. "Of Mimicry and Man: The Ambivalence of Colonial Discourse." *October* 28 (1984): 125–33.

Blumentritt, Ferdinand. *Versuch einer Ethnographie der Philippinen*. Gotha: Justus Perthes, 1882.

Blumentritt, Mia. "*Bontoc Eulogy*, History and the Craft of Memory: An Extended Conversation with Marlon E. Fuentes." *Amerasia Journal* 24, no. 3 (1998): 75–90.

Boas, Franz. "On Alternating Sounds." *American Anthropologist* 2, no. 1 (1889): 47–54.

Bolter, Jay David, and Richard Grusin. *Remediation: Understanding New Media.* Cambridge, MA: MIT Press, 1999.

Bonitzer, Pascal. "The Silences of the Voice." In *Narrative, Apparatus, Ideology: A Film Theory Reader*, edited by Philip Rosen, translated by Philip Rosen and Marcia Butzel, 319–34. New York: Columbia University Press, 1986.

Bosch, David J. *Transforming Mission: Paradigm Shifts in the Theology of Mission.* Maryknoll, NY: Orbis Books, 1991.

Brady, Erika. *A Spiral Way: How the Phonograph Changed Ethnography.* Jackson: University of Mississippi, 1999.

Bruzzi, Stella. *New Documentary: A Critical Introduction.* London: Routledge, 2000.

Bull, Michael. *Sound Moves: iPod Culture and Urban Experience.* London: Routledge, 2007.

Campt, Tina M. *Listening to Images.* Durham, NC: Duke University Press, 2017.

Castelli, Elizabeth A. "Interview with Adele Horne, Director of *The Tailenders* (2006)." *Postscripts* 2, nos. 2–3 (2006): 316–27.

Chen, Nancy. "'Speaking Nearby': A Conversation with Trinh T. Minh-ha." *Visual Anthropology Review* 8, no. 1 (1992): 82–91.

Chion, Michel. *Audio-Vision: Sound on Screen.* Translated by Claudia Gorbman. New York: Columbia University Press, [1990] 1994.

– *Sound: An Acoulogical Treatise.* Translated by James A. Steintrager. Durham, NC: Duke University Press, [2010] 2016.

Chow, Rey. "Listening after 'Acousmaticity.'" In *Sound Objects*, edited by James A. Steintrager and Rey Chow, 113–29. Durham, NC: Duke University Press, 2019.

Clifford, James. "On Ethnographic Allegory." In *Writing Culture: The Poetics and Politics of Ethnography*, edited by James Clifford and George E. Marcus, 98–121. Berkeley: University of California Press, 1986.

Clifford, James, and George E. Marcus, eds. *Writing Culture: The Poetics and the Politics of Ethnography.* Berkeley: University of California Press, 1986.

Crary, Jonathan. *Techniques of an Observer: On Vision and Modernity in the Nineteenth Century.* Cambridge, MA: MIT Press, 1990.

Culbert, Jennifer L. "A Counter-Archival Sensibility: Picking Up Hannah Arendt's 'Reflections on Little Rock.'" In *Law, Memory, Violence: Uncovering the Counter-Archive*, edited by Stewart Motha and Honni van Rijswijk, 16–33. London: Routledge, 2016.

Das, Santanu. *India, Empire, and First World War Culture: Writings, Images, and Songs.* Cambrige: Cambridge University Press, 2018.

Daughtry, J. Martin. "Acoustic Palimpsests and the Politics of Listening." *Music & Politics* 7, no. 1 (2013): 1–34.

Deleuze, Gilles, and Félix Guattari. *Anti-Oedipus: Capitalism and Schizophrenia*. Translated by Robert Hurley, Mark Steem, and Helen R. Lane. Minneapolis: University of Minnesota Press, [1972] 1983.

Denning, Michael. *Noise Uprising: The Audiopolitics of a World Musical Revolution*. London: Verso, 2015.

Derrida, Jacques. *Archive Fever: A Freudian Impression*. Translated by Eric Prenowitz. Chicago: University of Chicago Press, [1995] 1996.

– *The Ear of the Other: Otobiography, Transference, Translation*. Edited by Christie McDonald. Translated by Avital Ronell. Lincoln: University of Nebraska Press, 1985.

– *Mal d'archive: Une impression freudienne*. Paris: Éditions Galilée, 1995.

– *Of Grammatology*. Translated by Gayatri Chakravorty Spivak. Baltimore: Johns Hopkins University Press, [1967] 1997.

Dettelbach, Michael. "The Face of Nature: Precise Measurement, Mapping, and Sensibility in the Work of Alexander von Humboldt." *Studies of History, Philosophy & Biomedical Science* 30, no. 4 (1999): 473–504.

Diamond, Beverley. "Purposefully Reflecting on Tradition and Modernity." In *Music and Modernity among First Peoples of North America*, edited by Victoria Lindsey Levine and Dylan Robinson, 240–57. Middletown, CT: Wesleyan University Press, 2019.

Doane, Mary Ann. *The Emergence of Cinematic Time: Modernity, Contingency, the Archive*. Cambridge, MA: Harvard University Press, 2002.

– "Ideology and the Practice of Sound Editing." In *Film Sound: Theory and Practice*, edited by Elisabeth Weis and John Belton, 54–62. New York: Columbia University Press, 1985.

– "The Voice in Cinema: The Articulation of Body and Space." *Yale French Studies* 60 (1980): 33–50.

Doegen, Wilhelm. *Bericht über mein Wirken und Schaffen in der Preussischen Phonographischen Kommission*. Berlin, 29 July 1919. Deutsches Historisches Museum (unpublished and unpaginated).

– "Denkschrift Über die Errichtung eines 'Deutschen Lautamtes' in Berlin." Berlin: unpublished manuscript, 1909. https://soundandscience.de/text /denkschrift-uber-die-errichtung-eines-deutschen-lautamtes-berlin.

– *Jahrbuch des Lautwesens 1931*. Berlin: Lehner, 1930.

– *Kriegsgefangene Völker: Der Kriegsgefangenen Haltung und Schicksal in Deutschland*, Vol. 1. Berlin: Dietrich Reimer, 1919.

– *Unter fremden Völkern: Eine neue Völkerkunde*. Berlin: Otto Stollberg, 1925.

Dolar, Mladen. "The Burrow of Sound." *Differences: A Journal of Feminist Cultural Studies* 22, nos. 2–3 (2011): 112–39.

– *A Voice and Nothing More*. Cambridge, MA: MIT Press, 2006.

Elsaesser, Thomas. *Film History as Media Archaeology: Tracking Digital Cinema*. Amsterdam: Amsterdam University Press, 2016.

– "Media Archaeology as Symptom." *New Review of Film and Television Studies* 14, no. 2 (2016): 181–215.

El-Tayeb, Fatima. "The Universal Museum: How the New Germany Built Its Future on Colonial Amnesia." *Journal of Contemporary African Art* 46 (2020): 72–82.

Erlmann, Veit. "But What of the Ethnographic Ear?" In *Hearing Cultures: Essays on Sound, Listening, and Modernity*, edited by Veit Erlmann, 1–20. Oxford: Berg, 2004.

Ernst, Wolfgang. *Digital Memory and the Archive*. Edited by Jussi Parikka. Minneapolis: University of Minnesota Press, 2013.

– *Sonic Time Machines: Explicit Sound, Sirenic Voices*. Amsterdam: Amsterdam University Press, 2016.

Errington, Joseph. *Linguistics in the Colonial World: A Story of Language, Meaning, and Power*. Malden, MA: Blackwell, 2008.

Evans, Andrew D. *Anthropology at War: World War I and the Science of Race in Germany*. Chicago: University of Chicago Press, 2010.

Fanon, Frantz. *The Wretched of the Earth*. Translated by Richard Philcox. New York: Grove Press, [1960] 2004.

Feaster, Patrick, and Jacob Smith. "Reconfiguring the History of Early Cinema through the Phonograph, 1877–1908." *Film History* 21 (2009): 311–25.

Featherstone, Mike. "Archive." *Theory, Culture & Society* 23, nos. 2–3 (2006): 591–6.

Feld, Steven. "Acoustemology." In *Keywords in Sound*, edited by David Novak and Matt Sakakeeny, 12–21. Durham, NC: Duke University Press, 2015.

Feng, Peter X. *Identities in Motion: Asian American Film and Video*. Durham, NC: Duke University Press, 2002.

Fewkes, J. Walter. "On the Use of the Phonograph in the Study of the Languages of American Indians." *Science* (1890): 257–8.

Foucault, Michel. *The Archaeology of Knowledge and the Discourse on Language*. Translated by A.M. Sheridan Smith. New York: Vintage Books [1969] 1972.

Freshwater, Helen. "The Allure of the Archive." *Poetics Today* 24, no. 4 (2003): 729–58.

Friedrichsmeyer, Sara, Sara Lennox, and Susanne Zantop, eds. "Introduction." In *The Imperialist Imagination: German Colonialism and Its Legacy*, 1–32. Ann Arbor: University of Michigan Press, 1998.

Fuentes, Marlon. "Extracts from an Imaginary Interview: Questions and Answers about *Bontoc Eulogy*," in *F Is for Phony: Fake Documentary and Truth's Undoing*, edited by Alexandra Juhasz and Jesse Lerner, 116–29. Minneapolis: University of Minnesota Press, 2006.

Fuhrmann, Wolfgang. "Ethnographic Films from Prisoner-of-War Camps and the Aesthetics of Early Cinema." In *Doing Anthropology in Wartime and War Zones: World War I and the Cultural Sciences in Europe*, edited by

Reinhard Johler, Christian Marchetti, and Monique Scheer, 337–52. Bielefeld: Transcript, 2010.

– "Filmaufnahmen in Afrika: 'Lebende Bilder' aus den deutschen Kolonien." In *Geschichte des dokumentarischen Films in Deutschland*, vol. 1: *Kaiserreich 1895–1918*, edited by Uli Jung and Martin Loiperdinger, 149–60. Stuttgart: Reclam, 2005.

– "First Contact: The Beginning of Ethnographic Filmmaking in Germany, 1900–1930." *History of Anthropology Newsletter* 34, no. 1 (2007): 3–8.

– *Imperial Projections: Screening the German Colonies*. New York: Berghahn Books, 2017.

– "Propaganda und Unterhaltung: Kolonialismus im frühen Film." In *Deutsche Sprache und Kolonialismus: Aspekte der nationalen Kommunikation 1884 und 1919*, edited by Ingo H. Warnke, 349–64. Berlin: De Gruyter, 2009.

Gaines, Jane M. "Introduction: 'The Real Returns.'" In *Collecting Visible Evidence*, edited by Jane M. Gaines and Michael Renov, 1–18. Minneapolis: University of Minnesota Press, 1999.

Gellen, Kata. *Kafka and Noise: The Discovery of Cinematic Sound in Literary Modernism*. Evanston, IL: Northwestern University Press, 2020.

Ginsburg, Faye. "Shooting Back: From Ethnographic Film to Indigenous Production/Ethnography of Media." In *A Companion to Film Theory*, edited by Tony Miller and Robert Stam, 295–322. Malden, MA: Blackwell, [1999] 2004.

Gitelman, Lisa. *Scripts, Grooves, and Writing Machines: Representation Technology in the Edison Era*. Stanford: Stanford University Press, 1999.

Goh, David P.S. "States of Ethnography: Colonialism, Resistance, and Cultural Transcription in Malaya and the Philippines, 1890s–1930s." *Comparative Studies in Society and History* 49, no. 1 (2007): 109–42.

Gordon, Avery F. *Ghostly Matters: Haunting the Sociological Imagination*. Minneapolis: University of Minnesota Press, [1997] 2008.

– *The Hawthorn Archive: Letters from the Utopian Margins*. New York: Fordham University Press, 2018.

– "'I'm Already in Sort of a Tomb': A Reply to Philip Scheffner's *The Halfmoon Files*." *South Atlantic Quarterly* 110, no. 1 (2011): 121–54

Graf, Walter. "The Phonogrammarchiv der österreicherischen Akademie der Wissenschaften in Vienna." *The Folklore and Folk Music Archivist* 4, no. 4 (1962): unpaginated.

Greene, Sarah. "Jeremy Dutcher's Innovative 'Wolastoqiyik Lintuwakonawa' Is Really About the Future." *Exclaim*, 16 April 2018. https://exclaim.ca /music/article/jeremy_dutchers_innovative_wolastoqiyik_lintuwakonawa _is_really_about_the_future.

Grierson, John. "From 'First Principles of Documentary' (UK 1932)." In *Film Manifestos and Global Cinema*, edited by Scott Mackenzie, 453–9. Berkeley: University of California Press, 2014.

Griffiths, Alison. *Wondrous Difference: Cinema, Anthropology, & Turn-of-the-Century Visual Culture*. New York: Columbia University Press, 2002.

Groo, Katherine. *Bad Film Histories: Ethnography and the Early Archive*. Minneapolis: University of Minnesota Press, 2019.

Gunning, Tom. "The Cinema of Attractions: Early Film, Its Spectator, and the Avant-Garde." *Wide Angle* 8 (1983): 63–70.

– "Doing for the Eye What the Phonograph Does for the Ear." In *The Sounds of Early Cinema*, edited by Richard Abel and Rick Altman, 13–31. Bloomington: Indiana University Press, 2001.

Hagood, Mack. *Hush: Media and Sonic Self-Control*. Durham, NC: Duke University Press, 2019.

Hainge, Greg. *Noise Matters: Towards an Ontology of Noise*. New York: Bloomsbury, 2013.

Hanslick, Eduard. *Vom Musikalisch-Schönen: Ein Beitrag zur Revision der Ästhetik der Tonkunst*. Leipzig: Barth, [1854] 1902.

Harvey-Brown, Richard, and Beth Davis-Brown. "The Making of Memory: The Politics of Archives, Libraries and Museums in the Construction of the National Consciousness." *History of the Human Sciences* 11, no. 4 (1998): 17–32.

Henley, Paul. *Beyond Observation: A History of Authorship in Ethnographic Film*. Manchester, UK: Manchester University Press, 2020.

Himrod, David K. "The Syncretism of Technology and Protestantism: An American 'Popular Religion'?" *Explor: A Journal of Theology* 7 (1984): 49–60.

Ho, Joseph W. *Developing Mission: Photography, Filmmaking, and American Missionaries in Modern China*. Ithaca: Cornell University Press, 2021.

– "Imaging Missions, Visualizing Experience: American Presbyterian Photography, Filmmaking, and Chinese Christianity in Interwar Republican China." In *China's Christianity: From Mission to Indigenous Church*, edited by Anthony E. Clark, 52–85. Leiden: Brill, 2017.

Hochman, Brian. *Savage Preservation: The Ethnographic Origins of Modern Media Technology*. Minneapolis: University of Minnesota Press, 2014.

Hoffmann, Anette. "Introduction: Listening to Sound Archive." *Social Dynamics* 41, no. 1 (2015): 73–83.

– *Kolonialgeschichte Hören: Das Echo Gewaltsamer Wissensproduction in Historischen Tondokumenten aus dem Südlichen Afrika*. Vienna: Mandelbaum, 2020.

Holt, Hamilton, ed. *The Life Stories of Undistinguished Americans*. New York: John Potts, 1906.

Hoorn, Jeanette. "Captivity, Melancholia and Diaspora in Marlon Fuentes' *Bontoc Eulogy*: Revisiting *Meet Me in St. Louis*." In *Body Trade: Captivity, Cannibalism and Colonialism in the Pacific*, edited by Barbara Creed and Jeanette Hoorn, 195–207, London: Routledge, 2001.

Hornbostel, Erich Moritz von. "Formanalysen an siamesischen Orchesterstücken." *Archiv für Musikwissenschaft* 2, no. 2 (1920): 306–33.

Hui, Tingting. "Cosmopolitan Hospitality and Accented Crossing: Forging an Ethics of Listening with Lawrence Abu Hamdan's Artworks." In *New Cosmopolitans, Race, and Ethnicity: Cultural Perspectives*, edited by Ewa Barbara Luczak, Anna Pochmara, and Samir Dayal, 328–43. Warsaw: De Gruyter, 2018.

Humboldt, Alexander von. *Reise auf dem Río Magdalena, durch die Anden und Mexico, Teil 1: Texte*, edited by Margot Faak. Berlin: Akademie-Verlag, [1801] 1986.

Hutchens, Benjamin. "Techniques of Forgetting? Hypo-Amnesic History and the An-Archive." *SubStance* 36, no. 2 (2007): 37–55.

Jones, Heather. "Imperial Captivities: Colonial Prisoners of War in Germany and the Ottoman Empire, 1914–1918." In *Race, Empire, and First World War Writing*, edited by Santanu Das, 175–93. Cambridge: Cambridge University Press, 2011.

– *Violence against Prisoners of War in the First World War: Britain, France and Germany, 1914–1920*. Cambridge: Cambridge University Press, 2011.

Kahana, Jonathan, ed. *The Documentary Film Reader: History, Theory, Criticism.* Oxford: Oxford University Press, 2016.

Kalibani, Mèhèza. "The Less Considered Part: Contextualizing Immaterial Heritage from German Colonial Contexts in the Restitution Debate." *International Journal of Cultural Property* 28 (2021): 43–53.

Kane, Brian. *Sound Unseen: Acousmatic Sound in Theory and Practice.* Oxford: Oxford University Press, 2016.

Kaplan, Judith. "'Voices of the People': Linguistic Research among Germany's Prisoners of War during World War I." *Journal of the History of the Behavioral Sciences* 49, no. 3 (2013): 281–305.

Kim, David D. "The Task of the Loving Translator: Translation, *Völkerschauen*, and Colonial Ambivalence in Peter Altenberg's *Ashantee* (1897)." *TRANSIT* 2, no. 1 (2005). https://transit.berkeley.edu/2006/kim/.

Kirn, Gal. *The Partisan Counter-Archive.* Berlin: Walter De Gruyter, 2020.

Kittler, Friedrich A. *Discourse Networks 1800/1900.* Translated by Michael Mettler and Chris Cullens. Stanford: Stanford University Press, [1985] 1990.

– *Gramophone, Film, Typewriter.* Translated by Geoffrey Winthrop-Young and Michael Wutz. Stanford: Stanford University Press, [1986] 1999.

Koepnick, Lutz. *Fitzcarraldo.* Rochester, NY: Camden House, 2019.

Kuster, Brigitta, Britta Lange, and Petra Löffler. "Archive der Zukunft? Ein Gespräch über Sammlungspolitiken, koloniale Archive und die Dekolonisierung des Wissens." *Zeitschrift für Medienwissenschaft* 20, no. 1 (2019): 96–111.

Landry, Olivia. "Searching for a Storyteller, Remediating the Archive: Philip Scheffner's *The Halfmoon Files*." *New German Critique* 36, no. 3 (2019): 103–24.

Lange, Britta. "Archiv." In *Handbuch Sound: Geschichte – Begriffe – Ansätze*, edited by Daniel Morat and Hansjakob Ziemer, 236–40. Stuttgart: J.B. Metzler, 2018.

– *Gefangene Stimmen: Tonaufnahmen von Kriegsgefangenen aus dem Lautarchiv 1915–1918*. Berlin: Kulturverlag Kadmos, 2019.

– "South Asian Soldiers and German Academics: Anthropological, Linguistic and Musicological Field Studies in Prison Camps." In *"When the War Began We Heard of Several Kings": South Asian Prisoners in World War I Germany*, edited by Franziska Roy, Heike Liebau, and Ravi Ahuja, 149–84. Delhi: Social Science Press, 2011.

– "'Wenn der Krieg zu Ende ist, werden viele Erzählungen gedruckt warden'. Südasiatische Positionen und europäische Forschungen im 'Halbmondlager.'" *Südasien-Chronik – South Asia Chronicle* 5 (2015): 10–41.

Lange, Britta, and Philip Scheffner. "'The Halfmoon Files': Text Montage Based on a Lecture (2007) by Britta Lange and Philip Scheffner." Translated by Marcie K. Jost. EIPCP: European Institute for Progressive Cultural Policies, May 2007. https://transversal.at/transversal/0708/lange-scheffner/en.

Leimbacher, Irina. "Hearing Voice(s): Experiments with Documentary Listening." *Discourse* 39, no. 3 (2017): 292–318.

Levin, David Michael, ed. *Modernity and the Hegemony of Vision*. Berkeley: University of California Press, 1993.

Lionnet, Françoise. *Autobiographical Voices: Race, Gender, Self-Portrait*. Ithaca, NY: Cornell University Press, 1989.

Löffler, Petra. "Medienarchäologie und Film." In *Handbuch Filmtheorie*, edited by Bernhard Groß and Thomas Morsch, 1–16. Wiesbaden: Springer, 2016.

Mahrenholz, Jürgen K. "Recordings of South Asian Languages and Music in the Lautarchiv of Humboldt-Universität zu Berlin." In *"When the War Began We Heard of Many Kings": South Asian Prisoners in World War I Germany*, edited by Franziska Roy, Heike Liebau, and Ravi Ahuja, 187–206. Delhi: Social Science Press, 2011.

Marcus, George E., and Michael M.J. Fischer. *Anthropology as Cultural Critique: An Experimental Moment in the Human Sciences*. Chicago: University of Chicago Press, 1986.

Marks, Laura U. *The Skin of the Film: Intercultural Cinema, Embodiment, and the Senses*. Durham, NC: Duke University Press, 2000.

Massumi, Brian. "Working Principles." In *The Go-To How-To Book of Anarchiving*, edited by Andrew Murphy, 6–7. Montréal: The Senselab, 2016.

Mbembe, Achille. *Critique of Black Reason*. Durham, NC: Duke University Press, 2017.

– "The Power of the Archive and Its Limits." In *Refiguring the Archive*, edited by Carolyn Hamilton, Verne Harris, Jane Taylor, Michele Pickover, Graeme Reid, and Razia Saleh, 19. Cape Town: David Philip, 2002.

Mignolo, Walter D. *The Darker Side of the Renaissance: Literacy, Territoriality, and Colonization.* Ann Arbor: University of Michigan Press, 1995.

– "Delinking: The Rhetoric of Modernity, the Logic of Coloniality and the Grammar of De-coloniality." *Cultural Studies* 21, nos. 2–3 (2007): 449–514.

Mignolo, Walter D., and Catherine E. Walsh. *On Decoloniality: Concepts, Analytics, Praxis.* Durham, NC: Duke University Press, 2018.

Moore, Rachel. "Marketing Alterity." In *Visualizing Theory: Selected Essays from Visual Anthropology Review, 1990–1994,* edited by Lucien Taylor, 126–42. New York: Routledge.

Moten, Fred. *In the Break: The Aesthetics of the Black Radical Tradition.* Minneapolis: University of Minnesota Press, 2003.

Muñoz, José Esteban, "The Autoethnographic Performance: Reading Richard Fung's Queer Hybridity." *Screen* 36, no. 2 (1995): 83–99.

– "Ephemera as Evidence: Introductory Notes to Queer Acts." *Women and Performance: A Journal of Feminist Theory* 8, no. 2 (1996): 5–16.

– "Feeling Brown: Ethnicity and Affect in Ricardo Bracho's 'The Sweetest Hangover (and Other STDs).'" *Theatre Journal* 52, no. 1 (2000): 67–79.

Naficy, Hamid. *An Accented Cinema: Exilic and Diasporic Filmmaking.* Princeton: Princeton University Press, 2001.

Nagl, Tobias. *Die unheimliche Maschine: Rasse und Repräsentation im Weimarer Kino.* Munich: etk, 2009.

Nancy, Jean-Luc. *Listening.* Translated by Charlotte Mandell. New York: Fordham University Press, [2002] 2007.

Ngũgĩ wa Thiong'o. *Decolonising the Mind: The Politics of Language in African Literature.* Nairobi: East African Educational Publishers, 1986.

Nichols, Bill. *Ideology and Image: Social Representation in the Cinema and Other Media.* Bloomington: Indiana University Press, 1981.

– *Introduction to Documentary.* Bloomington: Indiana University Press, 2017.

– *Representing Reality: Issues and Concepts in Documentary.* Bloomington: Indiana University Press, 1991.

– "The Voice of Documentary." *Film Quarterly* 36, no. 3 (1983): 17–30.

Nietzsche, Friedrich. *Beyond Good and Evil: Prelude to a Philosophy of the Future.* Translated by Walter Kaufmann. New York: Random House, [1886] 1966.

Novak, David, and Matt Sakakeeny, eds. *Keywords in Sound.* Durham, NC: Duke University Press, 2015.

Ochoa Gautier, Ana María. *Aurality: Listening and Knowledge in Nineteenth-Century Colombia.* Durham, NC: Duke University Press, 2014.

Okslioff, Assenka. *Picturing the Primitive: Visual Culture, Ethnography, and Early Cinema.* New York: Palgrave, 2001.

Oliveros, Pauline. *Deep Listening: A Composer's Sound Practice.* New York: iUniverse, 2005.

Palis, Joseph. "The Ethnographic Spectacle of the 'Other' Filipinos in Early Cinema." *GeoJournal* 74 (2009): 227–34.

Parikka, Jussi. "Archival Media Theory: An Introduction to Wolfgang Ernst's Media Archaeology." In *Digital Memory and the Archive*, edited by Jussi Parikka, 1–31. Minneapolis: University of Minnesota Press, 2013.

– "Mapping Noise: Techniques and Tactics of Irregularities, Interception, and Disturbance." In *Media Archaeology: Approaches, Applications, and Implications*, edited by Erkki Huhtamo and Jussi Parikka, 256–77. Berkeley: University of California Press, 2011.

– *What Is Media Archaeology?* Cambridge: Polity, 2012.

Patrick, Peter L. "Language Analysis for the Determination of Origin (LADO): An Introduction." In *Language Analysis for the Determination of Origin: Current Perspectives and New Directions*, edited by Peter L. Patrick, Monika S. Schmid, and Karin Zwaan, 1–19. Cham, Switzerland: Springer, 2019.

Pratt, Mary Louise. *Imperial Eyes: Travel Writing and Transculturation*. London: Routledge, [1992] 2008.

Quijano, Aníbal. "Coloniality and Modernity/Rationality." *Cultural Studies* 21, nos. 2–3 (2007): 168–78.

Rabelais, François. *Five Books of the Lives, Heroic Deeds, and Sayings of Gargantua and his Son Pantagruel*. Chap. 4.LVI. 1552. https://www.gutenberg.org /files/1200/1200-h/1200-h.htm#link42HCH0056.

Radano, Ronald, and Tejumola Olaniyan, eds. *Audible Empire: Music, Global Politics, Critique*. Durham, NC: Duke University Press, 2016.

Rangan, Pooja. "Audibilities: Voice and Listening in the Penumbra of Documentary: An Introduction." *Discourse* 39, no. 3 (2017): 279–91.

– "Immaterial Child Labor: Media Advocacy, Autoethnography, and the Case of *Born into Brothels*." *Camera Obscura* 25, no. 3 (2011): 143–77.

– *Immediations: The Humanitarian Impulse in Documentary*. Durham, NC: Duke University Press, 2017.

– "The Skin of the Voice: Acousmatic Illusions, Ventriloquial Listening." In *Sounds Objects*, edited by James A. Steintrager and Rey Chow, 130–48. Durham, NC: Duke University Press, 2019.

Rehding, Alexander. "The Quest for the Origins of Music in Germany circa 1900." *Journal of American Musicology Society* 53, no. 2 (2000): 345–85.

Reik, Theodor. *Listening with the Third Ear: The Inner Experience of a Psychoanalyst*. New York: Farrar, Straus and Giroux, [1945] 1975.

Reill, Peter Hans. *Vitalizing Nature in the Enlightenment*. Berkeley: University California Press, 2005.

Rieger, Joerg. "Theology and Mission between Neocolonialism and Postcolonialism." *Mission Studies* 21, no. 2 (2004): 201–27.

Robinson, Dylan. *Hungry Listening: Resonant Theory for Indigenous Studies*. Minneapolis: University of Minnesota Press, 2020.

Rony, Fatimah Tobing. "The Quick and the Dead: Surrealism and the Found Ethnographic Footage Films of *Bontoc Eulogy* and *Mother Dao: The Turtlelike*." *Camera Obscura* 18, no. 1 (2003): 129–55.

– *The Third Eye: Race, Cinema, and Ethnographic Spectacle*. Durham, NC: Duke University Press, 1996.

Roy, Franziska. "South Asian Prisoners of War in First World War Germany." In *"When the War Began We Heard of Several Kings": South Asian Prisoners in World War I Germany*, edited by Franziska Roy, Heike Liebau, and Ravi Ahuja, 53–95. Delhi: Social Science Press, 2011.

Russell, Catherine. *Archiveology: Walter Benjamin and Archival Film Practices*. Durham, NC: Duke University Press, 2018.

– *Experimental Ethnography: The Work of Film in the Age of Video*. Durham, NC: Duke University Press, 1999.

Rydell, Robert. *All the World's a Fair: Visions of Empire at American International Expositions, 1876–1916*. Chicago: University of Chicago Press, 1987.

Said, Edward W. *Orientalism*. New York: Vintage Books, 1978.

– *Reflections on Exile and Other Essays*. Cambridge, MA: Harvard University Press, 2000.

Salzmann, Sasha Marianna. *Außer sich*. Frankfurt am Main: Suhrkamp, 2017.

Sarr, Felwine, and Bénédicte Savoy. "The Restitution of African Cultural Heritage: Toward a New Relational Ethics." Report, 21 November 2018. http://restitutionreport2018.com/sarr_savoy_en.pdf.

Schaeffer, Pierre. *In Search of a Concrete Music*. Translated by Christine North and John Dack. Berkeley: University of California Press, [1952] 2012.

– *Treatise on Musical Objects: An Essay across Disciplines*. Translated by Christine North and John Dack. Berkeley: University of California Press, [1966] 2017.

Schafer, R. Murray. "On the Limits of Nationalism in Canadian Music." *Tamarack Review* 18 (1961): 71–8.

– *The Soundscape: Our Sonic Environment and the Tuning of the World*. Rochester, NY: Destiny Books, [1977] 1994.

Scheer, Monique. "Captive Voices: Phonographic Recordings in the German and Austrian Prisoner-of-War Camps of World War I." In *Doing Anthropology in Wartime and War Zones: World War I and the Cultural Sciences in* Europe, edited by Reinhard Johler, Christian Marchetti, and Monique Scheer, 297–310. Bielefeld: Transcript, 2010.

Schmidt, Hannah. "Rassismus in der Klassik: Die Kolonisierung unserer Ohren." *Die Zeit*, 11 May 2021, https://www.zeit.de/2021/20/rassismus -klassik-phil-ewell-klassische-musik-europa-usa-deutschland.

Schneider, Rebecca. *Performing Remains: Art and War in Times of Theatrical Reenactment*. London: Routledge, 2011.

Schwarz, David. *Listening Awry: Music and Alterity in German Culture*. Minneapolis: University of Minnesota Press, 2006.

Scott, Colin. "The Global Recording Network's Response to *The Tailenders*."
Accompaniment to PBS premiere of *The Tailenders*, 26 June 2006. http://
archive.pov.org/tailenders/film-update/2/.

Sedgwick, Eve Kosofsky. *Touching Feeling: Affect, Pedagogy, Performativity*.
Durham, NC: Duke University Press, 2003.

Seider, Tanja. "Postcolonial Historiography in the Essay Film: 'De-Colonizing'
Sound and Image." *InterDisciplines* 1 (2013): 127–51.

Sengupta, Rakesh. "Towards a Decolonial Media Archaeology: The Absent
Archive of Screenwriting History and the Obsolete *Munshi*." *Theory, Culture
& Society* 38, no. 1 (2021): 3–26.

Serge, Victor. *Men in Prison*. Translated by Richard Greeman. Oakland, CA:
Spectre PM Press, [1931] 2014.

Serres, Michael. *Genesis*. Translated by Geneviève James and James Nielson.
Ann Arbor: University of Michigan Press, [1982] 1995.

– *The Parasite*. Translated by Lawrence R. Schehr. Minneapolis: University of
Minnesota Press, [1980] 2007.

Shilina-Conte, Tanya. "Black Screen, White Page: Ontology and Genealogy
of Blank Space." *Word & Image: A Journal of Verbal/Visual Enquiry* 31, no. 4
(2015): 501–14.

Silverman, Kaja. "Dis-Embodying the Female Voice." In *Revision: Essays in
Feminist Film Criticism*, edited by Mary Ann Doane, Patricia Mellencamp,
and Linda Williams, 131–49. Los Angeles: University Publications of
America, 1984.

Singh, Julietta. *Unthinking Mastery: Dehumanism and Decolonial Entanglements*.
Durham, NC: Duke University Press, 2018.

Smith, Jacob. *Eco-Sonic Media*. Berkeley: University of California Press, 2015.

Sobchack, Vivian. "Afterword: Media Archaeology and Re-presencing in
the Past." In *Media Archaeology: Approaches, Applications, and Implications*,
edited by Erkki Huhtamo and Jussi Parikka, 323–34. Berkeley: University of
California Press, 2011.

– *Carnal Thoughts: Embodiment and Moving Image Culture*. Berkeley: University
of California Press, 2004.

Sommer, Doris. *Foundational Fictions: The National Romances of Latin America*.
Berkeley: University of California Press, 1991.

Spivak, Gayatri Chakravorty. "Can the Subaltern Speak?" In *Colonial Discourse
and Post-Colonial Theory: A Reader*, edited by Patricia Williams and Laura
Chrisman, 66–111. New York: Columbia University Press, 1994.

Stadler, Gustavus. "Never Heard Such a Thing: Lynching and Phonographic
Modernity." *Social Text* 28, no. 1 (2010): 87–105.

– "On Whiteness and Sound Studies." *Sounding Out!* (blog). https://
soundstudiesblog.com/2015/07/06/on-whiteness-and-sound-studies/.

Steedman, Carolyn. *Dust*. Manchester, UK: Manchester University Press, 2001.

Steintrager, James A., and Rey Chow, eds. *Sound Objects*. Durham, NC: Duke University Press, 2019.

Sterne, Jonathan. *The Audible Past: Cultural Origins of Sound Production*. Durham, NC: Duke University Press, 2003.

Stoever, Jennifer Lynn. *The Sonic Color Line: Race and the Cultural Politics of Listening*. New York: New York University Press, 2016.

Stoler, Ann Laura. *Along the Archival Grain: Epistemic Anxieties and Colonial Commonsense*. Princeton: Princeton University Press, 2009.

– "Colonial Archives and the Arts of Governance." *Archival Science* 2 (2002): 87–109.

Stumpf, Carl. "Tonsystem und Musik der Siamesen." In *Sammelbände für vergleichende Musikwissenschaft*, edited by Carl Stumpf and Erich Moritz von Hornbostel, 69–138. Berlin: Drei Masken, [1901] 1922.

Stumpf, Carl, and Erich Moritz von Hornbostel. "On the Significance of Ethnological Studies for the Psychology and Aesthetics of Musical Art." Translated by Gerd Grupe and Kristen Wolf. *Translingual Discourse in Ethnomusicology* 1 ([1911] 2015): 1–12.

Taussig, Michael. *Mimesis and Alterity: A Particular History of the Senses*. New York: Routledge, 1993.

Taylor, Diana. *The Archive and the Repertoire: Performing Cultural Memory in the Americas*. Durham, NC: Duke University Press, 2003.

Thomas, Richard. *The Imperial Archive: Knowledge and the Fantasy of Empire*. London: Verso, 1990.

Thurman, Kira. *Singing Like Germans: Black Musicians in the Land of Bach, Beethoven, and Brahms*. Ithaca, NY: Cornell University Press, 2021.

Tieke, Julia. "Das deutsche Kaiserreich und der Dschihad." *Deutschlandfunk Kultur*, 19 November 2014. http://www.deutschlandfunkkultur.de /geschichte-das-deutsche-kaiserreich-und-der-dschihad.976.de .html?dram%3Aarticle_id=303174.

Toop, David. *Sinister Resonance: The Mediumship of the Listener*. New York: Continuum, 2010.

Trinh T. Minh-ha. *When the Moon Waxes Red: Representation, Gender, and Cultural Politics*. London: Routledge, 1991.

Truth and Reconciliation Commission of Canada. *Honouring the Truth, Reconciling for the Future: Summary of the Final Report of the Truth and Reconciliation Commission of Canada*. http://www.trc.ca/assets/pdf /Honouring_the_Truth_Reconciling_for_the_Future_July_23_2015.pdf.

Tuck, Eve, and K. Wayne Yang. "Decolonization Is Not a Metaphor." *Decolonization: Indigeneity, Education & Society* 1, no. 1 (2012): 1–40.

Vergara Jr., Benito M. *Displaying Filipinos: Photography and Colonialism in Early Twentieth-Century Philippines*. Quezon City: University of the Philippines Press, 1995.

Weheliye, Alexander G. *Phonographies: Grooves in Sonic Afro-Modernity*. Durham, NC: Duke University Press, 2005.

Whitehead, Harry. "The Agency of Yearning on the Northwest Coast of Canada: Franz Boas, George Hunt and the Salvage of Autochthonous Culture." *Memory Studies* 3, no. 3 (2010): 215–23.

Whitney, Tyler. *Eardrums: Literary Modernism as Sonic Warfare*. Evanston, IL: Northwestern University Press, 2019.

Wolf, Nicole. "*The Halfmoon Files*: To Be Haunted." *The Halfmoon Files*, accessed 6 February 2021, https://halfmoonfiles.de/en/4/film/be-haunted.

Wolfe, Charles. "Historicising the 'Voice of God': The Place of Vocal Narration in Classical Documentary." *Film History* 9 (1997): 149–67.

Woloshyn, Alexa. "Reclaiming the 'Contemporary' in Indigeneity: The Musical Practices of Cris Derksen and Jeremy Dutcher." *Contemporary Music Review* 39, no. 2 (2020): 206–30.

Wurtzler, Steve J. *Electric Sounds: Technological Change and the Rise of Corporate Mass Media*. New York: Columbia University Press, 2007.

yamomo, meLê. *Theatre and Music in Manila and the Asia Pacific, 1869–1946: Sound Modernities*. Cham, Switzerland: Palgrave, 2019.

Youdelman, Jeffrey. "Narration, Invention, and History: A Documentary Dilemma." *Cinéaste* 12, no. 2 (1982): 8–15.

Zantop, Susanne. *Colonial Fantasies: Conquest, Family, and Nation in Precolonial Germany, 1770–1870*. Durham, NC: Duke University Press, 1997.

Ziegler, Susanne. *Die Wachszylinder des Berliner Phonogramm-Archivs*. Berlin: Staatliche Museen zu Berlin, 2006.

– "Historical Sound Recordings in the Berlin Phonogramm-Archiv and the Lautarchiv." *Translingual Discourse in Ethnomusicology* 6 (2020): 136–55.

Zielinski, Siegfried. "AnArcheology for AnArchives: Why Do We Need – Especially for the Arts – A Complementary Concept to the Archive?." Translated by Geoffrey Winthrop-Young. *Journal of Contemporary Archaeology* 2, no. 1 (2015): 116–25.

– *Variations on Media Thinking*. Minneapolis: University of Minnesota Press, 2019.

Zilcosky, John. *Kafka's Travels: Exoticism, Colonialism, and the Traffic of Writing*. New York: Palgrave, 2003.

Zimmerman, Andrew [Angela]. *Anthropology and Antihumanism in Imperial Germany*. Chicago: University of Chicago Press, 2001.